PLANNING AT THE LANDSCAPE S(

C000150150

Traditionally, landscape planning has involved the designation and protection of exceptional countryside. However, whilst this still remains important, there is a growing recognition of the multifunctionality of rural areas, and the need to encourage sustainable use of whole territories rather than just their 'hotspots'.

With an inter-disciplinary assessment of the rural environment, this book draws on theories of landscape values, people–place relationships, sustainable development, and plan implementation. It focuses on the competing influences of globalisation and localisation as they are expressed in the landscape: external forces lead to a uniformity of landscapes and a decline in those farming/forestry practices that sustain local distinctiveness, whilst at the same time many people crave local identity and cherish inherited patterns of land use.

This book sees the role of planning as that of reconciling these conflicting demands, reinforcing character and distinctiveness without museum-ising rural areas, and instilling a virtuous circle between economic production and the natural environment. Paul Selman here examines the 'unmaking' and 'remaking' of landscape character, taking a critical approach to the – often conflicting – values associated with multi-functional landscapes and giving equal attention to both valued heritage sites and de-valued urban sites.

Taking a 'landscape scale' approach to the topic, this book responds to the interest sparked by concern for rural landscapes and by recent local and national policy shifts in this area. It combines human perspectives with scientific and policy perspectives and provides a valuable resource for students, academics and professionals in environmental management and planning, landscape management and planning, town and country planning, land economy, landscape design and geography.

Paul Selman is Professor of Landscape at Sheffield University.

THE RTPI Library Series

Edited by Cliff Hague, *Heriot Watt University, Edinburgh, Scotland***, Tim Richardson,** *Sheffield University, UK***, Robert Upton,** *RTPI, London, UK*

Published by Routledge in conjunction with The Royal Town Planning Institute, this series of leading-edge texts looks at all aspects of spatial planning theory and practice from a comparative and international perspective.

Planning in Postmodern Times
Philip Allmendinger, University of Aberdeen, Scotland

The Making of the European Spatial Development Perspective
No Master Plan
Andreas Faludi and Bas Waterhout, University of Nijmegen, The Netherlands

Planning for Crime Prevention
Richard Schneider, University of Florida, USA and Ted Kitchen, Sheffield Hallam University, UK

The Planning Polity
Mark Tewdwr-Jones, The Bartlett, University College London

Shadows of Power
An Allegory of Prudence in Land-Use Planning
Jean Hillier, Curtin University of Technology, Australia

Urban Planning and Cultural Identity
William J.V. Neill, Queen's University, Belfast

Place Identity, Participation and Planning
Edited by Cliff Hague and Paul Jenkins

Planning for Diversity
Policy and Planning in a World of Difference
Dory Reeves

Planning at the Landscape Scale
Paul Selman

PLANNING AT THE LANDSCAPE SCALE

PAUL SELMAN

Routledge
Taylor & Francis Group

LONDON AND NEW YORK

First published 2006
by Routledge
2 Park Square, Milton Park, Abingdon, Oxon OX14 4RN

Simultaneously published in the USA and Canada
by Routledge
270 Madison Ave, New York, NY 10016

Routledge is an imprint of the Taylor & Francis Group, an informa business

© 2006 Paul Selman

Typeset in Akzidenz by Taylor & Francis Books Ltd
Printed and bound in Great Britain by TJ International Ltd, Padstow, Cornwall

British Library Cataloguing in Publication Data
A catalogue record for this book is available from the British Library

Library of Congress Cataloging in Publication Data
A catalog record for this book has been applied for

ISBN10: 0-415-35141-3 ISBN13: 978-0-415-35141-6 (hbk)
ISBN10: 0-415-35142-1 ISBN13: 978-0-415-35142-3 (pbk)
eISBN: 0-203-6960-5   ISBN13: 978-0-203-69690-3 (ebk)

CONTENTS

LIST OF ILLUSTRATIONS

FIGURES

TABLES

CHAPTER 1

INTRODUCTION:

THE CHALLENGE OF PLANNING AT THE
LANDSCAPE SCALE

Landscape needs little justification as a subject of importance in land use planning. For decades, in many countries, planning and cognate legislatures have sought to protect areas of exceptional scenic beauty. They have often also sought to safeguard locally important landscapes and to enhance the appearance of built development by retaining existing vegetation and creating new features.

Latterly, however, there has been a growing international awareness that landscape is far more than just another 'sectoral' interest. There has been recognition that the distinctiveness of places, regions and even countries relies heavily on landscape characteristics and that, ubiquitously and insidiously, powerful forces are eroding this. Further, we have become increasingly aware that landscape contributes centrally to people's quality of life, and thus requires a more systematic and geographically comprehensive approach than simply preserving the prettiest areas for those fortunate enough to be able to gaze on them. Perhaps most importantly, modern theories of landscape represent it as a holistic entity within which natural and human processes merge, and where economic, social and ecological objectives can be balanced in the pursuit of sustainable development.

Equally, ideas about the nature and role of land use planning have been evolving, and two relatively recent trends are of particular interest to the current discussion. First, is the increasing prominence of sustainable development since the early 1990s, and the recognition of planning as a key vehicle for its delivery. This innovation has been multifaceted, and not solely about relationships between the environment and socio-economy. Thus, planning has been seen more strongly as an instrument for spatial justice and for listening to the voices of all stakeholders whose quality of life may be affected by development decisions. It has further sought to regain the initiative on matters of design and 'place-making', so that people might identify with and have pride in their localities. Its role in regeneration has become increasingly important within a context of urban renaissance, as declining industrial cities have endeavoured to reassert themselves as vibrant nodes within global networks of intelligence and culture.

Second, especially but not exclusively in a European context, land use planning has become centrally associated with new conceptions of spatiality, to the extent that 'spatial planning' has now become the term of preference. This term is still in the process of stabilising, and definitions vary. Broadly, it appears to comprise two key characteristics. On the one hand, it is seen to replace an old style of development planning – one which, often as a consequence of statutory remit, was excessively focused on controlling change in the built environment. Spatial planning, whilst embracing this well-established field of activity, aims more explicitly to integrate sectoral responsibilities in the pursuit of quality of life. Thus, spatial plans sit alongside other plans and coordinating mechanisms to mesh policies for land use, community, economy and environment. Although many such policies are 'aspatial' in their conception, an important part of spatial planning is to seek their integration within the context of localities and regions. On the other hand, in a post-industrial, network society, new spatialities are seen to be emerging, reflecting flows and complementarities. Although the two perspectives share a great deal of common ground, we might suggest that the former emphasises integration within 'place' while the latter sees this occurring across 'space'.

The theory and practice of both landscape and spatial planning are thus in a state of flux from which new possibilities are evolving. Significantly, these new potentials are associated with the widely claimed capacity of landscape to afford a scalar basis for spatial intervention – in other words, a distinctive contribution of a landscape perspective is that of 'scale'. Principally, this implies that landscapes, as reasonably clearly defined terrains, possess innate scalar properties, and thus divide the earth's surface into spaces and linkages that have meaning for both human and natural systems.

This book makes a foray into the interface between landscape and planning in two respects. First, it considers emerging practices of stewarding the landscape itself. This is referred to as 'landscape planning', and may be thought of as planning *for* landscape units. Second, it explores the potential for landscape to provide an integrative framework for wider practices of spatial planning. This is recounted here as landscape scale planning, or planning *through* landscape units. We may thus argue that landscape furnishes a terrain in which 'place' and 'space' coincide. Regardless of their shape or extent, viable landscapes typically possess coherent qualities of 'place-ness' in their own right, as well as fitting within a wider physical and information network across space. They are specific nodes and vertices where culture, wildlife, environmental systems, social capital and economic activity are particularised. Yet, as well as displaying and deriving their distinctiveness from a measure of self-containment, they are also conduits for physical and information flows from and to adjacent areas.

'Cultural' landscapes, which are the focus of this book, are simultaneously 'real' (hosting physical and ecological systems) and 'imaginary' (recognised by people through their collage of images). Whilst, in its exploration of scale and functionality, this book draws inspiration from the domain of landscape ecology, it recognises that this has often been criticised for modelling people-less landscapes. Hence, there is an attempt to redress this skew, and to propose a trans-disciplinary approach that is concerned equally with the human and the natural.

PLANNING FOR AND THROUGH LANDSCAPE

As just noted, this book seeks to contribute both to the specialism of 'landscape planning', and to the conception of landscape as a framework through which policy can be delivered and actions integrated. It proposes that the land surface can be understood in terms of coherent units within which lives unfold and environmental systems interact. The notion of 'planning' used in this book is a generic one, as many legislatures have defined development or land use planning in rather narrow terms, excluding many topics of interest to the landscape. Here, a broader view is taken, corresponding more closely to the European Landscape Convention's (ELC) definition of planning as 'forward-looking action to enhance, restore or create landscapes' (Council of Europe, 2000). This definition is similar to the long-standing notion of 'stewardship', embracing anticipatory care aimed at securing the sustainable development of natural and cultural resources.

The practice of landscape planning has principally focused on 'cultural' landscapes, wherein the use of land reflects an amalgam of environmental possibilities (such as gradient, climate and soil fertility) and human endeavour. This has produced classic landscapes, which are acknowledged to be as important to heritage as are fine historic buildings and vernacular settlements. Noting that concern for such landscapes is now universal, and has broken away from its former obsession with the 'Old World', Phillips (1998) affirms a growing international awareness of the links between cultural diversity and natural diversity, and the vulnerability of both to outside processes. This is paralleled by a widespread reaction against ways in which the global economy and technological advance have created increasingly standardised and homogeneous environments. Thus, cultural landscapes are no longer being seen as a sectoral, elitist, 'western' topic, but rather as arenas for multifunctional planning across a wide range of environments.

In relation to planning for landscapes, a number of core issues have emerged over the years. A major objective has been to safeguard a top tier, deemed to be the finest representatives of their kind, and to designate these areas in ways that ensure a degree of safeguard against unacceptable change. Often, this has been based mainly on restrictive development planning policies, but increasingly there is an emphasis on positive land management and the creation of new ecological habitat and recreational opportunity. Beyond these most special areas, there has been an acknowledgement of the need to safeguard more local assets by supplementary designations, and even to reinforce the landscape character of all countryside. Within the urban fabric there has been a longstanding commitment to the preservation of some key functions and to the inclusion of designed landscape elements within the development process, but this is now maturing into more integrated measures for multifunctional green infrastructures.

These concerns of landscape planning, however, whilst hugely important in their own right, are now seen to represent only part of the story. The contention of this book is that the notion of 'landscape scale' should be mainstreamed into the practice of spatial planning. On the one hand, spatial planning is concerned with 'place-making', in the quest for distinctive and identifiable settings where synergies occur between community, economy and environment; on the other, it 'mediates space', through its focus on nested spatial units within dynamic networks, wherein participatory governance is supported by integrated datasets and transparent decision-making. It also requires the integration of different spheres of policy activity such as community, employment and biodiversity. Further, by emphasising the pursuit of liveable and sustainable environments, it is concerned less with inherited conceptions of 'urban' and 'rural', and more with the experiential and functional validity of places. Finally, it increasingly acknowledges a spatial dimension to 'justice', where the geographical distribution of desired resources may be uneven, but efforts are made to improve accessibility and availability to all. These trends can prove unsettling to the traditional pursuit of landscape planning, which has tended to be sectoral and elitist; yet they also offer exciting new possibilities for an integrative concept of 'landscape scale'.

Current conceptions of spatiality often distinguish between a 'territorial' space, i.e. distinct and bounded units with relatively self-contained socio-economies, and a 'deterritorialised' space of network relations, in which places are essentially understood as nodes within a globalised web. Whilst this book acknowledges this debate, the term 'territory' is used only sparingly. This is because the European Landscape Convention, which has been a major impetus to landscape scale planning, refers to 'territory' in a particular way – essentially as the land of a nation-state, over which a government has sovereign jurisdiction – whereas other discourses treat it more conceptually. Hence, the term 'territory' is only used here when particularly germane to a specific theme.

The term 'landscape' has multiple associations. Even within planning and design circles, it variously refers to aesthetic conceptions of sublime or polite scenery, ornamented urban environments, tracts of visually coherent land cover and land use, and areas associated with characteristic stories and customary laws. In Old World landscapes, the challenges are essentially those of finding new and self-sustaining means of retaining landscapes whose qualities are being under-mined by functional obsolescence; in the 'New World', the challenge is often one of adjusting colonial mindsets to discover new ways (or rediscover old ways) of sustainable living in fragile and over-exploited terrains.

Despite these manifold notions there are surprisingly convergent views about the importance of landscape as an organising framework for analysis of and pur-poseful intervention in the process of land use change. Distinctive landscape pat-terns and processes appear to manifest themselves in both space and in time, and they offer a context for integrated, participatory planning. A key argument of this book is that, in order to steward and inhabit landscapes sustainably, we must work in tandem with their innate rhythms and patterns, and respond to them at an appro-priate scale. Sometimes, this requires a technical jargon and a sophisticated frame-work for intervention; at other times, it resonates with intuitive feelings about landscapes as identifiable and distinctive loci, to which we may feel instinctive and emotional attachment.

THE CULTURAL LANDSCAPE

Landscape, as defined in the European Landscape Convention, can be understood as 'an area, as perceived by people, whose character is the result of the action and interaction of natural and/or human factors' (Council of Europe, 2000). This careful wording embraces a number of ideas: a landscape is a relatively bounded area or unit; its recognition depends on human perception, which often is spontaneous and intuitive in its identification with a coherent tract of land; and it results from a long legacy of actions and interactions. However, it contains one rather debatable yet intentional element – landscapes may derive from a combination of natural and human factors, but equally they can be purely socially or purely naturally produced, and in the latter case there need be no explicit cultural component. In the context of the current discussion, this book has only a passing interest in those landscapes which are 'purely built' or 'purely natural' in their origins – it is concerned with the intimate association of people and 'nature' in the production and reproduction of distinctive cultural spaces. However, the European Landscape Convention's defini-tion suits present purposes well for a number of reasons. First, it recognises the role of human construction and imagination in creating and interpreting units of the environment that nevertheless possess a functional as well as a visual coherence. Second, it assumes that a fundamental feature of landscape is its distinctive 'character', which has resulted from a complex pattern of actions and interactions, manifest in both historical legacy and contemporary dynamics. Third, it implies that distinctive places are frequently the outcome of a fortuitous combination of natural and human factors.

Much of our previous experience with landscape planning has been in relation to natural/pristine systems where the human imprint is very limited. Whilst there are lessons to be learnt from the preservation of such environments, our concern here is with 'cultural' landscapes. This is perhaps most helpfully and authoritatively expressed through IUCN's[1] Category V, 'protected landscapes/seascapes', defined as:

> ... areas of land, with coast and sea as appropriate, where the interaction of
> people and nature over time has produced an area of distinct character with
> significant aesthetic, ecological and/or cultural value, and often with high
> biological diversity.
>
> (IUCN, 1994a)

As an accompaniment to this definition, the IUCN observe that 'safeguarding the integrity of this traditional interaction is vital to the protection, maintenance and evolution of such an area'. Hence, the sustainable development of valued landscapes pivots upon the complex relationship between people and nature, and on well-modulated governance. However, whilst the IUCN may be concerned with outstanding landscapes, these principles have a more general significance, because sustainably managed protected areas can be seen as 'greenprints' upon which wise stewardship of land can more generally be based (MacEwen and MacEwen, 1987), and because all cultural landscapes deserve to have their qualities recognised, enhanced and stewarded.

This invites debate about where landscape begins and ends, and whether there is any longer a meaningful distinction between 'urban' and 'rural' in post-industrial countries. Whilst terms such as 'rural' and 'countryside' are used here where appropriate, this does not imply that landscape stops at the urban boundary, even if one could be identified. However, it is fair to say that the emphasis is not only on cultural landscapes, but particularly on (agri)cultural ones – the parenthesis here implying that farming has been a dominant force in landscape production, and that it is more broadly symbolic of the general modification of rural land by human activity. Indeed, many other terrains may appear agricultural, as they are maintained in a 'quasi-grazed' condition by practices such as mowing, burning or even recreational pressure. In other cases, forestry or nature conservation may be the dominant user of land. However, one of the main arguments of this book is that multifunctional landscapes are likely to replace the polarised ones induced by monofunctional policy objectives during the 20th century so that, for example, modern equivalents to wood pasture might replace blanket tree cover, and more diversified land uses be encouraged in wildlife priority areas.

Thus, although there is an almost inescapable and implicit bias to 'rural' areas in the ensuing discussion, this is principally to avoid straying into the very distinct scholarship domain that has developed around the 'urban landscape', and which is variously concerned with the design of the public and private realm, human behavioural patterns, and symbolic expressions of power and capital. In reality, the urban–rural divide is blurring in many countries, both physically and socially, and the 'landscape scale' can apply to the full spectrum of spatial contexts. In practice, this book focuses on landscapes that are less extensively modified by urbanisation; it addresses a spectrum from green spaces within cities, through the indeterminate landscape of the urban fringe, across intensively managed farms and forests, via more extensively managed land that still retains many pre-industrial features, to relatively wild landscapes that have either escaped 'improvement' or are reverting to 'nature' following economic and social marginalisation.

In respect of landscape, the term 'cultural' invites controversy, not least because all landscapes are cultural in some degree – not even Antarctica is exempt from human influence. However, in policy circles 'cultural landscape' has acquired a particular nuance, and refers to those areas whose extent people intuitively grasp and whose distinctive character derives from centuries of human activity. Some are distinguished by a character that is widely perceived as aesthetically satisfying and/or ecologically or geologically rare, and are consequently deemed worthy of some degree of protection. Some are relatively nondescript, but may nevertheless command a high level of personal attachment from their inhabitants. Some are generally agreed to be unattractive, usually as a result of industrial damage, and may require remedial treatment to re-create visual and functional coherence; yet even here, value judgements are risky, and the expert 'gaze' may overlook visible features and inscribed histories that are cherished by locals.

Cultural landscapes are 'synoptic' spaces where human and non-human elements are fused in a physical and social entity laden with individual and collective associations. In this regard, Phillips (2002) has referred to the cultural landscape as comprising:

- nature plus people;
- the past plus the present; and
- physical attributes (scenery, nature, historic heritage) plus associative (social and cultural) values.

Stewardship of the landscape must, therefore, be informed by an understanding of three interlocking facets (cf. Terkenli, 2001) – form (the visual), meaning (the cognitive) and function (biophysical processes and human uses). Piorr (2003) amplifies on this by suggesting the need to consider:

- *structures* or landscape *form*, such as natural physical, environmental land use and human-made features, often recognisable visually;
- *functions* associated with biophysical processes and human uses, such as environmental services and spaces for living, working and recreation; and
- *values* or *meanings*, including cognitive qualities such as the intangible and fluid values imputed by society to landscape attributes deemed actually and potentially desirable, and real monetary values such as the costs of maintaining traditional agriculture.

This tripartite nature of landscape is central to its capacity to serve as an integrative medium through which transdisciplinary spatial planning can occur (Figure 1.1).

A key attribute of cultural landscapes is that they are, in effect, palimpsests – ancient documents with overwritten but never fully erased successive inscriptions – of occupation, and can thus be 'read' by the trained eye (or intuitively understood by the sensitised 'insider'). This 'textual' quality of the landscape has been widely attested and explained (e.g. Meinig, 1979; Clark *et al.*, 2003), and 'intertextual' studies have sought to relate landscape features to their host society and culture (Cosgrove and Daniels, 1988). Terkenli (2001) observes how the long-standing use of landscape as a basic unit of analysis in geography has been joined by a cultural interpretation which emphasises multitextuality, multivocality and multisemity. We may summarise these terms respectively as the layered and legible inscriptions in the landscape, the many 'voices' or shared histories and narratives associated with a particular landscape setting, and the many meanings and 'signals' that can be perceived in a landscape by sensitised viewers. Critical to the recognisability of landscapes, therefore, is their degree of *legibility*, or the potential for us to 'read' their embedded stories.

Broadly speaking, we can identify the principal hallmarks of characteristic and distinct cultural landscapes as being:

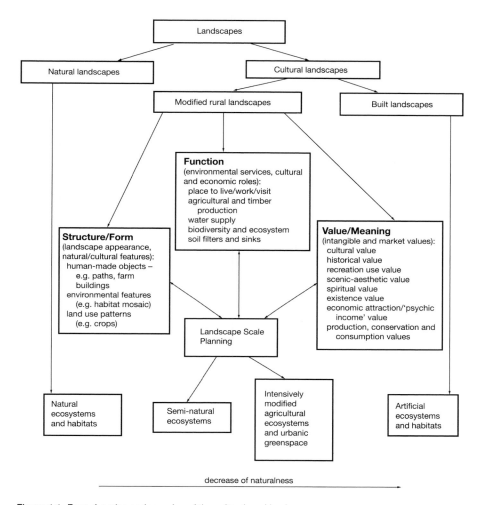

Figure 1.1 Form, function and meaning of the cultural rural landscape

Source: modified: based on concepts in Terkenli, 2001; Piorr, 2003; Bergstrom, 1998; Parris, 2004

- time-depth, often stretching back centuries or even millennia;
- traces of struggles and occupation, bearing imprints of survival and settlement;
- evidence of production, reflecting human toil and modern machinery, drainage, re-seeding, industry, water impoundment, and so forth;
- attributes that provide opportunities for enjoyment – aesthetic qualities of wilderness and the picturesque, for example, and settings for active and passive leisure;

Figure 1.2 An example of an important European cultural landscape: cultivation terraces in Spain

- natural qualities, particularly in relation to sustainable service functions[2] of soils, water, air and biodiversity; and
- 'customs and practices', where insider status may be associated with a 'secret' knowledge of places, traditions and customary laws.

Often, the rich textuality of highly legible landscapes will result in 'vernacular' vistas which are complex and pleasing to the human eye. However, it is also possible that they recall painful memories, perhaps of imperialism, war and 'dark histories' such as slavery and holocaust – though these also are hugely important to heritage. Similarly, the notion of 'associative landscape' (Gwyn, 2002) has been used to signify the capacity of places to articulate or evoke intangible acts of memory, imagination, belonging and alienation.

THE CHANGING LANDSCAPE

Despite the common human desire to retain the familiar, change in cultural land-scapes must be accepted as inevitable and endemic. The forces of change are often powerful and external. The key dilemma is that cultural landscapes, especially in Europe, are predominantly derived from past agricultural practices, and these are now progressively more obsolescent. For example, Piorr's (2003) analysis of current landscape evolution in Western Europe has alluded to three principal polarities, namely:

- *Expansion–withdrawal* where the area of land devoted to agriculture increases or decreases according to economic exigencies;
- *Intensification–extensification* where land is associated with high-input or low-input practices; and
- *Concentration–marginalisation* notably associated with the levels of enter-prise specialisation, such as conversion to arable farming.

The processes are linked, so that intensification and concentration in some areas may drive marginalisation and withdrawal in others. Whilst traditional practices can be prolonged through subsidies in selected localities, this is not a practical univer-sal solution in the long term.

Further, it has been suggested, mainly by continental European writers (e.g. Jongman, 2002; Antrop, 2004), that development planning has compounded the process of polarisation. The use of zonal plans to influence the location of future development, implemented through more or less flexible zoning ordinances and development control, has encouraged a segregation of land uses. Equally, the prevalence of different legislatures for natural resource planning and development planning has exacerbated polarising trends.

Thus, both government policies and global market forces have stimulated inexorable change. Yet retaining recognisability of landscapes often requires stemming this change, and re-affirming local qualities whose social and economic *raison d'être* may be vestigial. Some of the most challenging problems of landscape scale planning arise from this paradox. Thus, it is clear that landscapes are worked and inhabited places that are in a state of flux and cannot be fossilised. If we are to steward them in ways that retain and reinforce their character and distinctiveness, whilst serving as frameworks for multifunctional spatial planning, we must understand their elements and dynamics. Hence, whilst planners perforce often focus on the visible and perceivable parts of landscapes, it is essential that they also understand and address the underlying driving forces and processes (Palang, 2003).

Some landscapes are only lightly settled and exploited, if not bereft of humans, and can be managed as 'strict reserves': this book is not about such landscapes. Here, our concern is with landscapes in which people live and work, and whose distinctive features cannot be bubble-wrapped against change. Given that the drivers of change tend to be external, often originating far from an individual landscape unit, they are unlikely to be sensitive in their impact. Thus, characteristics that confer distinctiveness are widely being eroded and homogenised through processes of globalisation and modernisation. The French term *banalisation* has aptly been used to describe this trend. In recent years, a great deal of effort has gone into defining what it is that makes some landscapes distinct from others.

Distinctiveness appears typically to arise from a combination of innate visual harmony, the functionality of natural systems, the human scale of cultural features and time-depth. This synthesis of factors has generally evolved gradually and fortuitously. Even in industrial landscapes, historical change was often slow and comparatively manual, and the land still betrayed evidence of shared triumphs and tragedies. Now, however, these formative forces are obsolescent and the trend is towards industrial mass construction and intensive land management. The challenge is, somehow, to sustain the quintessential characteristics of an area without preserving a pretence. Living and evolving traditions must be maintained, via a judicious but not wholly contrived blend of controls and incentives, so that recognisably distinctive qualities are reproduced by succeeding generations.

The task of planning for and through landscapes, in essence, involves seeking ways in which they can evolve that are sustainable, and continue to support social vibrancy, economic opportunity, visual complexity and environmental resilience. Experience suggests that, in an era of space-time compression and rapid change, this no longer happens by fortunate accident: conscious intervention becomes necessary or else valued attributes are rapidly lost and cannot easily be recovered. 'Planning' in this sense is a form of local resistance to homogenising forces. Inadequate though it may at times appear against the tidal wave of globalisation, some attempt at localisation – or perhaps re-localisation – is widely sought (for a perspective on this, see O'Riordan, 2001). In part, this 'resistance' arises because of people's manifest (albeit sometimes self-contradictory) cravings for local identity and attachment; equally, though, it reflects a need to sustain the 'innovative milieux' (Camagni, 1995) and ecological processes invested in places.

LANDSCAPE: MULTIPLE MEANINGS AND MULTIPLE FUNCTIONS

Landscape is a concept of multiple meanings. Summarising Terkenli (2001), we may argue that it embraces three types of flow, two of which relate mainly to the physical environment (energy and material flows), and a third which affects people's perceptions, usage and values (information flows). These 'system flows' can, in turn, be understood in three ways: whether they are 'real' (e.g. physical fabric), 'perceived' (e.g. filtered in terms of utility and delight) or 'symbolic' (e.g. important to certain groups because of past associations).

Thus, some people refer to landscape as a physical entity produced by earth processes. Others see it as a social construction charged with cultural associations. It can be a thing of beauty or horror on a framed canvas. It can be a planner's spatial frame of reference. It can be recorded from a satellite or modelled from the perspective of an insect. It has been described as a 'hybrid' nexus of nature and culture in which dualities between people and their host environment dissolve. It is lived in, visited, cherished, protected and exploited. As a visually comprehended and perhaps relatively self-contained environmental unit, it can be used as a framework for analysis, synthesis, policy development and plan implementation. It is an area where different groups contest the meanings and significance of historical associations. It is a place of production, consumption and military engagement. Lowenthal (1997) has argued that rural landscapes may serve as ecological paradigms, citizens' realms, icons of collective identity, canvases for art, and wellsprings of heritage.

Equally, as the Countryside Agency and Scottish Natural Heritage (2002) have noted, landscape can mean a small patch of urban wasteland as much as a mountain range, and an urban park as much as an expanse of lowland plain. It results from the way that different components of our environment – both natural (the influences of geology, soils, climate, flora and fauna) and cultural (the historical and current impact of land use, settlement, enclosure and other human interventions) – interact together in both imaginary and material ways. Whilst the recognition of landscape is essentially a visual act, it also involves 'how we hear, smell and feel our surroundings, and the feelings, memories or associations that they evoke' (CA/SNH, 2002). As much as being a product of natural evolution, therefore, landscape is a social construction and – as has often been noted – it is people's perceptions that turn land into 'landscape'.

Landscape is thus quintessentially an inter-disciplinary concept, grounded in a wide range of scientific, social scientific, humanistic and artistic traditions (Phillips and Clarke, 2004). For us to plan effectively, different types of knowledge and expertise must be enrolled: both the insights of a range of experts and also, given that living in a landscape confers a deep understanding of it, the knowledge of lay individuals and communities. For many years there has been an awareness of the importance of *multidisciplinarity*. Multidisciplinary approaches typically comprise a patchwork of studies, each located in a well-defined discipline and 'stitched together' editorially at the end of a project (Winder, 2003). More recently, there has been a move towards *interdisciplinarity*, involving integration of several unrelated academic disciplines in a way that forces them to cross subject boundaries to solve a common research goal (Tress *et al.*, 2003). However, many commentators now advocate *transdisciplinarity*, which requires that projects integrate academic researchers from different disciplines with user-group stakeholders to reach a common goal (Tress and Tress, 2001; Tress *et al.*, 2004).

Similarly, *multifunctionality* has increasingly been proposed as a principal hallmark of landscape, strengthening its case for being at the heart rather than the periphery of integrated spatial planning (Brandt *et al.*, 2000). In essence, landscape is multifunctional in two key senses: from a cultural point of view it hosts many different human activities such as farming, settlement and recreation; and from an environmental point of view, it sustains multiple climatic, hydrological, edaphic and ecological processes. In respect of both of these, planners and managers aspire to ensure productivity, diversity, stability and integrity (Naveh and Lieberman, 1994). Haines-Young and Potschin (2000) have interpreted multifunctionality in terms of the three attributes of 'simultaneity' (different material processes in nature and society taking place simultaneously), 'co-existence' (embracing different spheres such as ecology, economics, culture, history and aesthetics) and 'inter-activity' (i.e. simultaneity, combined with an understanding of the interactions between environmental and socio-economic systems).

Landscape multifunctionality stands in sharp contrast to the dominantly 'single objective' planning of the past (Antrop, 1999; Pinto-Correia and Vos, 2004). During the 20th century, landscape functions – for instance, of nature conservation, natural resource management and leisure (cf. Klijn and Vos, 2000) – have tended to become segregated in most European landscapes, as a result of specialisation and intensification of production. Jongman (2002) considers this functional separation of land to be an underlying contributor to many environmental problems. Latterly, it has been argued (e.g. Brandt and Vejre, 2003) that new styles of spatial planning provide opportunities for promoting multifunctionality in space and time. Vos and Klijn (2000) consider that multifunctionality is highest when maintained at various levels – field, farm and landscape – and note that this was typical of traditional land use systems that combined arable, woodland and pastoral components in varying ways. Whilst there is little point in pretending that late-modern society can simply revert to pre-industrial mixed farm and forest, a key challenge for landscape scale planning may well be associated with recapturing the serendipitous balance between economic need, emotional attachment and ecological dynamics that appears to have transpired in many traditional, low-intensity landscapes.

SUSTAINABLE LANDSCAPES

A dominant paradigm of the past 20 years has been sustainable development, whereof multifunctional landscapes furnish a powerful expression. Understandings of sustainable development have moved on considerably since the 'Brundtland' definition of 'development which meets the needs of the present without compromising the ability of future generations to meet their own needs' (WCED, 1987). However, the myriad definitions and interpretations offered since then – whose perspectives have ranged from deep ecology to industrial promotion – merely serve to illustrate the complexity of the concept, and for the need to re-interpret it within particular contexts. Equally, however, it is now entering legislation, which to some extent denies us the luxury of endless philosophical debate and presents us with an immediate need for operational definitions and consistent, transparent methods of interpreting and implementing sustainable development in real-world decisions (cf. Kelly et al., 2004). In a landscape context, Hill (2000) identified three principal arguments in the concept of sustainability: efficiency that still allows for new growth; conservation of resources; and the restoration of human health and environmental quality.

In a policy context, the UK government has articulated and repeatedly reaffirmed sustainable development as comprising:

- maintenance of high and stable levels of economic growth and employment;
- social progress which recognises the needs of everyone;
- effective protection of the environment; and
- the prudent use of natural resources (DETR, 1999).

Whilst these principles are widely incorporated into official orthodoxies, they need to be seen as selective interpretations of a contested issue. Their implications for landscape will be similarly partial. For example, they reflect a strong reformist emphasis on policies related to social inclusion: these may lead to the promotion of large-scale housing and more diverse uses of the countryside, and will thus challenge protectionist attitudes towards 'polite' landscapes and their traditional modes of consumption. The UK government's pragmatic and policy-oriented interpretation of sustainable development is widely mirrored internationally, and has significant implications for landscape change. In particular, it is unlikely – even if it were desirable – that landscape stewardship can be pursued principally in ways that constrain 'sustainable growth'. Some speculations on the implications of 'ecologically modernist' sustainability principles for the landscape are set out here:

TABLE 1.1 POSSIBLE PRECEPTS FOR SUSTAINABLE LANDSCAPES FROM AN 'ECOLOGICALLY MODERN' PERSPECTIVE

- Cultural landscapes are as much about people – both insiders and outsiders – as they are about natural systems;
- landscapes must, by and large, 'pay their way' rather than having obsolescent land uses permanently shored up out of general taxation – whilst acknowledging that 'loss-making', in a landscape context, may be a myth of accounting conventions that undervalue the worth of natural capital and environmental service functions;
- land and water resources will normally be economically managed in cultural landscapes, but such use must be 'prudent' and 'wise';
- the purpose of planning for sustainable landscapes will vary according to setting, and will lie somewhere on a continuum from strong protection to creative development and regeneration, depending on current landscape condition;
- sustainable growth implies the need to build sustainable settlements, and these need to sit within coherent, multi-functional green infrastructures;
- landscapes contribute strongly to human quality of life and well-being, and thus need to contain sufficient levels of 'information' to both challenge and calm the human spirit;

- landscapes which are already in favourable condition and sustainably managed should be treated, not as set-apart reserves, but as exemplary 'greenprints' for wider adoption; and
- if sustainable development means moving along a sustainability transition, then we need to be able to measure and monitor whether landscapes are becoming more or less sustainable and thus whether we are heading in the right direction.

Sustainable development is commonly described in terms of achieving a balance between economy, environment and society. Landscape provides an arena in which this balance may be pursued. Thus, emergent views of landscape conceptualise it in terms of a number of interrelated elements, which may be summarised as visual identity, environmental integrity, vibrant socio-economy and legible time-depth. In order to sustain these attributes, the underlying 'capital' assets (e.g. Pearce, 1993; Ekins *et al.*, 2003) of the landscape resource will need to be interpreted and nurtured. A cultural landscape can therefore be thought of as comprising the following elements:

- *Natural capital* – its geomorphology, hydrology, soils and ecology, which provide irreplaceable service functions and are, effectively, life-support systems. Wise use of natural capital entails knowledge of its functions (particularly in terms of sustainability and renewability) and form (land use/cover, physical structural units), and seeks the safeguard of distinctive scenery and indigenous wildlife, and the integrity and regenerative capacity of natural systems and service functions.
- *Social capital* – which refers to the people living in and using the landscape, and the links and dependencies between them. Typically, the social capital comprises the general public (both residents and visitors), particular stakeholder groups representing various production and consumption interests, the constellation of interests that constitute governance structures (including private and voluntary organisations that are drawn into governance partnerships), and the formal and informal network relations within and between these.
- *Economic capital* – both locally based production and wider trading and investment linkages. Within sustainable landscapes, it is likely that the local economy will display a high degree of embedding, that is, there will be endogenous economic vitality with many internal linkages, leading to retention of added value in goods and services that may well display 'distinctiveness' and 'traceability'. Production and trading practices should also be 'just'.

Historically, agriculture has constituted the dominant economic capital of cultural landscapes, but this situation is changing markedly as rural and urban economies become more similar.

- *Cultural capital* – the living legacy of shared histories and human-made artefacts. Sometimes this is only apparent through historical and archaeological resources, but normally it will be continued and reflected in wider practices, and in shared stories and associations.

Landscape is thus a nexus where these capitals congeal and thus where multiple objectives of spatial planning can be pursued (see Figure 1.3).

LANDSCAPE GOVERNANCE

Given that landscapes are the material expressions of human actions and ideas, and that they afford opportunities for integration of sustainable policies and practices, some writers believe that they can serve as a framework for governance. This is reinforced by the argument that landscapes appear to be composed as units, often nested within larger units, providing intrinsic scales at which activities can be organised. Further, these units display a degree of self-containment: whilst landscape will inevitably be 'leaky' in terms of energy, material and information flows, they nevertheless can possess degrees of internality, coherence and character that render them highly effective vehicles for the pursuit of focused and integrated policy with which people and organisations can identify. Indeed, it may be hypothesised that landscapes – as intimate amalgams of natural, human and built capital – reflect the quintessential spatial frame for the governance of sustainable development. Such arguments have at times been assertive and simplistic, but this book considers the evidence for a landscape scale perspective at least contributing to emerging practices of spatial planning.

One of the key difficulties for landscape-centred planning – yet one of the main areas in which it can facilitate new solutions – lies in the 'dis-integrated' nature of much of our government and administration. A characteristic feature of 20th-century government has been the functional principle, which has been very cogent in focusing effort on clearly defined policy domains and pursuing carefully bounded criteria of effectiveness and efficiency. However, it has tended to create policy 'silos', unconducive to integrated policy development and delivery (Selman, 2000). In such circumstances, a 'governance' approach is required, based on achieving public goals through partnerships and flexible delivery instruments, rather than top down from a single government department. Potentially, the landscape

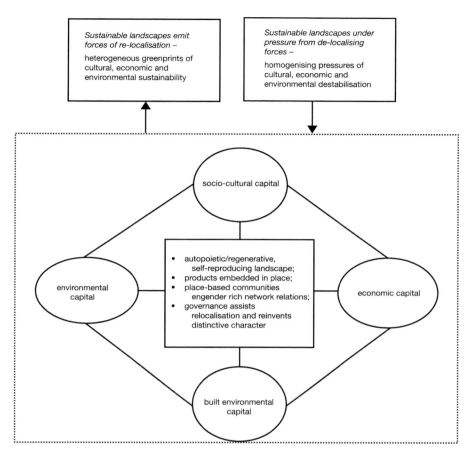

Figure 1.3 Landscape as a nexus for natural and social capitals

furnishes an effective setting for the operation of area-based partnerships which can intervene in a more integrated, seamless and place-sensitive manner.

These are issues which will be explored more fully in due course but, initially, we may note that governing at the landscape scale will require a basis in sustainability, cohesion within appropriate spatial units, and a flexible and inclusive use of complementary intervention measures. Achieving this synthesis requires spatially and institutionally joined-up approaches to governance that seek both to restrain undesirable change and promote positive change. Thus, landscape scale governance will need to draw upon a blend of strategies and tactics whereby partnerships of actors work together to protect and re-create distinctive places and spaces. In due course, the range of potential governance instruments will be elaborated more fully, but it is useful, at the outset, to note the markers set down by the European Spatial Development Perspective (ESDP) (Faludi and Waterhout, 2002) and the contemporaneous moves towards spatial planning in the UK, and the European Landscape Convention (ELC) (Council of Europe, 2000).

The ESDP is a non-binding but highly influential policy framework for improving the coordination of spatially important activities within the EU (DETR, 2000). Two key aspects may be noted: there is a blurring of urban and rural, with proximal and distant places linked in complex ways; and there are distinct types of region, namely, those dominated by a large metropolis, polycentric city-regions with high urban and rural densities, networks of medium and small towns, and remote rural areas. The main policy aims of the European Spatial Development Perspective incorporate a number of ingredients that are potentially sympathetic to a landscape scale synthesis. Thus, the theme related to 'Polycentric Spatial Development and a New Urban-Rural Relationship' includes the promotion of: a more balanced system of metropolitan regions, city clusters and city networks through closer cooperation between structural and urban policies; wise management of urban ecosystems; diversified development strategies, sensitive to the indigenous potentials of rural areas (e.g. the promotion of multifunctionality in agriculture); and sustainable agriculture and environmentally friendly tourism. The theme of 'Urban-Rural Partnerships' promotes cooperation between towns and countryside, aimed at strengthening functional regions and improving urban quality of life.

In particular, the theme of 'Wise Management of the Natural and Cultural Heritage' seeks the:

- continued development of European ecological networks including links between sites and areas of regional, national, transnational and EU-wide importance;
- integration of biodiversity considerations into sectoral policies (agriculture, regional policies, transport, fisheries, etc.) as included in the Community Bio-diversity Strategy;
- preparation of integrated spatial development strategies for protected areas, environmentally sensitive areas and areas of high biodiversity;
- greater use of economic instruments to recognise the ecological significance of protected and environmentally sensitive areas;
- promotion of transnational and interregional cooperation for the application of integrated strategies for the management of water resources and wetlands, including areas where cultural landscapes are prone to drought and flooding;

- preservation and creative development of cultural landscapes with special historical, aesthetical and ecological importance;
- enhancement of the value of cultural landscapes within the framework of integrated spatial development strategies;
- improved coordination of development measures which have an impact on landscapes; and
- creative restoration of landscapes which have suffered through human intervention, including recultivation measures.

In the UK, new planning legislation in 2004 introduced a style of spatial planning based on Regional Spatial Strategies (RSSs) and Local Development Documents (LDDs). Future approaches to planning are thus likely to include policies which can impact on land use, for example by influencing the demands on or needs for development, but which are not capable of being delivered solely or mainly through the granting or refusal of planning permission and which need to be implemented by diverse means. In particular, whilst the control of development is guided through a Local Development Framework, this can be supported by other, duly produced and sustainability proofed, 'documents'. It has been suggested that this facilitates an important opportunity for the incorporation of an integrative landscape perspective within the statutory planning process (Selman, 2002).

The ELC sets out a basis for landscape 'protection, management and planning' of the 'entire territory' of signatory countries. The Convention came into effect in 2004 following ratification by ten Council of Europe member states, and the number of signatories continues to increase. In the ELC's terms, *landscape protection* includes actions to conserve and maintain the significant or characteristic features of a landscape (those justified by heritage values associated with natural configuration and/or human activity). *Landscape management* refers to actions, set within a sustainable development perspective, that ensure the regular upkeep of a landscape, so as to guide and harmonise changes arising from social, economic and environmental processes. Such measures may relate to the whole landscape or to its components, and are aimed at harmonious evolution in a way that meets economic and social needs. *Landscape planning and landscape design/architecture* involve strong forward-looking action to enhance, restore or create landscapes. Landscape planning is defined as the formal process of study, design and construction by which new landscapes are created to meet people's aspirations. It is considered to entail framing planning projects, particularly in those areas most affected by change (for example suburbs, peri-urban and industrial areas, coastal areas), a key purpose being to radically reshape damaged landscapes.

CONCLUSION

Whereas landscape has, within land use planning, generally been seen as a specialist and sectoral interest, it is becoming a framework for understanding and guiding multidimensional change across 'entire territories'. Planning at the 'landscape scale' provides important opportunities for sustainable development and for improving people's quality of life. Whilst landscape as a term has multiple and contested meanings, the main emphasis of the current study is on cultural landscapes, many of which are experiencing strong pressures for change. This change is frequently leading to loss of coherence and functionality due to the obsolescence of their traditional economic base and exposure to globalising forces.

A recurrent theme is that cultural landscapes possess distinctive character, deriving from an amalgam of natural and human assets. The extent to which this character has been retained and is readily comprehended determines the 'legibility' of the landscape. Regrettably, various factors are reducing this legibility, leading to incoherence and anonymity. There is a widespread consensus that ecological and visual distinctiveness and complexity are being lost due to homogenising forces, and 'traditional' multifunctional landscapes are deteriorating, as their economic *raison d'être* is lost. In much of the post-industrial world, we are thus producing landscapes that are neither legible nor sustainable. Equally, though, landscapes cannot be fossilised – change, of a sustainable nature, must be embraced. In addition, landscapes are characterised by the health of their physical-ecological environments. Thus, landscape units are innately multifunctional, and they form the natural spaces within which environmental, economic and social processes intersect. Yet our previous use of the landscape has often been founded on land use simplification, in which land use activities are conducted in relative isolation and governance occurs on a sectoral basis.

An argument of this book is that we not only need integrated governance *for* the landscape, concentrating on its multiple dimensions and long-term sustainability, but we can also pursue the possibility of governance *through* the landscape, using multi-attribute units as a spatial framework for the delivery of integrated planning objectives. In this manner, the topic of landscape is moving from a sectoral to a mainstream feature of spatial planning, reflecting our increasing awareness of the need for joined-up action in the quest for sustainable development and quality of life. The contention here is that landscape can contribute pivotally to the theory and practice of spatial planning through its identification of innate scales for comprehension and action, its potential for integrating human and natural entities within defined geographic spaces, its peculiar capacity for facilitating transdisciplinary discourse and intervention, and its fundamental contribution to identity and 'place-ness'. However, the potential for landscape to play a central role in spatial planning is hampered by the esoteric nature of much of its underlying scientific theory and its legacy of being perceived as a minor, rural, sectoral interest. It is the purpose of this book to explore ways in which this potential might more fully be realised.

Having introduced the range of factors that impinge on a landscape approach to spatial planning, this book now moves onto an exploration of the nature and importance of 'scale'. This distinctive and diagnostic feature of the landscape perspective is clearly fundamental to the current discussion. The multiple scales at which landscape attributes occur are mirrored by the multiple levels at which planning takes place – from the transnational to the locality. However, scale is seen to involve more than 'space', and it is suggested that the passage of time and degrees of modification also combine to create rich and complex scalar frameworks. A landscape-centred approach affords the possibility of delivering policy through governance units which are related to the innate qualities of space and place. A frequent criticism of landscape approaches, however, is that they privilege land and wildlife over people, and so the third chapter considers the integral role of communities, stakeholders and individuals. This is followed by a review of the kinds of information we gather about landscapes, particularly the ways that these comprise both qualitative and quantitative data, and thus reflect both facts and values about places. Again, this is fundamental to the discussion, as new ways of generalising about and visualising landscape help us to comprehend this multi-attribute and multidimensional phenomenon in ways that are conducive to effective spatial planning. In Chapters 5 to 7, the book addresses the various ways that landscape scale planning occurs in practice, recognising that the powers to control change are often weak and fragmented, and need to be deployed imaginatively if powerful forces of globalisation are to be deflected to territorial advantage. Finally, the book suggests that spatial planning should aim to instil a 'virtuous circle' between biophysical conditions and the socio-economy, so that each drives sustainability in the other through a mutually beneficial and self-reinforcing relationship.

CHAPTER 2

WHY THE LANDSCAPE SCALE?

INTRODUCTION

A repeated claim about landscape, particularly in relation to policy and science applications, is that its distinctive hallmark is that of 'scale'. In other words, landscapes
display inherent patterns, closely related to underlying processes, permitting the
identification of distinctive 'units' within which environmental and socio-economic
interactions can helpfully be framed. This claim has been particularly associated
with landscape ecology, where the emphasis is on recurrent patterns and processes
across space (Pickett and Cadenasso, 1995). One of the most enduring (if regularly
contested) definitions in this regard, is Forman's (1997) description of a landscape as
a 'kilometres-wide' mosaic over which local ecosystems recur. This reflects the view
that research and decisions often need to be based on a wider area than the immediate site or locality. 'Scale' in this context refers to the spatial or temporal dimension
of an object or process, characterised by both grain and extent – that is, by the degree
of resolution and the size of the geographical area in question (Turner et al., 2001).

Other fields than landscape ecology have also attached great significance to
the issue of scale, and the 'landscape unit' is more widely canvassed as a framework for analysing inter-relationships and delivering joined-up policy within a comprehensible and identifiable space. Bioregionalists, for example, have argued that
'nature' defines its own integral systems and that, historically, sustainability in
human systems has been a consequence of close alignment between socio-economic practices and environmental capacity. This leads to arguments, discussed
more fully below, that natural, rather than political, boundaries could form the basis
of many planning and management choices. Fairclough (2006), writing from an
archaeological perspective, argues that attention to the issue of scale enables
time-depth in landscapes to be imagined in different ways, depending on the grain
and extent adopted. Further, he suggests that scale not only possesses spatial
dimensions, but also dimensions of time, perception, expertise and management.
Writers concerned with issues of aesthetics, political identity and emotional attachment have also expressed comparable views. A key property of landscapes –
whether perceived in scientific or humanistic terms – is that they are 'areas that
can be viewed at a glance' (Jackson, 1984, in Terkenli, 2001), and thus represent
intuitive spatial units in which multiple patterns and processes congeal.

A central assumption of this book is that landscape has shifted from being a sectoral interest associated with amenity, to a core, integrative concept enabling the delivery of sustainable development from a multifunctional perspective. Hence, we have moved beyond an important but limited understanding of landscape as a collection of visual 'set pieces', to a possibility that it serves as a frame for responding to complex future challenges. Whilst the dominant approach to landscape and conservation planning has centred on special areas, this selective focus is necessary but insufficient. The fact that we are now starting to see landscape policy as something which applies in different ways to the 'entire territory' (to use the European Landscape Convention's phrase) requires us to address the complete mesh of inter-locking units rather than elite selections often demarcated on the basis of administrative convenience. These scalar and holistic attributes of landscape represent the conceptual and geographical basis on which it can be mainstreamed into spatial planning.

In the context of landscape planning, the notion of scale has often been closely linked to that of the 'wider countryside', a term that has been used in various policy discourses. First, it has been used to refer to land beyond strictly protected reserves. Thus, some 'protected landscapes' such as the Anglo-Welsh Areas of Outstanding Natural Beauty (AONBs) have been referred to as the 'wider countryside', as they cover large areas and include settlements and diverse economic activities. Second, it has been applied to land beyond protected areas more generally, reflecting the fact that 'the rest' and not only 'the best' of the countryside have important functions and values. Third, in a similar fashion, it sometimes refers to the 'matrix' of land surrounding patches of ecological and visual significance, reflecting the importance of buffering key sites and enhancing their coherence and inter-connectedness. Consequently, scale has been related to arguments that both exceptional and unexceptional areas are important within the wider mosaic; increased landscape connection and cohesion can enhance the natural capital underlying critical services; and effective planning and management can spread the benefits of core protected areas.

However, whilst the 'scalar' properties of landscape have often been equated with geographical extent, we have briefly alluded to the fact that there are additional dimensions of 'landscape scale'. As previously noted, a temporal dimension is essential to the comprehension of historical or archaeological attributes, traditions and memories, and ecological dynamics. Further, it is important to include some indication of the degree of transformation of a landscape, and to understand the dynamic forces driving its change. Hence, scale is here related to three dimensions:[1]

1   a spatial dimension – the most commonly cited component of landscape scale,
     based on both a rational and an intuitive recognition of distinct physical units;
2   a temporal dimension – implying a continuum from the earliest human use of
     a landscape into the sustainable use by future generations; and
3   a modification dimension – from intensely urbanised areas, through farmland and
     other types of natural resource use, to pristine or wilderness areas, with some
     areas possessing such intense degrees of alteration that the landscape requires
     human assistance to accelerate the recovery of its 'regenerative' properties.

These dimensions are illustrated in Figure 2.1.

SPATIAL DIMENSION

Particularly in the landscape ecological literature, 'landscape scale' has entered
widespread parlance. As noted above, some landscape ecologists have referred to

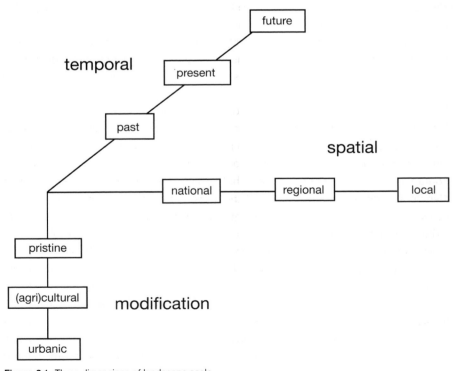

Figure 2.1 Three dimensions of landscape scale

the need to base analyses and strategies on zones that are at least 'several kilo-metres wide' (cf. Dramstad *et al.*, 1996; Forman and Godron, 1986; Forman, 1997). Differing views prevail on this but, based on pragmatic experience and from a multifunctional perspective, the 'several kilometres wide' principle holds consid-erable, if not always elegantly justifiable, appeal. However, the essential message is the need to consider the 'wider countryside' in terms of integrative landscape units, in addition to fragments of countryside singled out for supposed special qualities.

Many commentators have suggested that it is the spatial perspective that makes the landscape a distinctive organising framework. In most variants of 'the landscape' we refer to something framed at the human scale. However, this is revised upwards to reveal patterns from satellites, and downwards to reveal mosaics related to the life-spaces of meso- and micro-organisms. McPherson and DeStefano (2003), writing from an ecological perspective, identify landscape studies as being those undertaken at quite an extensive spatial scale: less exten-sive than the 'biome' (often continental) or 'biosphere' (global), but larger than (in descending order) the ecosystem, community, population, organism or cell.

Often, it is intuitively easy to recognise a 'scale factor' – for example, some landscapes are clearly distinguishable by their intimate and informal features whilst others comprise expansive tracts of montane wilderness. However, it is much more difficult to agree a definitive statement of what spatial 'scale' actually means, or whether landscapes nest within hierarchical spatial units. Three key perspectives may be used to gain an insight into this question.

First, we may note an *aesthetic* or *painterly* view in which the landscape is something that can be comprehended and organised into a meaningful whole by the human eye. Perhaps the most elegant expression of this is the framing of a landscape on an artist's canvas or in a photograph, though there is also an increas-ing tendency to use the landscape (both rural and urban) itself as a location for outdoor art. Artists, in this respect, help shape our aesthetic experience of the land's surface. A principal quality of this perspective is the notion of 'sublime', in which the landscape is imputed with qualities that transcend mundane experience. The landscape as framed represents a coherent space which can delight, inspire, evoke or disconcert in terms of its awe, harmony, associations or threats.

The painterly view of landscape is an extremely profound one that is difficult to relate to a rational planning approach, but is nonetheless at the heart of much of its instinctive appeal. In practice, much of our understanding and use of land-scapes is based on an intuitive visual grasp of their nature and extent. Moreover, eliciting people's responses to landscape change, and their involvement in spatial discourses and decisions, can be strongly aided by artistic and photographic land-scape representations (e.g. O'Riordan *et al.*, 1993).

Second a *physical geography* view has long prevailed, and is most closely associated with the Sauerian notion of landscape as a perceived segment of the earth's surface (Sauer, 1925). The idea of 'landform' is, to many scientists, synonymous with landscape, reflecting the influence of geology, fashioned by geomorphic processes, in controlling the essential appearance of land and strongly influencing soil type and vegetation cover. Within the physical geography perspective, the idea of a river basin or water catchment is a key organising principle.[2] It is one that divides the landscape into relatively self-contained units, separated by watersheds. Whilst these system boundaries are highly permeable, the watershed is nonetheless widely considered to impose a primary shape and functionality on the earth's surface.

Third, the *ecological* view has strongly influenced the whole enterprise of landscape scale planning. A major characteristic of this perspective is its use of landscape ecology metrics, discussed later in this chapter, to quantify spatial and topological physical attributes. Thus, as Botequilha Leitão and Ahern have noted:

> Scale is a key issue in sustainability planning. Due to the interdependencies of ecosystems, a planning approach is needed that examines a site in its broader context ... Landscape ecological concepts and applied metrics are likely to be useful to address the spatial dimension of sustainable planning.
>
> (2002: 68)

A particularly important notion alluded to in this statement is that of understanding the *site in context* (e.g. MacFarlane, 2000) – in other words, a landscape feature cannot be understood either visually or functionally in isolation from its wider environment. This principle can be applied to historic, social and economic perspectives as well as aesthetic and physical ones. The landscape ecological aspect of spatial scale has received so much attention in the literature that it merits separate attention in a subsequent section.

A widely attested feature of spatial scale is the phenomenon of 'nesting', or of small units with a fine-grain geometry sitting within coarser-grained ones. For example, in relation to 'seascapes', Hill *et al.* (2001) have proposed that there are 'national', 'regional' and 'local' scales. They define 'national units' as extensive sections of the coast with an overriding defining characteristic such as coastal orientation and landform, typically bounded by major headlands of national significance. Given their size – perhaps 100 km in length – they cannot be said to relate to visual criteria but rather are related to the orientation and topography of the coast. Various types of data are collated at this level as a context for the assessment of smaller scale units, and include the 'Zone of Visual Influence', unique or rare geomorphic or landscape features, major access points to the coast and the sea, marine and coastal recreation, and key policy designations. The authors define regional units as the appropriate working level for seascape assessment, based on regional headlands, islands or coastal features. Unlike national units, they are essentially visual, the determining factor usually but not always being shared inter-visibility. This level of assessment and evaluation is appropriate to the formulation of strategic and area-based planning policies on a county or sub-regional level, and to substantial coastal developments such as large offshore wind farms, oil or gas fields, or similar projects. Local units may be defined in more complex areas of coast, and typically deal with intimate or local areas of coast and sea. This type of detailed assessment is also appropriate to the impact appraisal of specific coastal or marine-based developments.

TEMPORAL DIMENSION

The second key dimension of landscape scale is that of 'time'. It is somewhat artificial to separate this out from 'space', as a key precept of landscape studies is that multifunctional systems are inherently in a state of flux, and thus temporal change and dynamism are fundamental to an understanding of present patterns and processes. However, this section considers the particular importance of understanding relationships between past, present and future in landscape.

Landscape units are important for their integrative properties not only in terms of synthesising spatial processes, but also of reflecting a present tension between a palimpsest of past inscriptions and a future arena of emergent nature–society relations. The permanence of the landscape 'present' is to some extent an illusion, and protectionist strategies should not attempt to fossilise it but, rather, should base prescriptions on a sound understanding of inherited features and stories, current dynamics and future potentials. Particularly in view of the pressure of change arising from urbanisation, deindustrialisation and globalisation, 'stability' in cultural landscapes is often superficial. Fairclough (2002), writing from an archaeological perspective, suggests that the present-day landscape should be seen as material culture, to be analysed, interpreted and read in order to explain both the past and the present.

The significance of time-depth has been well articulated in the European Pathways to the Cultural Landscape programme, conducted in nine countries between 2002 and 2003 (Clark et al., 2003). This comparative investigation by a group of archaeologists into culturally rich areas drew attention to six important ingredients of historic landscape character, which may be summarised as:

- *passage of time*, represented by the length of time reflected in an area's development;
- *change*, notably the importance of processes and the process of change itself;
- *multiple interpretations*, reflecting the complexity of landscape, as the product of a combination of many factors, posing ambiguities in interpretation;
- *the construction of nature*, in terms of the degree to which most landscapes – even deserted and ostensibly natural ones – are often more 'cultural' than they seem;
- *answers but more questions*, as perceptions of the 'meanings' associated with area can pose complex issues continually needing to be re-appraised; and
- *scale and magnitude*, such that, whilst past human actions have frequently modified whole landscapes, evidence for this often sits within individual sites.

Whilst archaeological and historical geography studies have mostly been concerned with artefacts and sites, more recently they have turned attention to the complex issue of the ways that historic features can accumulate to produce a 'landscape scale' effect. Traces left on the landscape by previous generations can obviously be associated with very different periods, and it is important not to confuse propinquity in space with proximity in time. However, we may assume that some landscapes are peculiarly rich either because they contain many relict features from the same period, or display a record of human progression by virtue of remains from successive periods. The realisation of a need to record and protect this phenomenon, and hopefully to integrate it with other landscape scale planning concerns, has been relatively recent.

The ways in which a historical/archaeological dimension can be mainstreamed into spatial planning are illustrated by two recent practices. First, in Europe, Historic Landscape Characterisation (HLC) has been developed progressively since the 1990s. Clark *et al.* (2004) suggest that a five-step 'enhancing and safeguarding' approach should build upon the initial HLC, comprising:

- *undertake survey* – identify historic heritage assets, i.e. archaeological sites, palaeo-environmental resources, built heritage and historic landscape;
- *conserve* – priority based on period, rarity, documentation, group value, survival/condition, fragility/vulnerability, diversity and future potential;
- *improve management* – encourage positive management, for example through agri-environment schemes;
- *avoid damage* – related to development, agriculture, etc.;
- *enhance interpretation*, whilst at the same time deflecting visitors from sensitive historic attributes.

Figure 2.2 'Time depth' in the landscape: extensive parts of Galloway (Scotland) are characterised by a
rich historical and archaeological record

They advocate the production of 'Historic Environment Action Plans' based on assessing character and analysing forces for change, leading to management strategies for conservation, enhancement or regeneration.

Second, the Countryside Council for Wales and Cadw (2003) have successfully developed a somewhat different approach through the 'Assessment of the Significance of the Impact of Development on Historic Landscape Areas on the Register of Landscapes of Historic Interest in Wales', known as 'ASIDOHL'. This draws upon the decision to identify distinct landscape areas whose character was deemed to derive heavily from their imprinted history, and to map and record them in a *Register* (CCW/Cadw, 2001). The first step in this method involves summarising the context of the proposed development. Next, the physical (direct) and non-physical (indirect, e.g. visual) impacts of the proposed development are identified, and these are measured against the footprint of the proposal and the main HLC Character Area on which it impinges. Then, the importance of the elements of the historic environment likely to be affected is established; this is inferred from the *Register* and its accompanying map and text-based HLC characterisations. Finally, overall impact is determined, based on pre-set criteria.

A particularly influential reflection on the treatment of the temporal dimension in landscapes has been provided by Adams (2003), whose case for 'future nature' rests on the well-established aim of striking a balance between the preservation of the best of the old and the creation of the new. Drawing an analogy from urban capital he notes that, whilst old buildings and townscapes are valued, it is also accepted that new buildings and new built environments can enhance the capital stock without necessarily needing to replace the old in a direct sense. This argument may be extended to the natural environment. Thus, whilst a degree of preservation is essential – for example, in relation to key biodiversity sites whose interest has taken centuries or millennia to develop – the old must be complemented by the new. Adams argues that, just as discourses about the conservation of the built environment have moved on from narrow debates about 'architectural heritage' to ones where new buildings are created and celebrated, so landscape planning needs to become receptive to well-modulated change. In this regard Adams argues that conservationists need to have the courage to build as well as defend, advocating a far more extensive and effective programme of creation and restoration of habitats and landscapes across the wider countryside.

In consequence, we might argue that the environment will display, in varying combination:

- *past nature* – the historical ecology of the landscape, reflecting a balance between natural vegetation cover and geomorphology, and representing a relatively 'low energy' style of landscape management;
- *present nature* – the current pattern of greater and lesser 'valued' land covers, of varying degrees of sustainability and distinctiveness, often subject to high-input farming and forestry; and
- *future nature* – the consciously or unintentionally deflected future pattern of land covers and their multifunctionality.

The role of future nature opens up possibilities of returning to more naturalistic designs in the management of our land and water spaces.

The current interest in 'future' landscapes can be related to four key factors. First, it is clear that simply 'holding the fort' in the face of strong external processes is not a large-scale option. In practice, landscapes would merely degenerate slowly if we sought exclusively to preserve them and failed to accommodate the inevitability of change. Thus, strict preservation is likely only to be successful in very particular settings. Second, we now widely acknowledge that some of our former land and river 'improvements' were, on balance, environmentally unsustainable, and there is interest in reverting some of them to a more 'natural', or at least less intensively controlled, condition – for example, undoing the effects of coniferisation on native deciduous woodlands or stripping the 'concrete overcoat' from stretches of river. Third, environmental conditions – notably climate-related – are themselves changing, and landscape intervention may in places be necessary to anticipate the consequences of change. 'Managed retreat' of parts of the coastline reflects this circumstance. Finally, some land-scapes are now so fragmented or damaged that conscious reconstruction is desirable, such as the need to re-imagine the urban fringe or to create community forests. However, these options all require the anticipation of how 'nature' might respond to intervention: a degree of unpredictability must be accepted here, both because of inherent uncertainties associated with environmental responses to anthropogenic and natural processes, and also because we are increasingly aware of the ethical problems of controlling nature through an excessively posi-tivistic style of conservation science. Consequently, we accept that there will be a 'future natural' which can to some extent be predicted and directed, but which will differ from 'past natural' and 'present natural' states to which planners often aspire (cf. Adams, 2003).

An illustration of the opportunity for future nature is provided by the Royal Society for the Protection of Birds' proposed programme of 'futurescapes' (RSPB, 2001). In this, they advocate that by 2020, some 160,000ha of the UK should be in 're-creation management' as heathland and downland, reedbed and other fresh water wetlands, heather moorland, woodlands and coastal wetlands, including mudflats and saltmarshes. Whilst supporting continued vigilance in protecting existing high-quality habitats, they argue for a complementary investment in large-scale habitat restoration, enhancing the viability of existing wildlife sites and increasing the habitat available for threatened species currently restricted to small, fragmented sites. The range of potential benefits accruing from such 'futurescapes' might include:

- *biodiversity* – alleviating pressure on threatened sites and species;
- *access* – providing additional open country habitats for public enjoyment;
- *health* – providing land for spiritual refreshment and physical activity;
- *education* – giving children more opportunities to experience nature and wild places;
- *local economies* – attractive landscapes benefit local economies through tourism and possibly inward investment, whilst habitat re-creation and man-agement themselves contribute to local employment;
- *reducing flood-risk* – working with nature rather than against it, for example through the creation of new wetlands to store floodwater, reducing the risk of flooding in urban areas;
- *addressing climate changes* – providing room for wildlife to move as lowland and southern areas of Britain become warmer and drier.

Inevitably the creation of 'future natural' entails a landscape scale approach rather than one solely restricted to local sites, important though these may be as part of the overall jigsaw.

THE MODIFICATION GRADIENT

Many writers on environmental systems have argued that, undisturbed, these achieve dynamic equilibrium or homeostasis, at least when viewed over certain time frames. Such a circumstance is not equivalent to 'unchanging'; rather, it implies an intact state in which natural flows of energy reproduce persistent physical and biotic conditions through fundamental processes. On different temporal and spatial scales, and in highly active environments, a more chaotic model might be appropriate; Naveh (2000), for example, promotes a non-equilibrium view of biosphere landscapes, based on Prigogine's theories of dissipative structures (e.g. Prigogine and Stengers, 1984). However, for many of the environment types and time frames addressed by landscape planners, dynamic equilibrium remains a useful abstraction. An extension of this argument is that plagioclimax systems – hybrid (people–nature) systems where natural conditions have been modified into semi-natural ones as a result of low intensity human management – can also become very stable, provided the management regimes of 'deflected stability' are maintained by a viable socio-economic infrastructure. Whilst these 'stable' models of landscape remain helpful for many management and planning purposes, it is important to recognise that, in natural systems, permanence is something of an illusion.

Given that this 'dynamic-but-persistent' state reflects the natural reproduction of essential 'life-support systems', it is also often considered to be an allegory for sustainable development. The position of a landscape on the modification gradient can, therefore, be indicative of its sustainability, or the degree of remediation involved in re-establishing sustainable conditions. Here, it is helpful to refer to Naveh's (2000) integrated approach to understanding environmental, ecological and human systems based on the 'self-organising' models associated with physico-chemical theories of dissipative structures, and biological models of catalytic networks of 'self-creating' living systems. He argues that these models have far-reaching implications for natural and semi-natural landscapes (*biosphere* landscapes in Naveh's terminology), which can be viewed as adaptive self-organising systems, internally regulated by natural information and having the capacity to maintain their organisation and structural integrity. This process of continuous self-renewal is termed *autopoiesis*. Applying these principles to other, more modified, landscapes Naveh identifies:

- *Traditional agro-ecotopes* which, although regulated and controlled by human cultural information, have still retained a great amount of their self-organising capacities and thus continue to behave as *regenerative systems* (Lyle, 1994).
- *Urban-industrial techno-ecotopes*, comprising human-made, artificial systems, driven by fossil and nuclear energy and their technological conversion into low-grade energy. Lacking multifunctionality and self-organising and regenerative capacities, they produce high outputs of entropy, waste and pollution.
- *High-input agro-industrial ecotopes* which, whilst still depending on photosynthetic energy, come close to 'throughput systems' and require high ecological and economic subsidies.

In essence, Naveh is identifying a modification gradient, in which landscapes become progressively less multifunctional or self-regenerative. East European landscape ecologists have described this trend as '*hemerobia*' – the degree to which land has been modified, fragmented and damaged. Bioregionalists have sometimes alluded to the purpose of planning as being that of promoting landscape conditions which are inherently autopoietic or regenerative.

A characteristic view of European landscape ecologists is that changes typically arise from *marginalisation* of less economic farmland and forests, and *intensification* of highly productive land (Jongman, 2002; Fry and Gustavsson, 1996), leading to *polarisation* of land use. Alongside polarisation is the concurrent process of fragmentation. Jongman (2002) illustrates this in relation to the urban fringe, where intensive agriculture used to be a mainstay but is now giving way to other functions such as horse keeping, garden centres and recreation, compounded by the construction of roads, railways and other linear industrial features. Whilst this results in greater diversity, the new elements are commonly described as being alien and hostile to existing structures, species and land uses. In less value-laden terms, we may propose that land use intensification and urbanisation tend to be associated with a decline in systems 'balance' and visual legibility, leading to landscape homogenisation through the diminution of regional difference and regenerative capacity. Antrop (2000, 2004) and Klijn and Vos (2000) similarly emphasise the key forces of polarisation between intensification and extensification, and an erosion of the distinction between urban and rural. In this perspective, new landscape elements and structures emerge which possess no link – and may even conflict – with the 'specificity of the place'.

In general, European commentators on landscape change draw attention to: the complexity, dynamism and frequent incoherence of the urban fringe; the difficulties of sustaining a suitable land management presence in the remoter areas; and the homogenising pressures upon the agricultural heartlands. They also emphasise the erosion of landscape structure and biodiversity as a continental phenomenon. Four key effects are thus recognised (Vos and Klijn, 2000):

- intensification and increasing scale of agricultural production, leading to habitat transformations;
- urban sprawl, growth of infrastructure and functional urbanisation;
- specific tourist and recreational forms of land use, particularly in coastal and montane regions;
- extensification of land use and land abandonment affecting remote areas with poor accessibility and less favourable and declining social and economical conditions.

Accessible landscapes, in particular, tend to be highly dynamic and multifunctional, but in the negative sense that a multiplicity of new landscape functions coexist in a more or less unrelated manner, creating a complex and highly fragmented mosaic of different forms of land cover and a dense transport infrastructure (Antrop and Van Eetvelde, 2000).

Two schemata depicting change and response can illuminate the modification gradient and its consequences for spatial planning of the landscape. One is the suggestion by McIntyre and Hobbs (1999) that a consideration of the relative degree of habitat destruction and modification provides a starting point for defining wider countryside objectives for planning purposes. Specifically, they draw attention to the processes of 'maintenance', 'improvement' and 'reconstruction' of the landscape ecological elements (core areas, corridors, etc.). The degree of alteration is deemed to derive from gradients of destruction and modification, the

Table 2.1 Landscape scale planning objectives related to landscape alteration level

Landscape planning objective	Landscape alteration level			
	Intact 10% destroyed Low level of modification	Variegated 10–40% destroyed Low–high modification	Fragmented 40–90% destroyed Low–high modification	Relictual 90% destroyed Mostly high modification
Maintenance Improvement	Matrix –	Matrix, Patches Connecting / Buffer	Fragments Fragments	– Fragments
Reconstruction	–	–	Connecting / Buffer	Buffer areas

Source: adapted from Watts, 2001, based on McIntyre and Hobbs, 1999 former resulting in loss of all structural vegetation features and loss of the majority of species, and the latter creating a more subtle texture of variation. The framework defines four distinct levels of habitat destruction, with 'intact' and 'relictual' landscapes representing the extremes, in which less than 10% or over 90% of the area of habitat is destroyed, respectively. In between these extremes, the matrix of a 'variegated' landscape is still formed by habitat, whereas in a 'fragmented' landscape, the matrix consists of 'destroyed habitat' (Table 2.1).

The second schema is that of Warnock and Brown (1998), echoed by Wood and Handley (2001) and elaborated by Simpson (2004), who draw attention to the importance of character and condition in defining landscape health and distinctiveness. These, they argue, are undermined by 'dysfunction', where land uses are introduced that are inappropriate to the landscape's functionality, and 'obsolescence', where the economic drivers that have created the landscape are losing their viability. In areas where serious damage has occurred to the landscape, restoration may be necessary, whereas in areas of strong character and robust functionality, a conservation strategy is frequently appropriate. Intermediate areas may require a blend of measures, including enhancement or strengthening, depending on whether functionality or character is the key concern, or whether trends are positive or adverse (Figure 2.3). Whilst studies of the landscape have often been criticised for being value-laden and implicitly nostalgic or conservative, Warnock and Brown's use of relatively neutral terms regarding character and functionality can help restrain our tendency towards subjective judgement.

LANDSCAPE ECOLOGY AND SPATIAL SCALE

As previously noted, perhaps the single most influential impetus behind the issue of 'scale' has come from landscape ecology. Many definitions have been advanced of this somewhat controversial subject, but a classic one is 'the study of structure, function and change in a heterogeneous land area composed of interacting ecosystems' (Forman and Godron, 1986: 594). Thus, theoretical landscape ecology investigates patterns and processes of changing landscapes, their origin, and how they influence each other (Golley and Bellot, 1991). A more recent definition states simply that landscape ecology is 'the study of the interactions between the temporal and spatial aspects of a landscape and its flora, fauna and cultural components'.[3] However, the subject also incorporates the study of water movements, particularly insofar as these impact on ecosystem properties. An understanding of ecological and hydrological patterns and processes not only reveals the complex web of natural interdependencies, but also enrols economic and social systems as these strongly

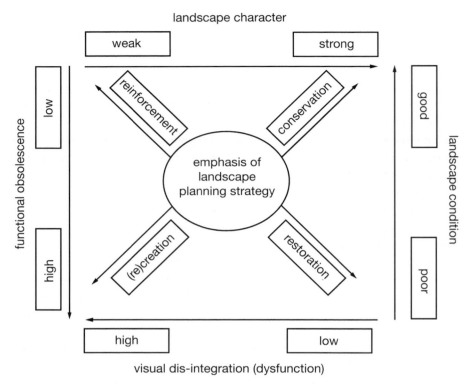

Figure 2.3 Relating landscape strategy to landscape status and trends

Source: adapted from: Warnock and Brown, 1998; Wood and Handley, 2001

modify the energy and materials inputs into cultural landscapes. Applied landscape ecology uses this knowledge to investigate environmental problems that have a spatial component, and to plan for landscape change in the future.

Landscapes are typically prone to a variety of disturbances – whether from natural or human sources – and, if not too severe, these result in heterogeneous patterns of diverse but complementary habitat. Heterogeneity is generally considered a positive attribute in supporting biodiversity as it not only provides conditions for a range of species with different requirements, but also supports the lifecycle requirements of species whose needs differ over time (e.g. insects whose food requirements differ between larva and imago phases). Where interventions (normally human-induced) become excessively frequent or destructive, however, habitats tend to become 'fragmented', which results in unfavourable ecological conditions. The breakpoint between a heterogeneous landscape and a fragmented one may be difficult to establish precisely.

A major reason why practitioners have become interested in landscape ecology is that it offers a powerful perspective on why, despite a century of scientifically robust nature conservation practice and increasingly strict planning and pollution controls, biodiversity has continued to decline sharply. Deterioration is often attributed to insidious problems associated with habitats becoming increasingly fragmented into isolated patches which are too small to be ecologically viable in the long term. Thus, whilst the classical approach to nature protection has been to 'ring fence' sites and manage them for key species, this does not address the 'wider countryside' problem of sites and species suffering from encroachment by increasingly hostile land uses.

Landscape ecologists are particularly interested in understanding the landscape as a heterogeneous mosaic of physical, hydrological and vegetation features that are of an appropriate functionality, size and condition to support lifecycle functions of endemic species. Thus, applied landscape ecology addresses three main challenges:

- to reduce the extent to which habitats and landscapes are fragmented into small areas by, for example, roads, intensive agriculture and urban development;
- to reduce the environmental impacts of human activities, such as pollution and noise; and
- to ensure as far as possible that human activities and land uses are compatible with the conservation needs of ecosystems, habitats, species and landscapes – for example, through appropriate forms of agriculture and forestry.

In so doing, applied landscape ecology typically seeks to protect or re-establish an ecological network comprising three general elements:

- 'core areas' to provide the particular mosaic of environmental conditions to conserve important ecosystems, habitats and species populations;
- 'corridors' to interconnect the core areas, although the rationale for these increasingly relies on a broader justification than supposed opportunities for dispersal and migration; and
- 'buffer zones' to protect the network from the potentially damaging impacts of activities outside the network, such as pollution or land drainage.

(CoE, 1998)

In order to effect this, a 'gap analysis' (Jennings, 2000) is often undertaken to identify missing links in the ecological infrastructure.

Given the level of complexity in understanding the multiple functions associated with patterns and processes at the landscape scale, researchers have
searched for some simplifying generalisations (Table 2.2). At a basic level, as previously noted, much of the justification for a landscape scale arises from humans'
intuitive grasp of visual 'set pieces': thus, simply being able to see the landscape
as a totality, notably through the advent of satellite imagery and geographic information systems, has greatly aided our comprehension. For example, Southworth *et
al.* (2002) mapped tropical forests in terms of spatial extent and processes of
change, and used remotely sensed imagery to discern landscape pattern, function
and change. In their study of forestlands in Western Honduras, a combination of
ground data, socio-economic information and satellite-derived classifications of
land cover enabled them to infer trends in landscape ecological patterns and to
relate the phenomena of reforestation and deforestation to social processes. This
study illustrates our recent capacity to 'see' whole landscapes through modern
information technology – visual perspectives which were not previously possible
but which have given a major impetus to the practice of landscape scale planning.

Landscape ecologists have also sought to generalise about processes and
patterns in the wider countryside by postulating general principles and summary
metrics. There have been numerous scientific reviews of these practices and much of
their underlying theory remains contested. For planning purposes, it is helpful to focus
on those core concepts over which there is relative consensus. Thus, whilst the scientific foundations are often controversial – for example, there is little direct evidence
of the widespread use of linear habitats as movement corridors – we are reasonably
safe in assessing some key arguments. First, lifecycle processes need to be sustained.
These comprise activities such as pollination, reproduction, feeding and migration,
and they need to be considered at the appropriate scale, which might require biological and hydrological connections over a large area. Further, populations in different core areas may interact in terms of their lifecycle processes; for example,
interbreeding between populations in two or more core areas may be essential to
maintain genetic diversity, otherwise isolated populations may become less robust
as a consequence of 'genetic drift'. This process may lead to the emergence of a
metapopulation (i.e. a 'population of populations') where local populations of a
species interact with each other in a persistent manner. Clearly, this requires a
landscape to be configured in ways that allow exchange between groups.

Moreover, a functional landscape should display permeability and porosity.
Core areas and corridors are surrounded by 'matrix' habitat, which favours or
inhibits their functions to a greater or lesser extent. If species are to cross the
matrix to behave as metapopulations or to satisfy their lifecycle processes, then
either it must be 'permeable' in terms of being reasonably conducive to traversal

and survival, or 'porous' in terms of having smaller areas of suitable habitat which serve as 'stepping stones'. The matrix is further enhanced if network connections are present, as it is generally considered desirable to join core areas by corridors, which may serve to increase an area's 'connectedness' (extent to which features are physically joined up) and 'connectivity' (degree to which corridors actually assist functions such as foraging and migration). Whilst there is very limited evidence that corridors *per se* demonstrably and uniquely assist lifecycle processes, especially in heterogeneous fine-grain landscapes where movement is relatively easy for mobile species, they do appear to perform several valuable roles. In practice, a key value of 'corridors' is that they frequently comprise relictual vestiges of formerly widespread habitat types, which can be used as nuclei for landscape restoration and biodiversity recovery.

Intensively exploited landscapes often display fragmentation, where patches of semi-natural habitat become progressively diminished and isolated. This creates several problems:

• a patch of habitat in which a species has become locally extinct cannot easily be recolonised by another local population of the same species;
• individual animals may not have access to a large enough area of habitat;
• migratory animals may be unable to move to those areas where they would normally stay for part of the year;
• genetic exchange between different local populations may be impeded;
• in a period of changing environmental conditions (e.g. climate change) it may be difficult for species to migrate to locations more suited to their 'range', or encounter some 'elbow room' in which to perform local coping strategies.

As previously noted, fragmentation should not be confused with heterogeneity, although the two are superficially similar insofar as they describe landscapes broken down into sub-components displaying features of core and matrix. Fragmented landscapes will tend towards visual and ecological incoherence; heterogeneous landscapes will tend to contain habitat patches which are complementary in the ways they support species' requirements, especially in relation to species' changing needs at different stages of their lifecycle (Selman, 1999).

Landscape ecology helps us to comprehend the landscape in ways which allow us to plan and manage its change without being overwhelmed by its infinite complexity and variability. Scientists have taken its general principles one step further and produced a range of summary metrics and geometric analyses as a consistent basis for analysing and designing landscape structures. Thus, McGarigal and Marks (1995) have reported how metrics provide information about the

---

**TABLE 2.2 SELECTED PHENOMENA WITH WIDE APPLICATION IN
LANDSCAPE STUDIES**

- *Connectedness* – a fundamental pattern, reflecting the extent to which important patches are spatially joined up.
- *Connectivity* – a fundamental process in landscape ecology involving movement of animals, plants or people through landscapes.
- *Corridors* – increase the flow of individuals between resource patches or suitable habitat, and contribute to the infrastructure of animals, plants and people.
- *Nodes* – important meeting places which have significance for the alternative ways individuals can move around the landscape.
- *Habitat supplementation and complementation* – ways in which individuals and populations sustain themselves with necessary resources in fragmented landscapes.
- *Heterogeneity* – a pattern property that ensures a wide range of resources to organisms in small-scale landscapes.
- *Continuity* – an aspect of the time depth of cultural heritage interests of landscapes and important for the species that live there.
- *Size and shape of habitat patches* – important variables affecting population viability and inter-patch movement.
- *Scale issues* – important to landscape ecology and landscape archaeology in respect of both spatial and temporal processes.

Source: Fry, 2004, modified

---

contents of a mosaic, notably in terms of the two basic components of *composition* and *configuration*. Composition metrics measure landscape characteristics such as proportion, richness, and evenness of different species or dominance by one or few species, and also diversity. Landscape configuration relates to spatially explicit characteristics of land cover, namely those associated with patch geometry or with the spatial distribution of patches. Many measures, from very simple to highly sophisticated, have been proposed as summaries of spatial properties but, based on an analysis of several landscape ecological studies, Botequilha Leitão and Ahern (2002) identified a core set of indicators to describe landscapes and plans, and to improve communication between planners and ecologists (Table 2.3). They considered that metrics could relate to several fundamental ecological processes of concern to planners – notably, loss of landscape diversity, fragmentation and disturbance – and were particularly useful in comparing the consequences of alternative planning options.

Landscape complexity can also be simplified and comprehended through generalised measures obtained from fractal geometry. Wu (2004) notes that

---

**TABLE 2.3 KEY LANDSCAPE METRICS FOR ASSISTING
COMMUNICATION BETWEEN PLANNERS AND
ECOLOGISTS**

Landscape composition metrics

- patch richness
- class area proportion
- patch number and density
- patch size

Landscape configuration metrics

- patch shape (perimeter-to-area ratio)
- edge contrast
- patch compaction
- nearest neighbour distance
- contagion

Source: Botequilha Leitão and Ahern, 2002, modified

---

spatial heterogeneity exhibits various patterns at different scales, and thus that patterns have distinctive 'operational scales' at which they can be best characterised (e.g. Lam and Quattrochi, 1992; Urban *et al.*, 1987). In a sense, this reveals how landscape is 'seen' by different organisms, and is a sophisticated insight into non-human perceptions and use of landscape.

If we assume that, within a particular space, there is some sort of regular and repeated pattern, then a 'fractal dimension' can be obtained summarising the nature of the pattern. In a heterogeneous landscape, we assume (hopefully correctly!) that characteristic physical and ecological features tend to recur in a non-random way that can be utilised by creatures living in that space. In its simplest terms, fractal mathematics can be thought of as a method of understanding self-similarity within patterns. A normal way of specifying a self-similar object is by using the exponent of the number of self-similar (or scale symmetric) pieces with magnification factor N into which the figure may be broken. For example, a square may be subdivided into N^2 pieces – thus, if the magnification factor is 3, the square will be subdivided into nine smaller squares. The definition of the fractal dimension of a self-similar object is then:

$$\text{fractal dimension} = \frac{\log (\text{number of self - similar subdivisions})}{\log (\text{magnification factor})}$$

The fractal dimension is a measure of the complexity of a self-similar figure. Much of the attraction of fractal geometry has been that it can be used to generate patterns which appear to be very similar to those found in nature, and embraces the property of 'recursive' design where scaled, self-similar patterns naturally occur, such as in branching trees or orders of streams in river catchments.

Confirmation of scale effects can be found in a number of studies, and these typically draw attention to the need for care in selecting the 'grain' and extent of the landscape. Thus, important effects will only be detected if an appropriate area of coverage and level of resolution are selected. Wu (2004), for instance, examined data from four different and heterogeneous landscape types – boreal forest, two contrasting landscapes from the US Great Basin, and an urban/agricultural landscape. An interesting if tentative finding was that landscapes do, within certain ranges, tend to display self-similarity. The various measures behaved differently in various respects, but tended to fall into three types: those which appeared to exhibit consistent scaling relations over a range of scales; those that displayed staircase-like responses with changing scale; and those that lacked any consistent scaling relations. Similar views are expressed by Bellehumeur and Legendre (1998), who note the importance of addressing size of sampling units and extent of area over which physical, geological, environmental and biotic processes operate.

A further important ecological reason to consider landscape scale is that 'thresholds' may exist below which loss of habitat cover precipitates extinctions, or above which regeneration of habitat cover provides conditions for species recovery (Fahrig, 2001). For example, work by Peterken (2002) points to landscapes behaving as if they were wooded once tree cover reaches 30% – this being the cover at which connectivity appears to occur in random simulations of landscape pattern. Elsewhere, Wiens (1997) has observed that landscapes covered by more than 60% of habitat are, in operational terms, not fragmented since they comprise a continuous cluster of habitat. In a study of the responses of woodland birds to landscape pattern in Victoria, Australia, Bennett and Radford (2004) found clear declines in species richness of woodland birds as wooded cover decreased, and that there was evidence for a threshold response, with a steep decline in richness in landscapes having less than 10% tree cover. However, these results were very generalised and the authors pointed to the need for further research into the demographic status of populations in modified rural environments, to assist in planning for their long-term persistence.

Studies using computer-based Neutral Landscape Models (NLMs) to simulate landscape pattern, however, indicate that the more 'realistic' the simulation, the less it tends to display simple thresholds. Thus, whilst 'random' landscape models suggest the possibility of simple threshold rules, more realistic simulations – based on fractal landscapes with high spatial correlation – display complex variations due to habitat quality and surrounding land uses. Thresholds probably exist, but are not susceptible to neat generalisation once all the complexities of dynamic landscapes have been considered. Further, some researchers consider that where thresholds are transgressed, biodiversity declines may be delayed as species 'cling on' in unfavourable conditions – hence, if restoration is proposed, a significantly higher percentage cover than the apparent threshold may be necessary to create conditions conducive to species recovery (Latham *et al.*, 2004; Ray *et al.*, 2004; Watts and Griffiths, 2004).

Although the literature has tended to emphasise vegetation cover, an equally important scalar arranging principle within landscape ecology is that of hydrology and the water catchment. Thus, the degree of wetness or dryness of an area, and the presence of secure and healthy water supply, strongly affects its vegetation, land uses and settlement patterns. Processes of flooding, sedimentation and erosion are major influences on the changing appearance and human occupancy of landscapes, often contributing to landscapes being perceived as 'hazardous' or 'hospitable'. Further, the processes of sediment and chemical transfer in both surface and ground waters greatly influence the nutrient status of habitats, often far from the initial source of inputs.

In terms of anthropic change, one of the most striking impacts on lowlands in many countries has been the systematic lowering of surface water tables – by techniques ranging from bankside planting of thirsty tree species such as willows, to sophisticated arterial pumping schemes – and associated straightening of river channels. As part of this taming process (Purseglove, 1989), many lowland rivers have been transformed in terms of the increasing dominance of linear flows over lateral flows: where once there would have been marshy fringes with complex patterns of rivulets flowing towards the main watercourse, now there is generally a sharp margin between the arterial channel and valley land.

River studies typically adopt a 'fluvial hydrosystem' approach in which the focus is on the downstream variation of flow, temperature, channel form and biotic communities, and fluxes of energy and material from the watershed towards the sea. By contrast, Petts and Amoros (1996) argue that, instead of viewing river ecosystems as simple linear features, they should be viewed as three-dimensional systems with longitudinal, lateral and vertical transfers of energy, material and biota. These systems can be understood in terms of a hierarchy of scales: from the primary unit of the overall drainage basin; through functional 'sectors' represented by sections of the basin with characteristic regimes of flow, water quality and sediment; to functional 'sets' of characteristic ecological units, such as pond, gravel bar and marsh; and functional 'units' of typical animal and plant communities.

These scalar properties of river basins are a principal reason why the water catch-ment has often been adopted as a 'natural' unit for landscape scale planning.

Various studies (e.g. Petts and Amoros, 1996; Ureña and Ollero, 2001) have drawn attention to the importance of the river margin zone in landscape scale plan-ning. A great deal of floodplain management, often in response to discharge and sediment problems associated with human land use in the catchment, has been directed at the progressive modification of channels by narrowing and straighten-ing. Hence, the 'riparian belt' – the interface between the aquatic and terrestrial ecosystems and the zone in which the river path moves – has particular signifi-cance. Vegetation in this zone is critical in producing a buffer or filter that can reduce the destructive potential of fluvial processes, so that land uses need to be compatible with lateral movements of the channel and with the maintenance of marshlands and riparian vegetation.

The importance of surface- and ground-water systems to landscape ecology has been noted by Ward *et al.* (2002), who argue that landscape refers to a spa-tially heterogeneous area, and that the riverine landscape or river corridor corres-ponds to the surface area composed of interacting terrestrial and aquatic units that are directly influenced by the river (i.e. aquatic habitats, floodplain surface and riparian zone). It is also complemented by a fluvial 'stygoscape' – a subterranean equivalent of landscape composed of aquifers beneath alluvial floodplains (Ward, 1997). In this perspective, strong links exist between spatiotemporal heterogeneity and hydrodynamic processes, including interactions between surface waters and ground waters (Table 2.4). Ward *et al.* (2002) consider there to be three phases of hydrological connectivity between the river channel and its floodplain:

- *disconnection phase* – in which distinct water bodies characterise the river-ine landscape, and are dominated by internal (autogenic) processes;
- *connection phase* – where river and floodplain are connected via subsurface pathways, and large amounts of nutrient-rich ground water enter and are retained in the floodplain, frequently stimulating algal production; and
- *surface connection phase* – when the river and its floodplain are intercon-nected by surface water, allowing hydrological exchange processes to domi-nate and high levels of particular matter to be transported.

Understanding these processes across the riverine landscape is important for two particular reasons in landscape ecology: they are critical to the success of river restoration strategies; and they strongly influence the supply of moisture and nutri-ents to habitat patches, even where hydrological connectivity may not be evident from the surface.

**TABLE 2.4 SOME KEY CHARACTERISTICS OF RIVER
LANDSCAPES**

- Floodplains and alluvial aquifers are integral functional components of river corridors.
- River corridors are non-equilibrium systems and their functional processes depend on natural disturbance regimes.
- Natural river corridors are characterised by multidimensional environmental gradients.
- Connectivity between landscape elements is crucial for sustaining functional processes.
- Hydrarch and riparian successional processes increase habitat heterogeneity, thereby contributing to the high levels of species diversity in intact river corridors.
- Effective conservation and restoration efforts require a strong conceptual foundation and a thorough understanding of natural processes.
- Ecosystem management of damaged river corridors involves reconstituting disturbance regimes and reconnecting landscape elements.
- Once functional processes are re-established, the river itself becomes the agent of restoration, so that natural processes are self-sustaining (i.e. 'letting the river do the work').

Source: based on Ward *et al.*, 2002

BIOGEOGRAPHIC UNITS – A BASIS FOR LANDSCAPE SCALE GOVERNANCE?

A widely advocated approach to landscape scale planning is to steward resources on the basis of biogeographic units: that is, segments of the earth's surface defined, not on the basis of traditional political and administrative boundaries, but according to intrinsic environmental properties. Very often, these units will also be associated with social traditions such as building styles, farming practices and food products, and may well be recognisable through literary and touristic images. There are three main reasons for the popularity of biogeographic units in landscape scale planning. First, natural systems, such as water catchments, often form logical units for many resource management decisions, and focusing on an integrative landscape unit may help reduce fragmentation of environmental processes and of policy delivery. Second, neither wildlife species nor hydrological systems recognise administrative boundaries, and their natural geographical range and extent must be taken into account in spatial planning, or even serve as its framework. Finally, people develop particular attachments to landscapes on the basis of both physical and cultural factors, and so may possibly identify with distinctive biogeographic spaces more than with, say, local government districts. Approaches based on these principles are often referred to as 'bioregional', and their underlying philosophies range from scientific arguments regarding energy and material fluxes, to psychological and religious grounds associated with attunement and responsibility towards nature (e.g. McGinnis, 1999; Thayer, 2003).

When extended to spatial planning, this line of reasoning has two key implications: first, that landscape governance is best addressed above the level of individual sites or land holdings; and second, that governance issues may more effectively be framed in terms of 'natural' units than traditional political-administrative ones. This logic is not, however, completely at variance with standard practice. The property of nesting, previously noted in relation to the general issue of landscape scale, is also important to landscape governance, as it ties in well with the principle of subsidiarity, where responsibility is delegated to the lowest appropriate level. Thus, 'nesting' of spatial units occurs in normal approaches to governance, and policy is developed and delivered at a range of levels, such as supra-nation, nation, sub-nation/region/state/province/territory, district or county, commune or 'parish', and neighbourhood (e.g. Bürgi et al., 2004). Thus, landscape scale planning can often be matched to appropriate tiers of governance, even where a strictly bioregional approach is not adopted.

Meadowcroft (2002) has critiqued a strictly bioregional approach to governance units, arguing that the notion of 'scale' is not simply a spatial one: environmental disturbances and policy interventions are social phenomena, so that scale dimensions relate not only to physical processes but also to social structures, practices and understandings. Meadowcroft emphasises two simultaneous processes affecting scale within environmental governance, closely mirroring our earlier observations about the tensions between globalisation and localisation. First, there is a scale-shift upwards in terms of the way in which we grasp and address complex environmental processes, and in the scale of social reforms envisaged. Thus, relatively recent concerns such as global warming and transnational ecological networks are leading to large-scale, multipartite solutions. Second, there is simultaneously a downward scaling, reflecting an increasing diversity, specificity and complexity of initiatives at more local levels. Furthermore, the initiatives to address environmental challenges tend to be layered on top of pre-existing structures and processes, rather than serving as replacements for them. Hence, he argues that there can be no simple redrawing of bioregional units for environmental governance, but instead advocates two types of 'pluralism':

- *a pluralism of institutions* – where different sorts of structures, with different scale pre-occupations, are charged with responsibilities for environmental governance; and
- *a pluralism of participating groups* – because groups experience environmental problems in different ways.

In practice, this closely mirrors the situation that has been emerging with biogeographic units such as Natural Areas, Character Areas, and similar schemes discussed in Chapter 4.

Whilst framing decisions within biogeographic units holds many attractions for landscape scale planning, a purist 'bioregional' stance may not be justifiable. Many landscape issues derive from an 'imaginary' geography – that is, they are products of our culture and perceptions, and do not exist independently of human thought and activity. Consequently, we must be cautious about relating them too inflexibly to 'intrinsic' environmental units. Further, a key argument for landscape scale planning is that the landscape offers a medium within which multiple activities and processes, and through which policy measures, may be integrated. Thus, it is the integrative potential of a landscape scale approach in terms of thematically and spatially joined-up action, rather than a strict adherence to landscape units, which is important. Nevertheless, biogeographic units can, as we shall see subsequently, provide a compelling basis for many aspects of spatial governance and are likely to exert an increasing influence.

CONCLUSION

Scale is a fundamental attribute in adopting a landscape-based approach to planning. Arguments for its adoption may be either elegant or pragmatic. Most fundamentally, some writers argue that the environment has self-organising properties, and these are likely to produce natural 'scale effects', with fundamental processes replicating themselves over consistent spatial ranges. Approaches such as fractal analysis can help identify the scales over which natural phenomena characteristically recur. In terms of achieving more sustainable landscapes, there is a strong argument that we ought to manage our own land use activities within spatial units that resonate with the self-organising properties of nature. This has led some proponents to argue for a bioregional approach to planning.

Equally, awareness of the temporal dimension to landscape planning is valuable in understanding the nature, direction and intensity of change. It also requires from us a degree of humility in recognising that we do not control the landscape, we can merely give nudges in the direction of what we believe to be the 'future natural'. Awareness of our current place in the long trajectory of landscape evolution reminds us of the importance of sustainability – of accommodating current needs, whilst having respect for our received heritage and our future shared space.

However, some of the writings about landscape scale have been rather assertive, and there is contention over what constitutes an appropriate size of planning unit. Some authors have suggested that 'several kilometres' is sufficient, whilst others indicate the 'region' as the appropriate level. In practice, we can argue that scale effects are likely to be nested, both in terms of natural processes and political-administrative units. Thus, whilst some landscape phenomena may most appropriately be considered at transnational or city-region levels, others can be analysed and managed more at a district or neighbourhood scale. It seems likely that future planning approaches will seek to address particular landscape objectives at different spatial administrative tiers, and that the delivery of some policies will be based on 'natural' units rather than traditional administrative ones. In this respect, whilst the identification of a planning scale appropriate to the resolution of particular issues – such as habitat reconnection – helps us to plan 'for' landscape, the use of 'natural units' as a substitute for or complement to political-administrative ones creates opportunities to deliver multiple sustainable development objectives 'through' landscapes.

Having addressed the central issue of 'scale', the next chapter considers another fundamental topic which will influence the agenda and practices of landscape-centred approaches – that of the social capital underlying cultural landscapes. Clearly, the character and condition of cultural spaces will be profoundly influenced by the past, present and future actions of people; yet contemporary planning is often conducted in a top-down manner, reflecting the selective preferences and values of particular social interests, and sometimes even implying that landscapes are better when unpopulated. Chapter 3 therefore looks at the links between people and place, particularly in relation to the ways in which we 'read' the stories underlying landscapes, attach ourselves to cherished localities, and acquire preferences for particular environments. It considers how these might vary depending on whether we inhabit a place, or 'gaze' on it from outside. It then touches on the complex questions surrounding human life and wildlife within landscapes, and the extent to which these lead to similar or divergent environmental preferences.

CHAPTER 3

PEOPLE AND LANDSCAPES

INTRODUCTION

In the Welsh language, there is an almost untranslatable notion of 'bro', referring to a quite extensive area of land with which people identify through shared endeavours and traditions, and is thus a landscape setting which reflects 'people' as much as 'place'. This ancient term reflects admirably the intuitive and instinctive quest for identity, distinctiveness and character at the landscape scale.

As Muir (2000) has noted, landscapes consist of places, and places have strong existential meanings, containing the memory of the past history of the land. In a similar vein, Lowenthal (1997) has argued that rural landscapes can be seen as '*lieux de mémoire*', places of collective memory. The 'identity' of a landscape can be seen to mean two closely related ideas: the visual identity which a professional or outsider might see, based on distinctive natural and acquired features; and a strong association between people and their terrain, so that insiders identify with a somewhat fluid but nonetheless definite area. A recognisable landscape is invariably associated with 'stories' – not only in the sense of legends and tales, but also in terms of underlying explanations of the landscape's condition and trajectory.

However, as we have noted, contemporary pressures are leading to the homogenisation of cultural landscapes, eroding the prospects for people to identify with distinctive and cherished localities. In this process, landscapes of multiple meanings are being displaced by ones of limited meaning or function, or by incoherent landscapes of diverse but confused meanings and transient functions. Antrop (2000) has commented that new landscape elements are often visually similar regardless of their location and they thus lack locational specificity, so that the history and memory of places are gradually erased and the *genius loci* lost. Once the links with the past have been broken, it is rare for a new distinct identity to emerge; indeed, Vos and Klijn (2000) suggest that new landscapes can actually produce sentiments of alienation.

From the mid-20th century onwards, it could be argued that changes have been so profound and rapid that the gradual sedimentation of locally distinctive character has not been possible. Instead, communities have become more mobile and diverse, local economies have been absorbed into national and global markets and their enterprises subsumed by external capital. Also, intensive technology and the diffuse effects of artificially introduced chemicals have impacted environments. In our practices, knowledges, moralities and reference points, we have become attuned to global cultures, so that people and places become progressively more alike. In particular, landscape elements have been subjected to intense transformations which remove their distinctive properties, whilst communities have acquired universal and predominantly urban outlooks in their attitudes and preferences. The net result has been a homogenisation of people and place, impelled by seemingly relentless and irresistible forces. A loss of local population, local knowledge and stories, local production and distribution facilities, and local breeds of animals and crops have matched the rapid erosion of characteristic landscape features.

Landscape planning has traditionally been concerned with the designation of valued areas so that special qualities can be safeguarded, whilst having regard to localities' social and economic vibrancy. There has been a noticeable shift in emphasis in recent years away from preservation, towards the promotion of sustainable development and a greater recognition of the needs of host communities. This must be balanced by noting that rural populations have long been in a state of flux, so that 'local' people are more heterogeneous and possess many attributes that are similar to those of 'outsider' professionals.

Many landscape plans (especially those of landscape ecologists) have been criticised for being 'people-less'. At the same time, development plans have often been accused of superficiality in relation to landscape issues. New practices of spatial planning have the potential to remedy these deficiencies by mediating measures for community, economy and ecology within areas with which people identify. In essence, this can be thought of as the sustainable development of 'peopled' landscapes. This chapter, therefore, considers a number of recurrent facets of the ways in which we inhabit, steward, value and visit landscapes. These are:

- what people see in landscapes – gazes, symbols and stories – and why understanding these is important to spatial planning;
- the paradoxical but creative tension between people's identification with the local, whilst inexorably and often willingly being mainstreamed into the global;
- people's preferences for particular landscape settings, and whether these are biologically or culturally determined;
- the differing perceptions and values held by those who are 'inside' or 'outside' a landscape;

- the relationships between people and nature, and how these elide within the hybrid space of landscape; and
- the social capital underlying landscape, leading to subsequent consideration (Chapter 5) of how stakeholders and the wider public may be enrolled into landscape designs, decisions and usage.

Landscape scale planning has generally centred on expert analyses of physical and ecological properties. If the landscape scale is to become a medium for practising spatial planning, we need to recognise the ways in which people relate to, and see themselves as part of, imageable physical spaces. It is clear that different people see different things in landscapes, and that landscape planners need to be sensitised to these diverse meanings and associations.

READING AND SEEING

Understanding the 'story' of a cultural landscape is central to our ability to comprehend its distinctive character. This story changes over time, and a succession of stories may be inscribed in a landscape, awaiting interpretation by those skilled in reading their inscriptions. Typically, the stories relate to people's relationship with nature, and to living within and visiting distinctive spaces. Thus, landscapes possess 'semiotic' properties – in other words, they contain signs in them that can be decoded by those with intimate knowledge of them. The capacity for a landscape's stories to be read may be thought of as its 'legibility'. Distinctive character thus derives not only from natural attributes such as relief and drainage, but also from the imprints that have been left by previous and present occupants. If impacts on the land have been too intense and destructive, previous traces become largely illegible, leaving only the most recent story to be read; if ecosystems and hydrosystems have been overwhelmed and residualised by human activity, the principal story to be read is that of unsustainable development.

The historical inscriptions in a landscape largely reflect people's need to gain a living from relatively nearby resources, supplemented in some cases by seasonally exploited resources (such as summer pastures) connected by habitual tracks. In order for this to occur, economies and communities needed to be reasonably self-contained and stable – notwithstanding the effects of migration, trade, epidemics, famine, climate change, technological innovation, war and political enterprise. Whilst Muir (2003) has shown how change is endemic in its nature and unpredictable in its consequences, its rate normally has been gradual enough for each phase to leave legible traces in the palimpsest. Accumulated effects have generally bequeathed landscapes of great interest, and frequently of considerable beauty.

Consequently, landscapes are considered to possess 'associative' values – the importance and signification that people attach to them. These values need to be understood, accommodated and nurtured. Planners need to be able to read landscape, not merely as an exploitable resource, but also as a dialectic between the identities, values and needs of individuals, and the potentials and capacities of the physical environment. This dynamic exchange between individuals and their environment results in a process of 'culturation'. Buchecker et al. (2003) considered contemporary processes of culturation within a rural district, and found that, whilst most residents cared about their local landscape, they did not feel responsible for its development and delegated the whole responsibility to local authorities. The authors suggested various reasons for this trend, but particularly noted alienation (a move from agricultural economy to urbanisation), and people's growing desire for individual identity. As a partial response, they proposed a more systematic involvement of residents in local landscape development through participatory measures.

LOCAL AND GLOBAL

Giddens (1991) has observed two simultaneous tendencies in contemporary society: increasing atomisation, so that society is becoming endlessly fragmented; and increasing homogenisation, so that we lack memory or solidarity, and clutch at new identities, typically derived from media images. Yet despite the seemingly inexorable trend towards a global culture based on the power of the image, there remain strong sentiments of place attachment. People appear to crave locational difference, and continue to view the countryside as a desirable place for life and leisure. This search for identity has most comprehensively been examined by Castells (2003), whose exploration of the tension between globalisation and localisation is central to the phenomenology of modern cultural landscapes. Castells notes how late-modern society combines the two extremes of extensionality and intentionality, namely, globalising influences and personal disposition. In other words, we might say that our information and outlooks are becoming internationalised, and our conduct and standards are based on (individual) preference and convenience rather than (collective) traditions and community norms; contemporary culture and economy thus draw simultaneously on personal identities and global phenomena. This produces a 'dialectical interplay' between the local and the global. Thus, Castells and Giddens aptly describe an intriguing paradox which is central to this book: that whilst we cannot deny the inevitability (and, in many respects, desirability) of globalising trends, we still display a craving for local identity and community. In negotiating our lifestyle choices, there is a pervasive tendency to reconstitute our living, working and leisure spaces based on familiar settings of community and locality. Recapturing 'legibility' at the landscape scale is a signal expression of late-modern search for individual and collective identity, and it represents a key endeavour in spatial governance and making distinctive places.

The link between legible landscapes and identity is a strong one, and operates at various levels, including the individual, the community, the region and the nation. The notion of identity is, however, complex. Castells (2003) has persuasively argued for a threefold distinction between legitimising identity, resistance identity, and project identity. These refer respectively – in brief and over-simplified terms – to our attachment to the official expressions of state and society, the use of protest based on a sense of common but vulnerable interest, and collective engagement in reform measures (often related to belief or values). If globalising pressures are diminishing landscape legibility and if re-making the integrity of places is to some extent dependent on re-localisation, then it is likely that all three aspects of identity will be enjoined. The reinforcement of landscape legibility is thus likely to involve a combination of statutory defence (through, for example, planning control), resistance by stakeholders to the loss of 'placeness', and 'projects' (both specific measures and broader social movements) to recover character and functional integrity. These activities are likely to be linked by a collective endeavour to move along the sustainability transition, which itself may form the basis of future landscape stories.

Thus, although some commentators have suggested that localism is a fundamentally flawed concept, based on a misguided belief that globalism could or should be arrested, there are some credible efforts by planners and non-governmental organisations to enhance and recapture the 'specificity' of place. Equally, re-localisation should not become a shibboleth. Place-making can at times be harnessed to opportunities afforded by globalism, for example in relation to new information technologies and patterns of consumption.

SOFT-WIRING AND HARD-WIRING

There has been a continuing debate in landscape studies about the extent to which our perceptions of and preferences for landscapes are innate (hard-wired) or are the products of our acculturation (soft-wired). On the one hand, our changing tastes for landscapes suggest that beauty is a culturally specific concept, and that judgements about landscape aesthetics will vary over time and space. On the other, the possibility of a deterministic or evolutionary component to our landscape perceptions indicates that we may store within our brains 'catalogues of images or patterns' which permit recognition of particular environments or habitats as 'safe' or 'welcoming' (Kaplan and Kaplan, 1989).

Arguing for a predominantly cultural basis, we might turn to Bourdieu's notion of 'habitus' (e.g. Bourdieu, 1977; see also Hillier and Rooksby, 2002). This suggests that people occupy a 'cultural habitat', and that their geographic and social space becomes internalised within routine frames of reference as habitual actions. As a result, the ways in which people believe it is appropriate to act, think and feel are strongly influenced by local norms. A geographic area, with its traditions, is thus likely to be a strong force of 'acculturation' on an individual, helping to create a milieu in which they feel 'at home' and able to 'perform' more confidently in everyday situations. This occurs to such a degree that we perform in a taken-for-granted fashion which we treat as normal. In respect of a landscape, therefore, those with inside knowledge of its topography and norms will be confident in negotiating their quotidian lifespace; equally, outsiders may fall foul of the norms of a landscape, and may feel excluded. Yet this relationship is itself dynamic and a particular habitus cannot be treated as sacrosanct and immutable, nor can a 'self-evident' way of behaving be assumed to be desirable or sustainable in the long term.

In terms of 'hard-wiring', evolutionary psychologists have argued for a biologically selfish element in the way we value landscapes. One useful idea is that of 'affordances', by which we refer to the capacity of landscapes to satisfy our needs and wants. The idea of affordances originates in psychology, where Gibson (1979) and subsequently Shephard (1984) identified our propensity to visually select those invariant features in the material world that are significant for us. Thus, affordances reflect what the environment offers, provides, furnishes and invites. According to this perspective, when perceiving the environment, we both register the invariant objects that we see, and filter them in terms of their values and meanings; further, we see the landscape both in terms of what it 'allows' relative to our capabilities as an organism. The term has become more generally used in landscape studies to refer to those properties of a landscape which the viewer perceives as 'affording' particular opportunities, for example in relation to economic production or specialist recreation.

Further, the hard-wired element of our landscape preferences may lead to an innate biophilia or topophilia. The idea of biophilia was popularised by Wilson (1986), who proposed that, because human beings have co-existed in close relationship with the natural world for many millennia, we have a natural sensitivity to the need for other living organisms. Whilst this claim might appear somewhat

unsubstantiated and assertive, there is some supportive evidence of people bene-
fiting physically and emotionally from 'green' surroundings – for example, some
research points to quicker recovery from surgery in well-landscaped hospital
grounds (Ulrich, 1997). An extension to this view is topophilia (Tuan, 1990), the
affective bond between people and place. Such studies, whilst by no means disre-
garding cultural influences, suggest that there is a biological basis linking human
psychology and landscape, and thus that place attachments and preferences for
certain types of landscape are innate. This view is reinforced by ideas such as
prospect-refuge theory, which hypothesises a preference for complex landscapes
that resonate with evolutionary needs (Appleton, 1996). Thus, diverse landscapes
might appeal to the ancestral hunter-gatherer in us by suggesting terrain in which
we could see without being seen, or feel secure, whilst open landscapes might
recall opportunities for grazing and cultivation. Finally, the even more controversial
and speculative field of ecopsychology suggests that there is a synergistic relation
between planetary and personal well-being, and that the planet's ecological health
is in some way related to the mental health of its inhabitants.

INSIDERS AND OUTSIDERS

We have noted the importance of the human capacity to 'read' the story of landscapes, and thus identify with them through their remnant inscriptions. But these
are read differently by insiders and outsiders. The former's lives have unfolded
there; the latter can selectively enjoy the more amenable aspects of a territory and
avoid the harsh or tedious ones. Outsiders – whose judgements have over the
past couple of centuries held the greatest weight in acclaiming landscapes – tend
to be influenced by touristic, environmental, artistic, literary and historical legacies.
Hence, landscape representations are often intended for outsiders' consumption,
although they may simultaneously have strong meanings for insiders. Landscapes
such as 'Thomas Hardy country' and the 'battlefields of northern France', for
example, evoke strong images, not always accurate, and thus exist as 'imaginary
geographies' as much as material entities.

However, culturally sanctioned perspectives are increasingly being ques-
tioned. As Brace (2003) notes, 'In recent years, the dual recognition of the visuality
of western culture and the importance of space to social relations has encouraged
academics from across the social sciences and humanities to rethink questions of
landscape representation.' Further, whilst landscapes may be 'cultural', that does
not mean to say that all people quickly feel at home in them: it is equally possible
to feel excluded. On the one hand, indigenous populations may feel dispossessed,

for example, if tenants are exploited by absentee landlords or if first nations have been expelled by settlers. On the other hand, 'landscapes of migration' may be settings where in-migrants experience hostility and discrimination, and suffer from not being able to read landscapes in ways that enable 'polite behaviour' within them.

'Power' (in the Foucauldian sense) is widely reflected in landscape. Urbanists have interpreted built landscapes in terms of the financial power of corporations and the central commanding position of governments, whilst ruralists have similarly revealed the power of landowners and external capital. Thus, cultural landscapes, whilst sometimes the spontaneous product of communal management and trust, are also often the outcome of unequal sets of power relations: they express the claims of some interest groups over others, as well as of people over animals and plants. In this respect, 'outsider' surveillance of a landscape has on occasion been likened to the battlefield, where control and conquest is exercised by occupying a commanding panoramic perspective on a scene (Olwig, 2002).

This idea of powerful gazes, mainly exercised by outsider interests, has been expanded by Macnagthen and Urry (1998) who depict different ways in which we 'consume' landscapes. In brief, they have suggested that our various modes of visual consumption comprise:

- *romantic* – where our gaze entails being immersed in a sense of awe;
- *spectatorial* – a series of brief encounters, where we glance at and absorb many different 'signs' of the environment;
- *possessive* – where we scan the familiar landscape as if it could be owned;
- *natural history* – a didactic viewpoint, involving scanning the landscape to 'surveille' and inspect nature;
- *anthropological* – where an investigator becomes immersed in a landscape to interpret local culture.

They suggest one more – the 'collective' – which is more appropriate to insider groups, who gaze on landscapes with a shared familiarity.

One key category of outsider is that of 'expert', whose requirements from a landscape may differ from the daily, lived experience of insiders, and who may overlook important 'lay' knowledge. Clark and Murdoch (1997) have shown how farmers in a Site of Special Scientific Interest in southern England possessed insights into the conservation importance and sustainable management practices of the habitat that were not fully appreciated by the statutory conservation agency. They argue that a notable reason for a disjuncture between the farmers' understanding of local nature and that of the conservation scientists was the virtual invisibility of many of the species deemed valuable and important by the conservationists, making farmers somewhat sceptical of 'official' knowledge. Thus, conservation scientists showed little interest in farmers beyond the basis on which they were enrolled into the networks (i.e. compliance with conservation management agreements), and disregarded their stocks of local knowledge and hence the possibility of learning from them. In a similar vein, Oreszczyn and Lane (2000) investigated the cultural dimensions and technologies of hedged landscapes through the collection and exploration of different stakeholder perspectives. Both insider and outsider stakeholders appeared to value hedgerows for a similar range of emotional, as well as rational, reasons. However, despite a high degree of commonality in different groups' perceptions, the authors found wide differences in relation to preferred management prescriptions and their goals for wildlife and aesthetics. They therefore advocated multi-stakeholder participation in relation to holistic landscape research, policy and decision-making processes.

Demographic and cultural churning is leading to more diversified types of insider and outsider interests, and the two groups are often no longer neatly separable. For example, in much of the European countryside, there has been a sharp shift of balance away from residents dependent on land-based activities – especially as those industries have increasingly substituted machines for people – to more affluent and somewhat more elderly incomers, especially in the accessible countryside. This is well reflected in England through annual *State of the Countryside* Reports (e.g. Countryside Agency, 2004), although the phenomenon is widespread in post-industrial, and even post-agrarian, economies. These Reports indicate that migration trends reflect people's lifecycles, with younger people moving away to work or study, and older people moving back into rural districts, either whilst working or to retire (albeit only around 10% of rural in-migrants are retired). Some studies suggest that in-migrants tend to be active, well-educated, younger than long-term residents and with higher incomes, and that they move (usually with families) for 'employment' and 'quality of life' reasons. By contrast, out-migrants tend to be under 25, and move for personal, employment or education reasons.

Thus, the 'insider' population of landscapes is in a state of flux, perhaps at odds with the permanence and continuity of past practices and memories. Some insider groups will gain their livelihood from within the landscape, often through land-based activities, so that their economic practices impinge directly on the functioning and appearance of the landscape. Such people are often also resident insiders, and thus may have social, kinship and emotional ties to the area. Others may be more recent incomers, or may travel into the area for activities such as agribusiness, mineral extraction or contract forestry. In some attractive rural areas, substantial farms are being purchased as country residences by people with city employment and who have little interest in the use of land beyond a few paddocks surrounding the main house. This trend is likely to have substantial consequences for landscape.

In broad terms, groups within landscape units can be seen to comprise:

- Outsider experts, such as land use planners and river basin managers, who may have particular interests in the landscapes and who may seek to prescribe social, economic and environmental policies and practices for the area.
- Outsider lay interests, such as conservation groups, which vary in the degree to which they are nationally or locally based. They may seek to achieve national objectives – such as conservation or recreation – through the local resources of particular landscapes, and thus argue for a 'national interest' to be reflected in their planning and management.
- Other stakeholders who have an interest in the state of a particular landscape, such as recreationalists, or homeowners exposed to flood hazards.
- Past and present insiders, who have moulded a cultural landscape and whose inscriptions help determine landscape distinctiveness and character, and whose stories and traditions persist. They are sometimes at risk of being forgotten or displaced – e.g. first nations, older residents being residualised by counter-urban migrants, and the producers of unfashionable or impolite landscapes such as coal miners. Their traditional perspectives and activities are also jeopardised by general globalising effects.
- Future people, including the present generation of children, on whose behalf resources are being stewarded and landscapes protected, enhanced and created.

Some key factors of importance to insiders and outsiders are summarised in Table 3.1.

In the following chapter, we will note how experts gaze on landscapes in order to perform measurement tasks such as: delineation and designation; mapping, inventory and evaluation; distinguishing between the supposedly 'enduring/permanent' and 'transient/ephemeral'; describing landscape in terms of inventory of land form, land use, artefactual and emotional qualities; and seeing in the landscape particular opportunities for protection and improvement. Given this variety of lenses through which we view landscapes, planners, at the very least, need to be aware of the partiality of their own insights, and the need to seek out the knowledge and aspirations of other stakeholders. The gazes of spatial planners may be very different in terms of their values, norms, perceptions and motivations than those of other groups.

Table 3.1 Some properties of landscapes sought by insider and outsider groups

Insiders	Outsiders (but also often valued by insiders)
quality of life	recreation and tourism
local employment and production	scenic beauty
facilities and services	biodiversity and environmental service functions
memories and associations	vicarious consumption of customs and traditions
way of life	architectural significance of buildings
symbols	safe food
living space	water, timber, minerals
safety, refuge, defence	military training and conquest

PEOPLE AND NATURE

There is a widely held view that 'modernist' (even 'Enlightenment') science has over-emphasised the 'duality' between people and nature, and treated them as independent domains. Thus, it is argued that science has behaved as if people were superior to other species and the physical environment, leading to a relationship of exploration, conquest, examination and exploitation. Dualism, it has been suggested, is responsible not only for an unequal way of understanding nature, but predisposes us towards unsustainable ways of using it.

A debate thus arises as to whether *Homo sapiens* are somehow separate from the remaining world order or are inseparable from it. This is of interest to many writers, who attribute our depredation of the world's 'resources' to distancing ourselves from nature and consequently seeing no ecological or moral problem in depleting and polluting it. The alleged weaknesses of this propensity include that:

- it leads to a loss of connection between society and nature, ultimately resulting in environmental dysfunction, both because of lack of understanding of complex environmental systems dynamics and a lack of humility for humans' place within the natural order;
- it leads to a 'colonial' or 'imperialist' view of nature, in which humans occupy a superior and controlling position, rather than a post-colonial view in which we accept the human risks and inconvenience associated with an unpredictable 'future nature';
- it neglects the many nature–society issues can only be understood by ascribing 'agency' to nonhuman elements, whether these are within nature (e.g. the potential of species to 'disobey' their expected behaviour according to conservation science) or are artificial and thus constitute a cyborg relationship

Figure 3.1 The Brecon Beacons National Park (Wales): a wild yet highly accessible landscape valued
by numerous inside and outside interests, including stock rearing, forestry, water catchment,
recreation, nature conservation and military training

with people (e.g. the way that personal computers modify our styles of thinking and problem solving);

• it under-values close associations between people and natural features, and
the ways in which nonhuman elements are charged with powerful socially
constructed meanings.

Hence, many observers now indicate the undesirability of referring to people and
nature as if they are unrelated. Nonetheless, in recording, monitoring, planning and
managing landscape, most practitioners and researchers find a continuing need to
rely on a reductionist and analytical approach. For practical reasons, as we shall
see, landscape research and planning remain strongly influenced by the western
tradition of scientific enquiry, and its separation of the world into subject (investigator) and object (observed organism or matter).

These ideas have led to the emergence of ideas about 'hybridity', and to the
adoption of ways of studying people–nature interactions through nondualistic
methods, such as actor-network theory (ANT) (e.g. Whatmore, 2001). ANT was
originally used to develop a sociology of science where scientific innovation and
paradigm shifts were exposed as social constructions, and human and nonhuman

components were accorded 'symmetry' (i.e. actors with equal importance); thus, discoveries and solutions were reported, not in terms of scientific rectitude, but of the promulgation of persuasive arguments by key human actors, and the cultures and capabilities of their laboratories. The method has since been used very widely to study situations in which human and nonhuman actors (scientists, policy-makers, computers, wild species, etc.) are coupled together in a network, and where practices and theories are based on socially constructed convergent worldviews, rather than objective scientific absolutes.

Understanding landscape decisions in this way can be helpful, as it reveals the complex ways in which distinctive places emerge, and collective actions occur, and displays full cognisance of the sometimes unpredictable and uncontrollable behaviour of nonhuman elements. In general, it is useful to understand landscapes as hybrid spaces whose specialness derives from intimate and risky associations between the human and nonhuman realms. A particularly notable study in this regard was Cloke and Jones' (2002) account of trees in various settings and their contribution to the meanings invested in territories. Here, the authors draw attention to: the *cultural* attributes (such as fear, spirituality and leisure) associated with trees and woods at different spatial scales and in different places; the *agency* exercised by trees and woods relative to how they are imagined and encountered, leading to a fecund 'between-space' wherein both humans and nonhuman agents become intertwined; and the ways in which trees help define *place*, which they see as an amalgam of 'the ecological and the cultural, the human and nonhuman, the global and the local, and the real and imaginary' (Cloke and Jones, 2002: 9).

One practical problem, which the 'nature–society' debate poses for landscape scale planning, is whether there are fundamental differences or similarities between the environmental requirements of wild species and the landscape desires of humans. For example, it could be argued that ecologists seek concentration into hotspots and corridors (de-fragmentation of the countryside), as big habitats are generally better for feeding ranges and reduce the 'edge effects' of fragmented habitats. By contrast, amenity conservationists often seek diversity, character and local difference. Further, nature often likes 'scruffiness' whereas people prefer tidiness, and nature requires disturbance (natural, e.g. landslides, fire), chaos and catastrophe, whereas people tend to avoid 'landscapes of fear' and seek stability and security from hazard.

Thus, there is a potential paradox for landscape scale planning that 'people' preferences for small-scale and safe environments, for example, may be at variance with 'nature' preferences for de-fragmentation and flux. However, this is not necessarily the case. In broad terms, we may speculate that visual complexity does not equate with incoherence, diversity does not necessarily lead to fragmentation, and massing of landscape elements does not mean that they need be unvaried – hence there may be grounds for compatibility between 'human' and 'natural' desiderata. There is also an 'aesthetic' view that landscapes are valued when they are perceived as places where the parts fit well together and are unified, whilst other places are apparently disjointed and difficult to understand (Leopold, 1949). Indeed, both ecologists and designers tend to share the view that alternatives must be sought to modern functional landscapes which lack visual and ecological integrity, coherence or validity. Kaplan and Kaplan (1982) consider that all highly rated aesthetic landscapes display coherence, complexity and mystery, and these qualities can be reconciled with ecological requirements of de-fragmentation, mixtures of patch/matrix/ecotone, and large 'core' habitats. Equally, aesthetically 'sublime' landscapes (where our comprehension is overwhelmed by the grandeur of a landscape, and perhaps where there is an element of risk and danger) chime in with patch magnitude requirements. However, there are still major challenges associated with the social acceptability of ecological objectives as illustrated, for example, by moves to re-create 'wildwoods' replete with wolves, or to breach coastal defences and allow farms to revert to wetlands. Landscape strategies based on ecological primacy and the 'future natural' might still be undermined by folk memories and their associated 'landscapes of fear'.

In one study of the interface between aesthetics and ecology, Palmer (2004) used landscape ecological metrics – i.e. wild species' requirements – to predict landscape quality – i.e. human preferences. A methodological problem in this kind of comparison is that many landscape metrics are sensitive to the chosen 'scale' of the study, as this varies relative to the needs of different organisms, including humans. Thus, the scalar property of 'extent' requires the investigation of an ecologically appropriate area, and this has been defined for wild species as 'the largest scale that an organism perceives' (With, 1994) and for humans as 'the range at which a relevant object can be distinguished from a fixed vantage point' (Kolasa and Rollo, 1991). In Palmer's study, frames were set in terms of the 'home range' (the area around an animal's home that is used during its daily activities), and the area that an organism can apprehend from a fixed viewpoint (in landscape assessment studies, the viewshed). Grain was operationally defined as 'the size of the individual units of observation' (McGarigal and Marks, 1995), though in more strictly ecological terms it is 'the finest resolution at which an organism perceives spatial heterogeneity' (With, 2002). In measuring landscape attributes, the study distinguished between measures of *composition* (types, naturalness) and *configuration* (homogeneity, heterogeneity, patch shape and patch diversity). Applying commonly used landscape spatial metrics, Palmer sought to explain the perception of scenic value in a landscape. Although the GIS-generated landscape metrics in this study only explained about half of the variation in landscape perception, there appeared to be a reasonable level of corroboration that human and wildlife landscape 'affordances' were broadly compatible.

SOCIAL AND INSTITUTIONAL CAPITAL AT THE LANDSCAPE SCALE

The essence of cultural landscapes is that they are the product of natural processes and human processes working in tandem. Consequently, whilst a great deal of attention has been paid to understanding the ways in which natural systems and their associated species behave within heterogeneous landscapes, an understanding of human systems is equally important to ensure the continuation of suitable conditions. Whilst nature, unaided, will find equilibrium, it will not reproduce innately cultural landscapes of high value.

The institutions, relationships, and norms that shape the quality and quantity of a society's social interactions are collectively known as social capital. This can be thought of as the glue which holds communities and wider society together through mutual trust and interdependence. Even though modern society is 'delocalised', people still live and work within relatively defined areas, and some important production and consumption activities are also likely to be localised and particularised. It is now widely held that social cohesion is critical for societies to prosper economically and for development to be sustainable. It has been argued that sustainable development thrives when representatives of the state, the corporate sector, and civil society create forums in and through which they can identify and pursue common goals. In addition to social capital, it is also important to recognise the 'human capital' composed of individual and collective practical knowledge, acquired skills and learned abilities. However, whilst planners increasingly seek to enhance and reinvigorate stocks of social capital, we need to acknowledge that much of it operates 'below the radar', and that many rural landscapes are sustained in no small part due to an 'informal' economy and often a counter-culture. These are areas in which planners should tread with caution.

Different commentators vary on what they term as 'social capital'. Some clearly relate it only to those interpersonal and inter-organisation dependencies that people produce independently of government. In other words, they see it as a spontaneous product of communities arising from their mutual need to share and trust. Others include the governance structures and institutional fabric of an area within their definition of social capital. Again, some include only the reciprocities between individuals, and between community-based organisations. Others include the business community, especially the non-economic linkages between firms, such as their shared knowledge and 'cluster benefits'.

Within a context of partnerships, these different elements – of interpersonal, inter-organisational, human, inter-firm, institutional and governance 'capitals' – in any case become imperceptibly merged. A key role of landscape governance is thus its capacity to assemble resources and regulate individual and collective conduct, 'construct' advantage for entrepreneurs, and deliver sustainable development. This goes well beyond the formal role of central and local government apparatus, and requires the recognition of three main facets: first, the role of local communities in managing sustainable landscapes; second, the intimate links between landscape quality and the economic and social entrepreneurship of an area; and third, the presence of a textured and flexible governance infrastructure that can find creative and innovative ways of delivering locally attuned policies. The first of these is addressed more systematically, under the topic of 'deliberative landscape scale planning', in Chapter 5. The second requires a concern for the business sector – not so much in terms of conventional competitive behaviour, but more in terms of common, regional and culturally based rules of behaviour, and accepted but tacit codes of conduct between firms. The third reflects the property of 'institutional thickness', in which accumulation of flexible and effective network relations between government, voluntary and business organisations – rather than heavier bureaucracies – are sought. Often this is constructed through formal partnerships, and increasingly is the focus of a regional level of governance (e.g. Morgan, 1997; Cooke and Morgan, 1998; Devine-Wright et al., 2001). Institutionally 'thick' milieux are particularly likely to display the collective learning capacity necessary for a transition to the multifunctional landscapes of tomorrow.

An illustration of regional institutional capacity in a landscape context is provided by Baker (2002), who examined the role of the Government Offices for the Regions and the Regional Development Agencies in respect of the coastal zone in northwest England. His particular focus was the integrated management approaches being promoted through the North West Coastal Forum, and its role in helping stakeholders reach consensus on various issues and promote collaborative approaches. Particular opportunities arose through brokerage, lobbying, bidding, influencing policy, and securing enhanced funding for more locally based activities in ways that some individual members would have found difficult acting in isolation. The Forum was also instrumental in setting a strategic framework for the development of integrated coastal zone management regionally, and it served as an arena for inter-organisational networking and information dissemination. Of particular importance was Baker's observation that it had the potential to strengthen future regional modes of governance, together with consequential opportunities for net-working, partnerships and regional institutional capacity building.

CONCLUSION

Sustainable cultural landscapes have strong character and are in favourable con-dition. As we have seen, they are undermined by factors such as dysfunction and obsolescence, often associated with strong external – even global – forces. Con-sequently, many landscapes are becoming 'illegible' and losing their associations with place and people. This is often paralleled by a loss of environmental cohesion and functionality. Addressing the problem of declining legibility poses serious chal-lenges because the drivers of landscape change are typically beyond local control.

To date, the idea of 'landscape scale planning' has been a rather technical issue involving debate between environmental scientists, designers and spatial planners. However, plans are unlikely to be sustainable unless they are sensitive to the attachments and aspirations of local people, and seek to engage communities in design and long-term management. In an anonymising landscape, subject to dysfunction and obsolescence, an important role of planning is to find ways of reconnecting people to their territory so that coherent stories and identities can be recovered. Although we cannot fully explain it, people appear intuitively to identify with particular territories, and landscape scale planning needs to relate to these imagined spaces just as much as it relates to visual-ecological units or water catchments.

Similarly, much landscape practice to date has relied on the expert 'gaze'. Whilst this continues to be crucially important, it is equally necessary that the privi-leged position of the expert does not over-ride 'insider' values and sensitivities. Active involvement of stakeholders – whether local 'lay' people or other categories and organisations within an area – is desirable for several reasons. For one thing, landscape proposals are often superior if they have engaged people with local knowledge. Indeed, some planning legislatures now require meaningful participa-tion by stakeholders. Further, only truly pristine landscapes 'look after themselves': cultural landscapes will require varying degrees of active input from humans, whether through everyday economic activities, organised community endeavours, specially appointed paid staff, or some combination of these.

The relationships between people and territory are complex and rather poorly understood. However, the difficulty of comprehending and acting upon them should not deter planners. Successful inclusion of communities in landscape scale plans can yield benefits not only in technical outcomes, but also in the more subtle process of recovering identities and quality of life. Lack of meaningful lay input into expert proposals and lack of effort in building social capital, by contrast, are likely to result in failure. Thus, effective participatory techniques are likely to generate more sustainable proposals 'for' landscapes; beyond this, however, the deeper and broader cultivation of people's attachment to place creates opportunities to plan 'through' landscapes, by delivering policy according to areas which people find recognisable and important.

A landscape-centred approach to planning evidently promises both to provide appropriately scaled frameworks for delivering policy, and to involve people more effectively in choices that affect the sustainability of their environments. However, it courts the risk that such an approach may be undermined by its sheer complexity and multifunctionality. Traditionally, we have tended to 'reduce' problems so that they can be understood and addressed effectively, a tendency which may be especially necessary when involving the lay public or their elected representatives – though even experts baulk at the overwhelming range of factors and issues within landscape systems. The next chapter therefore looks at the potential for comprehending landscape, that is, 'getting our heads round' its multiple and diverse attributes, in ways that enable us to embark on focused and deliverable planning strategies. It also considers the challenges of integrating data about the form and function of landscapes, with more subjective information about the values that we attach to them, and of tracking positive and negative changes in these multiple attributes.

CHAPTER 4

COMPREHENDING THE LANDSCAPE SCALE

INTRODUCTION

The main attraction of the landscape scale as a framework for spatial planning is its holistic nature, and its capacity to integrate human and environmental systems within identifiable and distinct places. However, this also makes for great, perhaps overwhelming, complexity. This chapter looks at ways in which we can comprehend – or 'get our heads round' – the qualities of landscape. It looks both at the emerging multi-attribute information base, and our capacity as humans to interpret whole landscapes.

Spatial information on environmental resources, such as soil and geology, has long been available. However, it is only relatively recently that landscape as a topic has been systematically monitored and reported, not least because of the problems of comprehending such a multifunctional feature and distilling it into simple mappable indices and of monitoring change consistently in something so subject to value judgement. An important landmark in reporting change in cultural landscapes was the Dobris Assessment on Europe's environment (Stanners and Bourdeau, 1995), which devoted a chapter to a typology and interpretation of European cultural landscapes and an assessment of the threats to them. Although problems of transboundary comparability and replicable measurement led to a hiatus in reporting landscape change, nevertheless this was a signal acknowledgement that provision of such information was both potentially desirable and feasible.

Spatial planning attaches great importance to high-quality information – increasingly referred to as an 'evidence base' – for two main reasons. First, effective decisions require a systematic knowledge of the quantities and properties of available resources. Second, adaptive environmental planning, which depends on flexible and testable methodologies, is fundamentally reliant on timely information about environmental changes to check whether a strategy is having its desired effect or whether (and in what direction) it needs to be modified. Thus, despite the difficulties of recording the multiple and often subjective features of landscape, of dividing the 'whole' landscape into separate parts, and of deciding whether any changes are leading to improvement or deterioration, some attempt at landscape scale information gathering and interpretation is essential.

The need to classify and evaluate landscapes faces the fundamental problem that the imagined landscape, particularly where perceptions of 'natural beauty' are involved, is inherently subjective and culturally specific. Perhaps for this reason, landscape assessments have never commanded the same authority as other natural resource evaluations, such as those for soil and biodiversity, and have often been difficult to defend in land use decisions. Furthermore, it has been extremely difficult to convey in equal measure the national importance of rare and exceptional landscapes, and the great value to local people of 'quotidian' landscapes. It is also intractable to separate out the importance of purely aesthetic qualities of land and water from their other properties, such as human affordances and environmental service functions.

The practice of landscape recording has had to satisfy a number of different requirements. First, planners have often needed to undertake 'elite' assessments, so that they can accord special measures to landscapes, which are widely acclaimed to be outstanding in their present condition, and are an important part of a nation's heritage and identity. Thus, one task of a landscape assessment system is to identify a top echelon of areas for special recognition, and thus not only map their boundaries but also (at least implicitly, and often explicitly) rank landscapes in terms of their relative merit. This leads to practices of both *description* and *evaluation*. Description is the more straightforward task, and may comprise relatively objective attributes of land cover, landform and documented cultural representations. Evaluation is more contentious, but is typically based either on statistical surrogates derived from observers' perceptions of either actual or photographed scenes, or on expert judgements.

A second task of landscape assessment is to understand the underlying character and functionality of an area, and what marks it as being special and distinctive. This has the merit of being relatively value-free and of recognising that all areas have a degree of distinctiveness, character and functionality, albeit possibly vestigial and not necessarily acceptable in their current condition. This type of mapping is appropriate to situations in which planners need to target landscapes for recovery by practices such as land restoration or agricultural stewardship, or to prevent types of development that would lead to an erosion of distinguishing features or sustainability. Thus, some mapping methods entail an interpretive landscape assessment which reveals the nature, vulnerability and condition of the elements of an area's character. Some concentrate particularly on time-depth aspects, and thus may identify landscapes which have been deliberately designed and are considered to be important exemplars of a particular designer or period, or which display broader historical or archaeological significance through the imprint of human occupation or abandonment. Finally, some approaches stress the functionality of landscapes in terms of natural services and goods, such as biodiversity and hydrology.

LANDSCAPE UNITS

It is assumed here that, in order for people to comprehend the hyper-complex totality of the earth's surface and land–water interface, and to apply policy strategies to its sustainable planning and management, some degree of 'reduction' is inevitable. A reductionist approach implies *inter alia* a division of the earth's surface into units that have more in common internally than they do with neighbouring terrains. The logic of this division is reinforced by observations of the ways in which plant and animal ranges, river basins, and emotional attachments often appear to relate to intuitively recognisable areas.

Despite consistent patterns emerging as a basis for 'natural' divisions, however, we must accept that all boundaries in nature are permeable and fluid, and that humans are 'compulsive organisers' who seek regularities even where they are barely discernible or differ between cultural traditions. Equally, some would oppose the practice of reduction itself, arguing that it leads to a detached, clinical and potentially exploitative gaze. Further, despite the multiple meanings of landscape, there is a consistent, basic distinction that tends to divide landscape traditions: a positivistic view, in which landscape can be codified and measured, and enjoyed in a leisurely fashion, typically by outsiders; and a humanistic view, taking a phenomenological perspective, in which 'insider' perceptions are especially significant. Thus, landscapes have importance to the scientist, planner and tourist; equally they have strong meanings to people who have lived in them, suffered in them, journeyed in them or fallen in love in them.

For the present, we assume that an awareness of positivistic approaches to landscape taxonomy is necessary in order to understand current efforts to assemble a systematic evidence base. In this perspective, a starting point is to sort the landscape into relatively homogeneous units, reflecting aesthetic and/or natural attributes. Cognate steps are then to consider whether some of these are of sufficient quality to deserve special custodianship or stewardship, to identify planning and management prescriptions that will reinforce distinctiveness and/or functionality on the basis of identifiable landscape attributes, and to report whether changes in these units are leading to an improvement or deterioration in distinctiveness and/or functionality.

For a long time, we have recognised the difference and distinctiveness of cultural landscapes. A revealing classification of the principal exemplars within Europe was produced by Meeus *et al.* (1990), and was used in the inaugural European State of Environment Report (Stanners and Bourdeau, 1995), noted above. This is useful for illustrating the richness and variety of the resource, and for signalling the valued and often threatened qualities that we wish to retain. It also reveals how particular features, such as cork-oak groves or heather moorland, form part of wider complexes that are special and distinctive (Table 4.1). However, as a taxonomy, it poses problems of precise definition and comparability across national boundaries. Thus, Bunce (2001) has argued strongly for selecting landscape units on a quantitative and objective basis. In particular, he argues that:

• Threatened landscapes need objective data to be recorded in order to assess whether the type of changes taking place are affecting the quality of characteristic component elements. Such procedures must be statistical, so that real changes can be distinguished from either opinion or background noise, thus signalling a need for multivariate statistical classification.
• Because the pressures on rural environments operate across national frontiers, it is necessary to have a standardised procedure for assessing landscape character, and the potential impact of policy scenarios on rural landscapes.

However, whilst strictly quantitative approaches perform an important role, the majority of effort is still directed towards mixed methods of landscape description and interpretation.

Thus, the systematic division of landscape into planning and management units, though contested by some critics for its reliance on subject–object dualism, is widely practised as a first step for policy intervention and evidence gathering. Whilst this appears to privilege a top-down, expert approach, there is a growing tendency to base such division on allegedly innate properties that reveal landscape units in terms of integral properties, and to embrace the knowledge and values of local stakeholders. The act of differentiating landscapes into units which are relatively internally homogeneous in terms of cultural and functional properties reinforces the need to plan at a landscape scale – it implies that units tend to self-organise and often have sub-units nested within them, and that these may serve as the intrinsic divisions through which spatial planning strategies can be applied.

Since the mid-1970s, multivariate methodologies have regularly been used as a means of objective landscape classification (Bunce *et al.*, 1996). In Britain, a Land Classification System has been used in a variety of contexts, based on the principle that the major significant ecological and landscape variables are

Table 4.1 An overview of landscape resources in Europe

Category	Sub-category	Selected adverse trends
Tundra	arctic tundra	
	forest tundra	fires, overgrazing
Taigas	boreal swamp	drainage, peat extraction
	northern, middle, southern and fringe taiga s (progression from relatively species -poor coniferous forests, to mixed forests with pasture and arable)	clear felling, increasing dominance of spruce
Uplands	northern highlands (rough, very open)	afforestation
	mountains (wild, mixture of enclosed/ cultivated in valleys and open on moors)	abandonment, afforestation, tourism impacts
Bocages	Atlantic *bocage*	field enlargement, hedgerow removal
	semi-*bocage*	abandonment, afforestation, extensification in Mediterranean areas
Openfields	Atlantic openfield s (large -scale, monoculture)	intensification and set -aside
	continental openfields (more diverse in scale)	
	'collective' openfields in former centrally - planned economies (large -scale, open)	water and wind erosion
	Mediterranean open land (contrasting h ills and valleys)	intensification, extensification, abandonment
Steppic/arid landscapes	puszta (treeless, extensive stock farming)	salinisation, water/ wind erosion
	steppe (treeless, dry, windy, very open)	overgrazing, salinisation
	semi-desert	changing levels of groundwater and seawater
	sandy desert	
Regional landscapes	kampen (enclosed field, mosaic)	increasing scale, extensification
	Polish strip -fields (small -scale diverse, labour intensive)	loss of labour, changing field patterns
	coltura pro miscua (heterogeneous, small - scale diverse)	homogenisation
	dehesa/montado (agr o-silvo-pastoral parkland)	degradation, shrub colonisation
Artificial landscapes	polder (flat, open, fertile, artificial)	intensification, set -aside
	delta—artificial forms (intensive, flat, open, fertile)	salinisation, intensification
	huerta (irrigation, terraces, orchards)	

Source: based on Meeus *et al.*, 1990; Stanners and Bourdeau, 1995 associated with and dependent upon environmental variables. The starting point is to record the presence of environmental attributes – such as geology, land use, altitude, tree cover and water features – from information assembled on a grid square basis, which is then classified by successively dividing squares from published maps. The approach successively divides squares into two groups on the basis of the similarity of their environmental data characteristics using a multivariate ordination technique. The approach has subsequently been extended to a European level (Bunce, 2001). Despite the fact that data describing even simple parameters such as geology are not consistent across frontiers and are very variable in quality, the approach has successfully used climatic and altitudinal data, together with limited locational information, to yield a statistical classification of European landscapes.

In the UK, a complete land cover census, based on field recording and satellite imagery, has been undertaken through the Countryside Survey 2000 (CS2000, http://www.cs2000.org.uk/ [accessed 28 June 05]). The methodology has involved detailed field observations in a random sample of 1 km grid squares, recording data such as habitat types, hedgerows, plant species and freshwater invertebrates. Many of the sample sites were first visited in 1978 and subsequently in 1984 and 1990, providing a time series of land use changes. Combining them with satellite imagery led to the Land Cover Map 2000 (Fuller *et al.*, 2000). Howard *et al.* (2000) point out how these quantitative data have been linked to other surveys including more subjective datasets based on interviews with landowners.

THE INGREDIENTS OF LANDSCAPE

Although possessing different emphases, the multiple attributes of landscape are at least implicitly, and increasingly explicitly, reflected in any landscape recording method. Thus, the natural systems and human imprints that make an area distinctive must collectively be intimated. This multifaceted task is apparent from the World Heritage Convention's (UNESCO, 1972) definitions of 'natural' and 'cultural' heritage and, whilst these have been designed for application to elite sites, they provide a succinct indication of the range of key landscape attributes. Thus, *natural* heritage is deemed to comprise: 'natural features', comprising physical and biological formations or groups of such formations of value from the aesthetic or scientific point of view; geological and physiographical formations, and plant and animal habitats of conservation value; and natural sites or precisely delineated natural areas of value from the perspective of science, conservation or natural beauty. In a similar vein, *cultural* heritage is composed of: monuments, such as architectural works and archaeological structures, of importance to history, art or science; groups of buildings which are valued for their architecture, homogeneity or their place in the landscape; and sites valued from the historical, aesthetic, ethnological or anthropological point of view.[1]

The attributes of natural heritage, as we have noted, have been extensively mapped in 'objective' scientific terms. Interpretive maps of drift and solid geology, soil, hydrology and vegetation have been compiled over many decades, in the cause of natural resource management. As we noted in the previous chapter, there is an increasing contribution made by landscape ecological maps to our understanding of patches, corridors and species' ranges across territories. However, our spatial coverage of 'cultural' features is less systematic, and yet is fundamental to our knowledge of the 'making' of landscape. Two key elements of this need to be considered – the artefacts of cultural heritage, and the intangible qualities that people associate with landscapes. In respect of the former, CEMAT (2003) has identified six key elements that 'make' landscapes, namely:

- spatial organisation
- agrarian landscapes
- communication channels
- buildings
- private space, and
- economic activities.

Using the CEMAT descriptions as a starting point, Table 4.2 summarises the main features of these categories. The intangible qualities are far more difficult to systematise than cultural elements, but a widely applied checklist of these has arisen from the programme of Landscape Character Assessment developed since the 1990s in England and Wales (see below) (CA/SNH, 2002). This suggests that human responses to landscape can be understood in terms of:

- aesthetic aspects – scale, enclosure, diversity, texture, form, line colour balance, movement and pattern; and
- emotional qualities – security, stimulus, tranquillity and pleasure.

The degree to which a surveyor considers these qualities to be present can in turn be related to lexicons of adjectives reflecting their presence or strength.

These varied components all accumulate towards unique and multifaceted landscapes. They can all be associated with 'integrating' and 'disintegrating' factors (the more widely used terms, 'positive' and 'negative', are avoided here in

TABLE 4.2 PHYSICAL ELEMENTS OF CULTURAL LANDSCAPES

Spatial organisation – the broad view of a landscape, e.g. whether it is harmonious and relatively unchanging, whether it appears recent and featureless, or whether it is in a state of flux with historical traces alongside new uses. The most extensive use of cultural landscapes is usually that of agriculture. Other spatial elements include: afforested lands (forests, woods, copses, etc.) and their associated ownership, management and users' rights; rivers, lakes and ponds, and their degree of alteration (or even creation) by human agency; and the form, scale and location of the built area, and how this has changed over time.

Agrarian landscapes – the most extensive feature of (agri)cultural landscapes, typically comprising a range of elements such as:

- open fields, and cropping patterns, regional typicality, boundary demarcation and patterns of rights of way;
- hedgerows – their density, *maillage* (grid/mesh), mode of construction, and alteration through land consolidation;
- marsh, once common but now increasingly rare due to land drainage, but sometimes remaining as permanently or seasonally wet areas, and sometimes having particular agricultural or community uses;
- terraces – particularly in parts of Europe and Asia – which have been laid out for various types of crop, and constructed in differing ways;
- orchards and vineyards, and their role and form in the countryside, and associated vegetation;
- mountain landscapes, and their characteristic montane flora and fauna (natural and domestic), buildings, and natural hazards.

Textured on top of these, patterns of land inheritance can also have profound influences on the form and matrix of agrarian landscapes.

Communication channels of various types over land and water, sometimes catering for particular, and sometimes general, traffic. Thus, roads and paths are distinguished by their organisation, hierarchy, edges (such as verges, ditches and hedges) and special features (e.g. holloways, green lanes). Modern high–capacity roads may be destructive and intrusive in landscape terms, but equally, through their scale and linearity, create new possibilities for strategic landscape creation. Navigation routes include canals and navigable rivers, along with their engineered reinforcements and associated works such as towpaths and warehouses, and railway structures. Given the inevitability of change in transport technology, the condition of communication channels varies greatly in terms of intactness and obsolescence. Although infrequent features, airports are associated with distinctive landscapes and shadow zones.

Buildings comprise permanent structures composed of walls and a roof (sometimes ruined), ranging from castles and houses to barns and factories. Whilst their form frequently reflects their original purpose, their detailed appearance is often attributable to local technology and skills, regional materials, site restrictions and traditions. Key types are:

- public buildings (some of which have subsequently been converted into private use), such as churches, town halls, markets and community facilities;
- farms and residential houses, of hugely varied affluence and architectural merit;
- craft, industrial and working buildings, such as factories and their associated structures, and a variety of farm-related structures;
- historical buildings, such as castles, abbeys, archaeological sites, whose usage may range from current and active to a long-forgotten mystery;
- neighbourhood constructions, such as signs, landmarks, water impoundment and distribution structures, commemorative items and memorials.

Private space covers private life (organisation of family life) and social life (relationships between family unit or individual and neighbours). Aspects even of these personal factors can express themselves in the landscape, perhaps in ways related to the different use of spaces by extended and nuclear families, and the ways in which people personalise private spaces such as gardens. More generally, the human and social capital of an area is essential to the vibrancy and sustainability of its landscape. Celebrations in communal life (e.g. religious festivals, fairs and holidays), local culture (costumes, music, dance, stories, games, etc.) and languages and place names are also pertinent.

Economic activities – which the CEMAT typology restricts to land- and water-based ones – comprise different methods of cultivation, stock rearing, inshore and freshwater fishing, and timber production. These have consequences for many factors, such as the colours and seasonality of land, species and breeds of livestock, intensity of use of machinery relative to human and animal power, and activity in harbours. The output of economic activity may also be reflected in typical local products, notably food.

Source: after CEMAT, 2003

order to reduce the use of value-laden terminology). Integrating qualities are essentially those where human activities are 'embedded' in their spatial setting – for instance, place-related customs and traditions or manufacturing activities that source their materials locally. Here, landscape represents a sustainable infrastructure for meeting physical and emotional needs, and people in turn invest physical and emotional energies in the landscape. Generally, landscapes with a predominance of integrative qualities also display aesthetic attractiveness, though – given that beauty is often in the eye of the beholder – only insiders may appreciate the warts-and-all beauty of some landscapes. Disintegrating attributes are typically described in terms of landscapes, which are chaotic, pockmarked or garish, rapidly trending towards uniformity, disfigured or abandoned,

and where inherited features are trivialised and unvalued and modern development lacks reference to older features (CA/SNH, 2002). Deteriorating landscapes often experience social dysfunction and withering of community ties and
memories, collective amnesia of local skills and stories, loss of biodiversity and
often loss of population. In essence, they are landscapes of convenience or
decline, in which socio-economic obsolescence and dysfunction are closely
linked to environmental disruption.

LANDSCAPES AS ECOLOGICAL–HYDROLOGICAL UNITS

A particular concern in biodiversity planning has been to identify ecological planning units, but a major problem has been their inherent complexity of composition
and indeterminacy of boundaries. Two main options have been proposed: taxonomic approaches based on vegetation classification, plant associations, and
habitat types (e.g. Rodwell, 1991, 1992, 1995); and approaches centred on a
limited number of 'flagship' species, where landscape features are matched to
species' lifecycle needs.

As an illustration of the former approach, Livingston *et al.* (2003) describe an
exercise undertaken within an urban area, where several micro-scale studies had
already been conducted and could be used as a source for rapid identification of
site characteristics such as type of vegetation, size of site and other site elements.
It also considered the larger-scale land cover mosaics and their connectedness, in
order to address potential relationships between wildlife habitats and urban sites.
Thus the study sought to link micro- and macro-scale data, and recorded four vegetative parameters – total vegetative cover, native vegetation, escape cover vegetation (i.e. for potential prey to make a get-away), and structural diversity – and on
this basis produced a 'wildlife habitats value' index. This exercise indicated how
mapping can contribute to land use proposals based on the inherent/intrinsic properties of landscape units. Its outcome was a series of planning recommendations
to:

- preserve an interconnected network of vegetated landscapes with the
  highest valued sites being retained as habitat for wildlife;
- restore the vegetative continuity of habitats, especially trying to link vegetative
  corridors to large suburban habitats;
- emphasise the use of native plant species; and
- utilise a diverse array of plant species and plant forms in amenity landscapes.

In respect of the second approach, there is, as Rubino and Hess (2003) have observed, a 'need to balance rigorous science with the need for expediency'; in practice, a number of 'short cuts' based on ideas of umbrella species, keystone species and focal species have proved influential. Species-centred analyses can quite effectively be linked to habitat patterns, as these are assumed to reflect the requirements of a wide range of organisms typically co-located with the target species. This approach can be a very valuable aid to landscape protection and reconstruction, and is discussed more fully in Chapter 5.

Attempts to generate more generic classifications of ecological planning units are illustrated by the definition of 'natural areas' in England during the 1990s. Although primarily based on natural environmental characteristics, they also incorporated cultural factors, such as socio-economic drivers and the views of local people. Natural Areas' boundaries reflected sub-divisions of England, each with a characteristic association of wildlife, landform, geology, land use and human impact, whose interactions resulted in a unique identity: thus, the units formed biogeographic zones reflecting geological foundation, natural systems, and wildlife, and providing a framework for setting objectives for nature conservation (Porter, 2004). Although mapped in terms of sharp boundaries, conservationists acknowledged that these were in reality fuzzy, both on land and between land and sea.

The key purpose of Natural Areas was to provide a wider context for nature conservation action, embracing the views of the people living and working in them. Various uses for Natural Areas were identified, notably:

- a framework for identifying suitable areas for site designation, habitat expansion, restoration and re-establishment;
- a framework for targeting agri-environment grants;
- identifying economic drivers;
- dividing up Biodiversity Action Plans into areas for targeting policy delivery;
- communication with stakeholders, other agencies and local communities for integrated delivery of nature conservation;
- identifying generic problems and solutions, which may be overlooked using single-purpose landscape frameworks; and
- allowing for nature conservation objectives to be considered alongside social, cultural and economic issues in the context of wider countryside planning and management.

A signal point was that Natural Area boundaries rarely coincided with administrative boundaries, as these often bear little relationship to the 'natural landscape'.

Hydrological systems have, along with ecological units, long been viewed as a natural basis for division of the earth's surface. Thus the 'watershed' or 'catchment' has often been proposed as the most appropriate division for landscape planning. Key reasons have been: its relative self-containment in terms of flows of water, other materials and energy; its relationship to geomorphic processes and the consequent recognisability of landforms characterising individual catchments; and the importance of water, often in short or excess supply, to human settlements. Increasingly, landscape ecologists also recognise the importance of water catchments in influencing the nature and functionality of ecosystems, through their role not only in supplying moisture but also moving chemical nutrients along rivers and through ground and soil water. Similarly, landscape design acknowledges the aesthetic and recreational issues associated with the fragmentation of river landscapes, caused by activities such as channel straightening, bankside vegetation removal, low flows caused by over-abstraction, and the imposition of a 'concrete overcoat' in areas of flood hazard.

There has been a good deal of convergent thinking in relation to environmental processes at the catchment scale, and recognition of the need to undertake integrated river basin management. In some quarters, there has been a growing preference for management solutions that incorporate 'naturalistic' designs for rivers and floodplains, rather than relying solely on 'hard' civil engineering solutions. Catchment ecosystems possess properties of self-regulation, and our practice of managing floods through engineered defence systems, though necessary in places, is expensive and carries a risk of pushing the system beyond the thresholds of recovery.

Hence, integrated river basin management often focuses on the level of catchment basin or sub-basin, and their associated natural 'regulators' (i.e. system components, such as vegetation cover, that regulate and buffer the quantity and quality of water movements). In essence, it addresses the interdependency of natural and human factors within a catchment, so that decisions can be based on the interaction of both sets of factors across the whole system. In England and Wales, the Environment Agency (and its predecessor, the National Rivers Authority) have progressively introduced the practice of Integrated River Basin Management (IRBM), most notably through Catchment Management Plans (early 1990s), giving way to Local Environment Agency Plans (late 1990s) and, in response to the EU Water Framework Directive, to River Basin Management Plans and Floodplain Management Plans (2003 onwards). A key purpose of integrated river basin management is to integrate land use planning and development control into managing the use of water. In the European Union, the Water Framework Directive (WFD) now requires all Member States to assign their land area to *river basin dis-*

tricts, to prepare management plans on a six-yearly basis, and to conduct a 'characterisation' of river basins.

LANDSCAPES AS SCENIC-CULTURAL UNITS

Most attempts at landscape taxonomy since the 1960s have tended, at least implicitly, to reflect aesthetics. This, however, is insufficient, as it fails to:

- acknowledge that landscape character is universal and not just restricted to sublime, harmonious or polite terrains;
- reveal the 'insider' values attached to places, and only considers the external, expert gaze;
- provide a systematic baseline for monitoring, anticipating and evaluating the effects of landscape change.

More recently, there has been an emergent consensus that we should principally consider landscape in terms of its specialness and character. Thus, contemporary approaches typically identify features essential to a landscape's socially and culturally constructed scenic qualities, and associated 'gazes' and 'stories'. Surveys are also likely to seek to detect those attributes that are fragile and vulnerable to intensive change.

The most common way of assessing and mapping landscapes has, in the past, been in terms of its visual attributes and relative aesthetic qualities. Such approaches may be thought of as Scenic Beauty Estimation (SBE) techniques (Terkenli, 2001). The emphasis has been on perceptual units and visual relationships between sites and topographic features, although symbolic meanings may also be incorporated. When we 'gaze' on the landscape, we do so either as professional outsiders or as lay insiders, and see essentially three types of attribute: its affordances, perhaps subliminally and instinctively in terms of survival, challenge or enjoyment; its scenic beauty, or aesthetic qualities; and its time-depth and shared stories.

In characterising visual units, there are a number of persistent difficulties. First, is the problem of drawing lines round essentially indivisible parts of the earth's surface. In some protected area systems, this has historically been on bases as arbitrary as following road boundaries. This is not as irrational as it may appear, as one of the prerequisites for firm protection of land is to know whether a particular site is inside or outside the designated area – in expansive and often unenclosed countryside, in the days before global positioning systems, this could be a significant feat. The need for precision of boundaries enabling protected areas to be administered and protected effectively endures, even though this approach to the division, naming and control of land may be increasingly unfashionable.

Further, in terms of estimating scenic beauty, there is the problem of finding features over which landscape professionals agree. For many years, and especially in the 1970s, the emphasis was on relative evaluation – what makes one area 'better' than another. During the 1980s, there was a popularisation of landscape assessment tools that separated the classification and description of landscape attributes from the evaluation of landscape. Subsequently, the criterion-based description of landscape features has tended to be distinguished from the task of ranking and rating (i.e. evaluating) landscapes.

An additional problem is that of understanding how local people identify with landscapes and place values on them, and of unravelling the stories that are woven into them. Landscape assessment has generally been based on expert judgement but, essential though this is for many purposes, it has significant weaknesses. Perhaps most notably, these judgements are generally made by outsiders, who gaze on landscapes with very particular professional sensitisations. By contrast, it is possible though more difficult to analyse landscape in phenomenological terms, with attention being paid to inscribed signs and symbols that can be understood by 'insiders' whose lifeworlds unfold locally. Thus, many writers see landscape perceptions as being mainly culturally determined. Cosgrove (1998), for example, emphasises landscape as a way of seeing which is linked to social, political and moral assumptions and taste. The influential research of Meinig (e.g. 1979) has been concerned with iconography, in which landscapes are seen as the embodiment of myths, meanings and values; they contain sets of coded symbols, understood properly only by those with particular insight into them. Hence, cultural landscapes possess semiotic properties (i.e. they contain symbols or signs), and thus are imbued with meanings that are inscribed into a landscape 'text'.

A further property allegedly associated with legible landscapes is that they are 'enchanting' places, perhaps for reasons only fully appreciated by insiders. Some enchanting places may be sublime or aesthetic, and a wide audience quickly grasps their appeal. Some may be scarred, yet those who have lived and loved in them, and have been navigated by their landmarks, can understand their value. Often, the significance of landscapes to insiders remains secret. A rather exotic but nonetheless telling illustration of place-enchantment is offered by He's (1998) study of Fengshui principles in villages of Southeast China. These principles rest on the belief that human events and natural processes (terrestrial and celestial) interact with each other, so that their beneficial Qi can be induced into human dwellings. Aspects such as site selection, key entrances, construction of pagodas, and arrangement of ancestral tombs are critical to this process of induction. For example, many villages face onto a meandering watercourse, surrounded on three sides by undulating mountains; archival studies reveal that they were typically built only after consulting a Fengshui Master who would seek places (e.g. mountain dragons, surrounding hills, watercourses and particular orientations) which accumulated the maximum terrestrial and celestial Qi. Thus, maps of villages, cities and temples show consistent relationships in key individual elements, which are presumed to be propitious, and landscape development has consciously sought to produce feelings of security, harmony, well-being and good fortune. Whether or not one is persuaded by Fengshui traditions, He's maps offer a fascinating insight into our subconscious attitudes to landscape. Whereas these lack cartographic precision, they are laced with depictions of favourable spirit features, in contrast to a typical western road map which depicts the landscape as neutral space to be crossed as quickly and conveniently as possible – truly a disenchanted view.

Particular difficulties arise where there is need to place relative values on visual units. This (if it is attempted) is generally undertaken in one of three ways. First, where there is a need to rank landscapes in terms of their priority for safeguard, scores can be allocated to them on the basis of aesthetic, biological, geological and geomorphological qualities. This approach typically involves either observing specific features of the land, or asking observers to rate actual or photographed scenes on a pre-determined scale. Second, experts can ask people to price landscape assets. Whilst this approach has been much criticised, it is often inevitable if Treasury funds are required to support a conservation, acquisition or restoration strategy. Normally, estimates of value are based on a neoclassical economic technique such as contingent valuation, where questionnaire respondents are asked how much they would be willing to pay for a non-market good or how much compensation they would need to accept for its loss (GB HM Treasury, 2003). However, some radically different methods, such as common-good approaches, have been proposed (Harrison and Burgess, 2000).

Further, landscape preferences may be influenced by 'identity' factors, such as ethnicity, gender, class and personal experience. Trained and seasoned observers of landscape may see an area as being attractive and comfortable, or inspiring and challenging. However, through most of time and place, people have encountered 'landscapes of fear' (Tuan, 1979), and relatively few cultures have selected landscape as a pleasing aesthetic for study, contemplation and artistic representation. Even within late modern societies, where nature has largely been 'tamed', some groups of people may fear particular landscapes. Woodland environments, as one important illustration, may create a sense of vulnerability or disorientation to certain users, and Burgess (1995) has convincingly demonstrated how woods can provide places where attackers can hide, and where users can experience entrapment and isolation. Such considerations are often absent from official and romanticised discourses of landscape attractiveness. More generally, whilst landscapes are often deemed remarkable for their aesthetic properties, this is a concept strongly influenced by 'educated' taste and values.

Moreover, debates over landscape preferences recall our earlier incursion into the 'hard- and soft-wiring' dilemma (p. 55–57). Hence, on the one hand, some would claim that landscape perceptions and preferences were entirely culturally determined, and that our primary effort should be directed to new acculturations that place people as intimate components within delicately balanced lifespaces or bioregions. On the other hand, some would argue for the possibility of certain land-scape archetypes being intuitively preferable on the basis of evolutionary biology, and that this should influence our principles of landscape design and planning. Whilst the debate is probably insoluble, it does point to the complexity of under-standing people's preferences for, and relationships to, landscapes.

An analogy may be drawn with fashion design, where certain items possess an 'acquired aesthetic' as a result of their association with changing social norms – commodities considered unfashionable at one time may become very trendy by association with people, events or ideas. Perhaps our tastes for landscape are sim-ilarly malleable? For example, a more ecologically-attuned society might cherish certain landscape types that currently are perceived as scruffy, such as permacul-ture settlements, or hazardous, such as floodplains. This dichotomy can be debated endlessly but, in all probability, our landscape tastes are a complex product of both biological and cultural factors, so that preferences for landscape types may change in detail whilst having a stable core. In this regard, there is some evidence from participatory planning/design that 'social learning' can help accus-tom us to alternative new landscapes. Also, consideration of the 'landscape modifi-cation gradient' (Chapter 2) may lead us to accept safer and more ordered landscapes close to centres of population, with larger-scale and riskier landscapes where they pose less threat to large numbers of people. Bell (1998) (echoing Whitehead's [1947] theory of aesthetics) sheds some light on this dilemma by observing that:

> Aesthetics begins with the pretty (the minor form of beauty) which leads to the
> major form of beauty and the strengths of the ecologically healthy landscape,
> expressed in its massiveness and intensity proper. This connects the natural
> and cultural patterns and processes with a most rewarding vein for aesthetic
> exploration. The link completes the circle from the structure of the landscape to

our basic perceptions of it; if we are able to make sense and orientate ourselves in the landscape, whilst appreciating the process involved, this can lead to the highest form of aesthetic experience.

This view gives us some hope in reconciling the aesthetic and ecological. If our cultural predispositions towards the landscape are at least partly acquired, then perhaps we can learn to enjoy ecological landscapes because we perceive in them the ultimate 'affordance' – the mechanisms of our life-support system. Ultimately, it could be argued that we will discover beauty in autopoietic and regenerative land-scapes even if at times they appear scruffy and hazardous to contemporary post-industrial tastes.

LANDSCAPE CHARACTER – A MORE DEFENSIBLE APPROACH?

Towards the end of the 20th century, there was an emerging consensus that land-scapes could most consistently and helpfully be described in relatively non-judgemental terms, based on recordable features that contributed to their distinctive-ness. Thus, the analysis and explanation of landscape character became the keynote, rather than evaluation of scenic beauty. Whilst issues of 'value' cannot be avoided, they can at least be based on explicit parameters and transparent procedures.

Three key attributes of visual landscape qualities are claimed to have emerged over time (CA/SNH, 2002):

1   character, or the human and natural features which make an area recognis-able and coherent;
2   distinctiveness, or the properties which make one area different from another; and
3   value, or the adjudged relative merit of landscape based on observable and generalisable properties of character and distinctiveness, rather than per-sonal sentiment and emotional attachment.

Latterly, there has been a view that all landscape has character, and thus war-rants protection and/or recovery, and this has led to the promulgation of Land-scape Character Assessment (LCA) (CA/SNH, 2002; Swanwick, 2004). Thus, LCA provides a structured basis for identifying character and distinctiveness on the one hand, and value on the other. The method entails a distinction between the tasks of 'characterisation' – involving identifying, mapping, classifying and describing landscape character – and 'making judgements' based on landscape character to inform a range of different decisions. In this approach, character is defined as 'a distinct, recognisable and consistent pattern of elements in the landscape that makes one landscape different from another, rather than better or worse'. An important implication of this definition is that all areas should be included within a landscape appraisal and policy, whereas hitherto the main purpose of landscape assessment has been to filter out 'the best' areas for special treatment. Hence, whilst selection and protection of premier sites remains important, Landscape Character Assessment is intended as a more systematic and inclusive approach with broader purposes (Table 4.3). These purposes comprise:

- identifying what environmental and cultural features are present in a locality;
- monitoring change in the environment;
- understanding a location's sensitivity to development and change; and
- informing the conditions for any development and change.

(CA/SNH, 2002)

The output of the LCA approach is the division of the land surface into 'landscape character types' and 'landscape character areas'. Landscape character types are 'generic' in nature and thus may occur in different parts of the country. Wherever they occur, however, they share broadly similar combinations of geology, topography, drainage patterns, vegetation and historical land use and settlement pattern. For example, chalk river valleys or rocky moorlands are recognisable and distinct landscape character types. Landscape character areas, by contrast, are 'unique' and are the discrete geographical areas of a particular landscape type. Thus, for example, the Itchen Valley, Test Valley and Avon Valley (all chalk rivers in Southern England) would be unique landscape character areas, of the generic chalk river valley landscape character type. Each has its own individual character and identity, even though it shares broad characteristics with other areas of the same type. The end product of characterisation will usually be a map of landscape types and/or areas, together with relatively value-free descriptions of their character. 'Forces for change' or 'key issues', such as agricultural innovations and types of development pressure, will often also be identified.

Landscape Character Assessment has been applied at a number of different scales, and it is intended that these should fit together as a nested series. Thus, a hierarchy of landscape character types and areas emerges in such a way that assessment at each level adds more detail to the one above. The three main levels

**TABLE 4.3 FEATURES AND PRINCIPLES OF LANDSCAPE
CHARACTER ASSESSMENT**

LCA is:

- a suite of tools to describe landscape character
- scientifically sound, region-specific and stakeholder orientated
- applicable at national, regional and local scales
- focused mainly on the more 'factual' aspects of landscape, in order to minimise value judgement.

Landscape Character derives from:

- a *combination* of factors such as geology, landform, soils, vegetation, land use, field and human settlement patterns
- past, present and/or future contexts
- interrelationships between biophysical and cultural factors.

Landscape Character can be seen as an expression of the way in which the natural and cultural elements of terrestrial ecosystems combine to create unique places with specific ecological, economic as well as social functions and values.

LCA involves making a distinction between:

Characterisation – a way of identifying areas of distinctive character, classifying and mapping them, and describing and/or explaining their character. It yields both:

- Landscape character types (usually, generic classifications or typologies)
- Landscape character areas (single and unique areas that may capture a 'sense of place' for people).

It is a staged process entailing: defining the scope of an exercise; desk study of published information; field survey of landscape elements; and classification and description of landscape character types/areas, and their key 'forces for change'. The end product of characterisation is normally a map of landscape character types and/or areas, together with relatively value-free descriptions of the character and the key characteristics that are most important for defining this character.

Judgements – using a transparent valuation system, and based on the results of the characterisation process. The nature of the judgements and the outputs that result from the process will vary according to the purpose of the assessment – such as landscape strategies, landscape guidelines, attaching status to landscapes, and landscape capacity.

Some key terms are:

- *Character* – a distinct, recognisable and consistent pattern of elements in the land-scape that makes one landscape different from another, rather than better or worse.
- *Characteristics* – elements, or combinations of elements, which make a particular contribution to distinctive character.
- *Elements* – individual components which make up the landscape, such as trees and hedges.
- *Features* – particularly prominent or eye-catching elements, like tree clumps, church towers, or wooded skylines.

Source: CA/SNH, 2002, modified

at which Landscape Character Assessment are carried out – each requiring progressively more detail – are:

- *National and regional scale* – comprising patterns that result from the underlying geology and landform overlaid with the influence of broad ecological associations and key aspects of settlement and enclosure history. This results in the identification of distinct landscape types and areas such as chalk downland or montane plateau, as well as the character areas where they occur.
- *Local authority scale* – having unity of character due to particular combinations of landform and land cover, and a distinct pattern of elements. They comprise discrete geographical areas conveying a sense of place, and might include river floodplains, plateau moorlands or enclosed farmland.
- *Local scale* – a detailed assessment may then be used either to map landscape types and/or areas at an even finer scale, or add detail by mapping and describing the individual elements which contribute to the character of the area, such as hedges, arable fields and farm buildings. Local assessments may consider the contribution made by the site to the character of the surrounding area as well as views into and out of it.

LCA also incorporates participation by stakeholders, that is, individuals and groups having an interest in the landscape through their direct involvement in land management, their knowledge of and interest in a particular subject, or their attachment to a particular place (either as residents or visitors).

A fundamentally similar approach has been taken in Scotland, although the top-level units are somewhat larger and referred to as Natural Heritage Futures.

These are deemed to comprise the 'habitats, species, rocks and landforms of Scotland, its natural beauty and amenity' (SNH, 2002). Whilst they are essentially biogeographic regions – identified on the basis of taxonomic, climatic, soil, land use and landscape character data – they are supplemented by public perception studies. Scientific information has been derived through a number of national assessments incorporating six 'themes', namely, coasts and seas, farmland, forests and woodlands, fresh waters, hills and moors, and settlements. The framework is proving useful in a variety of ways, but most notably as a basis for: the production of specific action plans and milestones; improving collaboration with key stake-holders at national and local levels; stimulating integrated policies for natural her-itage, both within government generally, and more specifically across the range of scientific and cultural responsibilities of Scottish Natural Heritage itself; targeting resources and actions; and improving internal collaboration, based on shared visions about what SNH is trying to achieve. Whilst these purposes are being met with varying degrees of success – for example, not everyone welcomes a 'conser-vation' body straying beyond a narrow remit – there is some evidence that the approach is linking economic and social agendas, and leading to improved action for the natural heritage and its associated stakeholders (Crofts, 2004).

The approach taken by CA and SNH is corroborated by the work of the Euro-pean Landscape Character Assessment Initiative (ELCAI) which reviewed a wide range of approaches employed within Europe. ELCAI's systematic review of state-of-the-art approaches in landscape character assessments found a consistent dis-tinction between:

- characterisation – the search for landscape types and/or unique areas; and
- judgements via transparent valuation systems – the selection of priority areas within particular landscape priority schemes.

However, adopting a standardised approach at the European scale is likely to raise considerable problems of transborder landscapes, where visually and ecologically similar landscapes may be severed by sovereign jurisdictions, with very different customary laws and land management practices, making management and protec-tion of contiguous units extremely difficult.

Similar approaches have also been used to define areas of significance for landscape history and landscape archaeology. Historic Landscape Characterisation (HLC) (Clark et al., 2004; MacInnes, 2004) was developed with the aim of viewing individual sites in a wider context, partly to move away from the traditional emphasis on single building or monument designation. In the early 1990s, initial work concen-trated on devising a mechanism to incorporate historic depth and characterisation into landscape assessment. This entailed the production of a series of overlain maps within a GIS, which illustrated changes within a landscape through time. Thus, unlike visual and ecological frameworks, HLC does not produce one fixed map identifying character areas, but provides layered depictions of landscape change. Equally, it dispenses with a simple definitive method in favour of an evolving and fluid one, dependent on project needs and availability of information. This flexible approach, in which the choice of methodological detail is devolved to local authority level, has been both applauded for its ability to accommodate local needs and circumstances, and criticised for lack of national consistency, thereby making comparisons and generalisations difficult. The method, though, has found various applications, and has ensured that considerations of time-depth complement other landscape classifications.

INTEGRATED APPROACHES

Despite the complexities involved, there is a clear case for developing integrated approaches to landscape information which more fully reflect multifunctionality. A notable attempt has been that of the Countryside Council for Wales (CCW), through their LANDMAP system (CCW/WLPG, 2001; Owen and Eagar, 2004). Although initially designed for flexible development at the local scale, this has gradually accumulated towards a national typology. It is essentially a landscape assessment framework incorporating both objective and subjective data, and comprises five components, or 'aspects', of the landscape, forming individual layers within a GIS. The aspects comprise:

- *culture* – human influence on, and the ways in which people apply meaning to, the landscape;
- *earth science* – geology, geomorphology and hydrology;
- *biodiversity* – vegetation and habitats, consideration of landscape ecological issues;
- *historical and archaeological historical* sites;
- *visual and sensory* – qualities perceived through senses, such as landform and land cover.

These combine to produce 'Aspect Areas'. Outputs from the system are arranged hierarchically into four levels, these providing in turn:

- Level 1 – basic description of landscape type
- Level 2 – description of major landforms

- Level 3 – sub-division of landforms, indicating basic physical descriptions including vegetation cover
- Level 4 – the most detailed level, at which individual features are identified and fully described.

Whilst the approach is data intensive and its full extension to Level 4 will require a long time horizon, its value as a multi-attribute data source is already helping to mainstream landscape scale thinking into spatial planning.

All of the approaches discussed so far have essentially been reductionist in nature, related to a range of applications in policy, protection, planning, measurement and monitoring. A radical alternative would be an interpretivist approach, seeking to comprehend and value landscapes in terms of their meanings to insiders, and to understand their evolving 'stories'. In contrast to the widespread 'official' approach, based on hypothetico-deductive or empirical principles, Oreszczyn and Lane (2000) have advocated a holistic, inductive approach. Their particular interest was in a *bocage* landscape, within which hedgerows were considered an integral part of a human activity system. A 'systems approach' was used to investigate the situation in terms of the connectedness and relationships between parts set in a particular context, as opposed to looking at parts in isolation (Ison and Blackmore, 1997). Although systems thinking, in its early years, was concerned with engineering and production systems, more recently researchers have extended it to the analysis of socio–technical or human activity systems. In these, humans, and indeed the researcher, are seen as part of a complex system rather than as external users of it (Oreszczyn, 2000). The authors imply that the challenge for future landscape planning and management is to consider the 'total human ecosystem', which entails including all stakeholder views on an equal basis, both emotional and rational, personal and professional, and objective and subjective. Such an approach, whilst enjoying some success within particular research applications, has not yet been extended to wider practices of spatial planning.

CHANGE AT THE LANDSCAPE SCALE

Whereas much of the development of landscape classification and evaluation since the 1960s has been concerned with mapping its relative qualities and attributes, there has been a more recent concern with identifying landscape change, particularly the loss and gain of features that contribute to landscape distinctiveness. Modern methods of characterisation make this a more feasible task, as they are based on the presence and condition of observable attributes, and thus furnish a relatively objective baseline for recording change. A well–established model for reporting environmental change is that based on cause-effect relationships between interacting components of social, economic and environmental systems, notably developed as part of the Canadian and European State of Environment Reporting systems (http://glossary.eea.eu.int/EEAGlossary/D/DPSIR [accessed 28 June 05]; Simpson, 2004), namely:

- Driving forces of environmental change (e.g. industrial production)
- Pressures on the environment (e.g. discharges of waste water)
- State of the environment (e.g. water quality in rivers and lakes)
- Impacts on population, economy, ecosystems (e.g. water unsuitable for drinking)
- Response of the society (e.g. watershed protection).

This is referred to by its acronym, *DPSIR* (Figure 4.1)

    A landscape equivalent of this model was proposed by Gobster *et al* 2000 (cited in Gobster and Rickenbach, 2004) (Figure 4.2). In one application, they reported on issues of parcelisation (subdivision of land into development sites) in Wisconsin, and summarised these in terms of:

- *Patterns* – visible patterns and sizes of parcelisation, where they are occurring and the degree to which the process is resulting in fragmentation or land development.
- *Drivers* – the characteristics and causes of parcelisation.
- *Effects* – problems, benefits and human/ecological impacts resulting from parcelisation.
- *Response Strategies* – nature of and responsibilities for solutions to parcelisation issues.

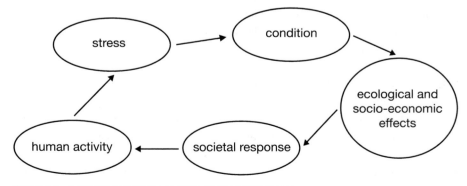

Figure 4.1 A simplified model for reporting environmental change

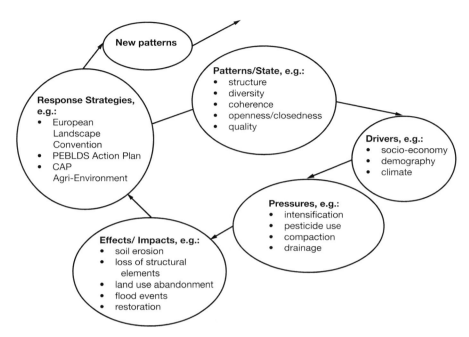

Figure 4.2 A model for reporting landscape change

Source: based on Gobster and Rickenbach, 2004; Wascher, 2004

Questionnaire results exploring these factors were used as a basis for discussion forums, which led to the derivation of a number of categories and themes, namely:

- *Patterns* – Movement; distribution; size; rate of change
- *Drivers* – Socio-economic; demographic; values and motivations; globalisation and technology; natural capital; policies
- *Solutions* – Planning and regulation; taxes and incentives; acquisition and funding; education and ethics.

In Europe, landscape monitoring is likely to be based on a suite of:

- Driving force indicators, focusing on the causes of change in environmental conditions in agriculture, such as changes in farm financial resources and pesticide use.
- State indicators, highlighting the effects of agriculture on the environment, for example, impacts on soil, water and biodiversity.

- Response indicators covering the actions taken to respond to the changes in the state of the environment, such as changes in agri-environmental research expenditure.

(OECD, 2001)

Given the complexities of defining and measuring the components of landscape change, however, the detail of these indicators has been much slower to develop than that of other environmental topics (OECD, 2003). Piorr (drawing upon Eiden, 2001) found that emerging approaches to landscape indicators generally appear to require identification of specific attributes, incorporating:

- landscape features: the elements composing a landscape and which can be described (biophysical objects);
- human perception: indicators dealing with the perception of landscape by different stakeholders; and
- landscape management and conservation: indicators reflecting landscapes as a subject for management, planning, conservation or protection.

At a finer grain, they generally include: formal, natural and cultural-historic landscape features; present anthropogenic landscape features; and protection/ conservation of cultural landscapes and nature. These may then be differentiated into specific attributes to obtain indicators of change (Wascher, 2004). Clearly, the costs of establishing a programme of landscape monitoring are considerable, and firm criteria for robust time-series data must be agreed (Table 4.4) (Howard et al., 2000).

In England, the 'Countryside Quality Counts' programme has produced indicators of change in countryside character and countryside quality, which input into the national series of indicators for sustainable development. These are based on a national Landscape Typology reflecting the combinations of factors that have the strongest influence on landscape, namely, physiography (altitude and geology), landcover (ecological character from the interpretation of soils, farm type) and cultural patterns (historic settlement and land use). Early results from CQC were obtained by assessing change in relation to woodland, boundary features, agriculture, settlement and development, semi-natural habitats, historic features, and river and coastal elements, which had already been mapped for the Joint Character Areas[2] of England between 1990 and 1998. Judgements about the significance of change were made in relation to a series of Character Area Profiles, based on the Character Area descriptions published by the Countryside Agency in the mid-1990s. The outputs indicated areas in which changes appeared either to be consistent with, or undermining, key attributes of existing countryside character. Overall, between 1990 and 1998 23% of landscapes in England had changes that were marked and inconsistent with descriptions, and 37% had changes that were inconsistent but of less significance for overall character.

TABLE 4.4 CRITERIA FOR LANDSCAPE MONITORING DATA

1   The extent and components of the landscape being monitored must be explicitly stated – the geographic boundary of the region of interest must be demarcated and the statistical confidence in any results or descriptions set. Once all these items have been taken into account, a campaign of data collection can be planned. While the information to be collected and the funds available will determine the methods of collection, it is important to be aware of the views of different users of the information in order to avoid criticism resulting from poor communication with different sectors.

2   Terms must be clearly defined and methods fully explained – clear communication is essential at all times, between surveyors/analysts and users of information.

3   Samples must be targeted carefully to maximise returns on effort – an appropriate stratification increases efficiency, but must be statistically rigorous.

4   Standard methods of recording must be utilised on each sampling occasion – any modifications or additions must be conservative and not jeopardise comparison with data already collected.

5   Subjective decisions must be avoided or minimised – decisions should be made in the field wherever possible, and appropriate training and clear definitions provided to surveyors.

6   A standard level of expertise must be set for surveyors/interpreters.

7   Different sources of information should be used to maximise their strengths – census techniques give excellent broad-brush descriptions, whereas field samples provide greater depth of environmental/ecological detail, for instance.

8   The time between surveys should be long enough to allow change – this is a compromise as processes operate on different time-scales, so seasonal fluctuations and dynamic processes may be confounding.

9   The same sample locations should be revisited so that real change can be recorded.

10   The accuracy of results should be tested through quality assurance exercises – information should be presented in a variety of ways but always qualified by descriptions of confidence.

Source: Howard *et al.*, 2000, modified

CONCLUSION

Planning for landscape sustainability must be informed by a rigorous evidence base, but must also be sensitive to the meanings and stories attached to distinctive territories. Thus, whilst mapping landscapes requires the extensive use of codified scientific evidence, it also needs to embrace lay knowledge and emotional responses. Considerable progress has been made in recent years in gathering information both about the properties of landscape, and about the nature and consequences of change. Much of this information is being collected on the basis of 'intrinsic' landscape units rather than traditional administrative territories, which often cut across the boundaries of environmental systems. However, it is important that such information is presented in ways that are useful to practitioners who operate within conventional political-administrative units. More ambitiously, landscape scale information permits planners not only to plan for landscape units, but also through them, as they become the basis for gathering and integrating multi-attribute spatial datasets.

Paradoxically, despite the fact that the landscape is valued as a framework for spatial planning precisely because it is holistic and integral, codified scientific knowledge relies on 'reduction'. In essence, the division of landscapes into recording units, and 'naming their parts' in terms of measurable attributes, is somewhat at variance with principles of integration and transdisciplinarity. However, data gathered on a systematic and rigorous basis appear to be essential to effective spatial planning, and a reductionist gaze may effectively be balanced by the overarching use of a 'landscape scale' as an integrative framework for place-making. In this regard, the current emphasis appears to be on gaining information on scientific and historic attributes of landscapes, and also on the less fully quantifiable topic of 'character'. Equally, though, the 'evidence base' must increasingly include issues such as local associations and people's perceptions of landscape change, and this will pose challenges for many years to come.

Having covered the various factors underlying a landscape-centred approach to spatial planning — the nature of 'scale', the relationships between people and place, and the evidence base required for effective intervention — we now consider the ways in which such an approach might actually be practised. A fundamental attribute of landscape-based approaches is their holistic and systemic nature, necessitating a perspective, which cuts across subject and professional disciplines, and across artificial divisions of the earth's surface. This poses a major and often unfamiliar challenge, and requires that planners have methods at their disposal which assist joint problem-solving and the production of integrative strategies. Whilst there has only been a limited track record in these matters, there is now a modest but growing body of experience, reflecting a range of natural and social science projects. It is difficult to claim that there is a single consensual 'landscape scale planning' method, but there is sufficient evidence from recent exercises that such an approach is becoming feasible.

CHAPTER 5

PRINCIPLES FOR LANDSCAPE SCALE PLANNING

INTRODUCTION

Drawing upon the ideas explored thus far, this chapter begins to bring together the emerging approaches to spatial planning for and through landscapes. Rookwood (1995) has argued that such an approach needs to bridge the rationalised, compartmentalised reality of science, and the emotional, interactive reality of politics. It therefore needs to be able to translate scientific theory into a vocabulary of planning objectives which can influence the decision-making process. A main aim of this chapter is to review means of bridging the science–society divide by identifying mechanisms for delivering environmentally robust solutions through appropriate spatial units in ways that are supported by institutional capacity. Reflecting this aim, three principal considerations are addressed: crossing boundaries, both disciplinary and geographical; normative spatial planning, based on scientific and management principles; and deliberative planning, drawing upon the social and institutional infrastructure.

CROSSING DISCIPLINARY AND ADMINISTRATIVE BOUNDARIES

One of the most recurrent observations about landscape scale practice is that it needs to draw upon multiple subject disciplines. Designers, ecologists, economists, planners and others need not only to work together, but also to talk together in mutually comprehensible terms, and communicate their ideas in ways that engage non-experts. After many years of attempting such practices, commentators have broadly identified three stances:

- *multidisciplinarity* – where experts of different professions work together on a particular project, each contributing their own specialisms;
- *interdisciplinarity* – where experts of different professions work within the same team and take a shared approach to problem-solving by gaining insights into each other's expertise and methods so that integrated solutions can be proposed; and

- *transdisciplinarity* – where an inter-disciplinary approach is taken, but lay stakeholders and policy-makers are actively engaged in problem formulation and design by integrating their knowledges and experiences with those of scientific experts.

These approaches are progressively more demanding, but are fundamental to the practice of effective spatial planning.

Uhrwing (2003) notes a number of potential problems, which need to be faced when working across disciplinary boundaries, particularly those arising from differences in conceptual and analytical frameworks. Whilst transdisciplinary approaches can be highly complex and frustratingly slow, Uhrwing argues that ignoring their problems may create confusion and conflict, whereas facing up to them often creates space for mutual learning. She advocates a number of areas for attention, which may be summarised as:

- *Problem solving* – problems and their solution spaces need to be defined with great care as different interested parties may conceptualise them in different ways. A systems analysis approach may be helpful here, but 'toolkits' may also be useful in helping inexperienced workers in inter-disciplinarity grasp shared concepts and approaches.
- *Leadership* – a programme leader can help instil a vision which motivates inter-disciplinary work. Necessary qualities are the ability to build bridges between subject 'cultures' and empathy for capacities of different team members.
- *Quality and critical mass* – focusing on a small number of fast-developing and promising projects, that have a critical mass of personnel and infrastructure, may help projects blend into existing structures, and create win-win partnerships beyond the immediate institutional setting.
- *Training* – interdisciplinary perspectives, problem orientation and a feeling for context need to be introduced to team members at an early stage, though it is equally important for members to have core competences and problem-solving abilities.
- *Quality control* – most quality control criteria, such as performance indicators, have been developed within individual disciplines, and more integrative targets need to be devised.
- *Exchanging experiences* – future improvements in interdisciplinary work will depend on clarification and replication of best practices, hopefully leading to a 'mainstreaming' of interdisciplinary methods and cultures.

Because they involve a strong public/stakeholder participation element, transdisciplinary approaches also require an integration of expert and lay knowledges. One means of bringing these together is through 'knowledge brokership'. Van Mansfeld (2002) has shown how such an approach was undertaken during a regional dialogue conducted in the Netherlands based on:

- an interactive transdisciplinary approach dealing with an inventory of opinions;
- innovative approaches towards sustainability solutions for complex problems;
- bridge-building between fundamental and applied research;
- rendering implicit knowledge explicit;
- creating, mixing, spreading and using different kinds of knowledge;
- gaining the active support and commitment of key parties to opinions and solutions;
- developing ideas on a cooperative basis between actors, in order to achieve agreement and minimise defensive reactions.

Critical to success was a knowledge broker, who played the pivotal role in making sense of a transdisciplinary approach and retaining the commitment of individual contributors (Table 5.1).

Of equal importance with the issue of crossing 'knowledge' disciplines is that of transcending administrative-political boundaries. Centring on the notion that a region might be aligned to the self-organising properties of environmental systems and embedded socio-economies, one argument has been to try and identify

---

TABLE 5.1 'PERSON SPECIFICATION' FOR A KNOWLEDGE BROKER

- Good communicator to bridge the gap between governors, policy-makers and citizens;
- instigator of 'magical moments' in the planning process;
- facilitator of participatory/workshop design approach;
- reformulator of the basic issues, to keep the working process transparent;
- intermediary between public and private sectors and scientific investigators;
- builder of 'process architecture', to plan the process and interactions;
- administrator, planner, conflict manager;
- creator of safe learning environment, mediator to create consent (as opposed to consensus), stimulator of open-mindedness of contributors, group builder stimulating joint identity;
- sectoral knowledge carrier on landscape issues;
- a learning attitude.

Source: based on Van Mansfield, 2003

'natural units' either as a generic basis for governance, or for the organisation of more limited spatial planning partnerships. Thus, the case has been made for integrative 'bioregions' or, more frequently, and as discussed in the previous chapter, for landscape units (such as Natural Areas) devised for particular purposes.

The desire to define 'bioregions' arises both from cultural and ecological motivations. We have noted previously how traditional identities have declined, and this 'detraditionalisation' has led, amongst other things, to a decline in the sense of attachment to sharply-defined national, regional and local identities. This has been synchronous with a 'hollowing' of the national state by supranational realignments (such as the EU) and transfers of responsibility to sub-national governance levels and private/voluntary organisations (Millward, 2000). Thus, faced with the erosion of traditional allegiances, there seems to be a cultural trend to invent new regional and local identities. Although differing from historical attachment to specific regional spaces, people now appear to identify with a particular locality because 'it pleases them, because it offers agreeable landscapes, a clement sky, well-serviced towns, or because it was celebrated in literature, poetry or the cinema' (Claval, 1993: 160; cited in Low Choy, 2003).

McGinnis (1999) has linked bioregional thinking to the relationships displayed between indigenous cultures and their landscapes: in this perspective, industrialisation and its associated economic, social, institutional and administrative structures are represented as the cause of our psychological and political separation from local/regional landscapes. Whilst early bioregional thinking emphasised the role of ecological systems in determining 'natural' boundaries, it now more typically reflects a belief that 'landscape units' should reflect not only environmental processes, but also a sense of place and a human identification with familiar landscapes (Brunckhorst, 2000). According to Low Choy (2003), a bioregion thus needs to be of such a scale that it facilitates maintenance of the integrity of a region's biological communities, habitats and ecosystems; supports important ecological processes; meets the habitat requirements of keystone and indicator species; and includes the human communities involved in management, use and understanding of biological resources. Whilst this implies quite a large area, it also needs to be small enough for local residents to consider it 'home'. However, although there may be a compelling 'systems' logic to the creation of bioregions, it is clear that, given the alleged prolonged separation between people and place in post-industrial societies, substantial effort must be invested in reconnecting people and their governance institutions with place. As Brunckhorst (2000) has cautioned, bioregional frameworks will only be useful if they have meaning to decision-makers and communities, and are recognised as valid by a range of sectoral interests.

According to McGinnis (1999), bioregions are based on four key principles, namely:

- *interdependence* – the recognition of a strong connection between natural and social systems;
- *autopoiesis* – a system's self-organising capacity, deriving from the unity and relationship between its component parts;
- *adaptability* – the bioregional boundaries should reflect the self-producing and self-withdrawing characteristic of living systems; and
- *self-regulation* – the system's capacity for self-organisation needs to be enhanced, and matched by the capacity of the social/governance system.

Brunckhorst (2000) has further suggested that a bioregional planning framework might centre on some core elements. These can be summarised as: the participatory identification of a number of hierarchical management units and assembly of associated information needs based on multi-attribute biophysical regions and watersheds; an exploration of local people's perception of their place and their relationship with the biophysical attributes; and a participatory reconciliation of the implications of outcomes from these two steps.

Building upon the ideas of Brunckhorst and McGinnis, we can suggest that a landscape scale approach needs to incorporate three facets, namely:

- *spatial* – the redrawing of political and economic boundaries on the basis of bioregionally oriented relationships such as biotic province, biome, ecosystem or watershed;
- *functional* – a move towards transparent, flexible transdisciplinary governance structures, aligned to the adaptive and open nature of natural systems; and
- *temporal* – the successful transition to a bioregional approach through the adoption of timeframes that transcend short-term political and economic cycles.

These writers also echo some elements of spatial planning which we have noted previously. Key elements include identifying information needs and hierarchical ('nested') management units based on multi-attribute biophysical regions and watersheds, involvement of all stakeholders (land management agencies, resource users, local government and key community representatives), an exploration of local people's perception of their place and their relationship with the biophysical environment, and a participatory process to examine the implications of future options. Brunckhorst notes that this will involve the collection and handling of multidisciplinary data, gathering and mapping community and social data, identifying the responsible agencies and their jurisdictions, using transdisciplinary planning approaches, examining the integrative capacity of the institutions and their existing processes, and promoting the transformation of existing social and institutional structures.

NORMATIVE LANDSCAPE SCALE PLANNING

This section addresses emerging possibilities for 'normative' planning approaches, that is, intervention to achieve defined goals based on notions of how things 'ought to be'. Whilst landscape scale planning has only a limited legacy of experience in this respect, much can be learned from cognate fields, notably that of 'ecosystem-based management'. This typically draws on scientific (particularly landscape ecological) principles, and is thus essentially normative in terms of working towards modelled goals. One of the chief commentators on the subject is Slocombe (1998), who notes that the need to respond to problems of fragmented management has been coupled with a growing interest in integrative management approaches based on sustainable development, biodiversity and ecosystem integrity. As with landscape scale planning, ecosystem-based management seeks to transcend arbitrary political and administrative boundaries, in order to achieve more effective, integrated management of resources and ecosystems at regional and landscape scales. Botequilha Leitão and Ahern (2002) consider that the key characteristics of ecosystem-based management are that it must be built on ecological science and on understanding ecosystem function, and that humans are integral components of ecosystems. The ecosystem-based management approach – of defining the management unit, developing understanding, and creating planning and management frameworks – has found widespread application in the USA, Canada and Australia.

This approach, however, is not purely expert-led and also recognises the importance of stakeholder inclusion. For instance, Szaro et al. (1997) emphasise the need for a participatory dimension, in which all stakeholders are involved in defining sustainable options for people-environment interactions. Echoing bioregionalism, they argue that its goal is to restore and sustain the health, productivity, and biodiversity of ecosystems and the overall quality of life through a natural resource management approach that is integrated with social and economic needs, and that place- or region-based objectives must be defined appropriately for each given situation. They also stress the importance of interaction between stakeholders and institutions, given the ways in which natural ecosystems typically cross administrative and jurisdictional boundaries.

Another leading exponent of ecosystem-based management, Yaffee (1999), has shown how it draws on the complementary traditions of 'environmentally sensitive multiple use', 'ecosystem approaches to resource management' and 'ecoregional management'. The first of these is based on an anthropocentric perspective that seeks to foster multiple human uses subject to an understanding of environmental constraints. An ecosystem approach is, by contrast, more biocentric in its view; here, ecosystems are understood as a metaphor for holistic thinking, and thus the approach requires a broad understanding of the dynamism and complexity of ecological systems, relationships between different scales, and the need for management across ownership boundaries. Ecoregional management takes an ecocentric perspective that focuses on the management of specific (i.e. geographically defined) landscape ecosystems, requiring a management shift away from the requirements of individual biota and towards ecosystem processes. Yaffee (1999) argues that, as particular cases vary, and the philosophies of planners and conservationists differ, it is unlikely that a single model will be found. Rather, we will tend to move along a continuum, and target policy prescriptions (such as legal instruments, incentives and information provision) according to the requirements of different contexts. Botequilha Leitão and Ahern (2002) seek to link the ecosystem-based management paradigm to landscape ecology. In so doing, they advance a conceptual framework for sustainable landscape planning based on landscape ecological principles and selective use of landscape metrics.

Given the breadth of information associated with landscape ecological models, it is impossible to produce normative prescriptions which are applicable to all types of species, environment or policy systems. Instead, a number of alternative approaches have developed in different countries relatively independently of each other. For example, Hawkins and Selman (2002) have identified three approaches which appear to have been used relatively widely and persistently, though they are by no means exhaustive. These are the 'landscape stabilisation' model popularised in Eastern Europe during a period of command-and-control planning; the 'focal species' model where futurescapes are based on generalisable habitat requirements of characteristic species; and linear features or 'greenways' that form a multifunctional interconnected green infrastructure.

The 'landscape stabilisation' approach entails conducting a landscape analysis, as a basis for comprehensive landscape planning at a range of scales. It emphasises the role of landscape elements in conserving and enhancing biodiversity and scenery, and places particular emphasis on their 'hygienic' functions such as water and soil protection, air purification, and soil erosion control. The understanding of 'stability' relates to the capacity of a landscape to remain unaltered or to regenerate quickly after anthropogenic or natural perturbance (Miklos, 1996), and stable landscapes most typically comprise those in a natural or semi-natural condition. The basis of this planning approach is to map at various scales those elements in the landscape that are inherently stable or unstable, and to determine from these maps a network of landscape elements to act as 'biocentres' and 'bio-corridors' (Bucek *et al.*, 1996). The existing network can then be analysed to identify where landscape creation or rehabilitation is necessary to fill strategic gaps. The basic concept involves retaining existing ecological infrastructure, and then creating 'more of the same' in deficient areas. The approach is often referred to as Territorial Systems of Ecological Stability (TSES) (Jongman, 2002; Miklos, 1996), and is based on selection criteria (representativeness, ecological significance, internal ecological stability, size and shape), location criteria (position and spatial arrangement of geo-ecosystems, requirements of soil and water protection, anti-erosion measures, filtration, micro-climatic, hygienic, aesthetic functions, ecostabilising measures) and realisation criteria (ecological quality of the current landscape structure, existing legal protection instruments).

This 'ecostabilisation' approach has most typically been applied where landscapes have been seriously damaged, notably during the communistic era in Eastern Europe where land use was subordinate to the rules of the planned economy, leading to large-scale technocratic projects, a monofunctional simplification of the collectivised agricultural landscape, widespread erosion and salinisation of soils, and other environmental problems (Jongman, 2002). The theoretical basis for this approach was developed by the Russian geographer, Rodoman (1974), who advocated the idea of a 'polarised landscape', which basically accepted intensive land use but compensated this with a functional zonation, including areas and elements where 'nature' can predominate. Thus, targeted landscapes were zoned into areas prioritised for nature and recreation (including appropriately restored sites) on the one hand, and urban-industrial and agricultural use on the other. Jongman argues that this approach has, however, not been restricted to centrally planned economies, and cites the Netherlands as one example where there has also been a polarisation of landscapes and land uses (through very different economic and political forces), accompanied by comparable planning methods such as the 'framework concept' (Vrijland and Kerkstra, 1994).

With regard to the focal species approach, we have already noted that a dilemma for landscape ecologists is the impossibility of defining an appropriate 'landscape scale' for each of a myriad of species. In practice, generalisations can be made about 'guilds' of species (groups of species that exploit the same class of environmental resources in a similar way) or 'focal' species (key species with which a characteristic ecological dependency web is associated) and whose habitat requirements are an effective proxy for numerous associated organisms. However, one of the most serious practical difficulties facing landscape ecologists when advising on the redesign of landscape elements is that there is no single optimum solution that suits 'biodiversity' generally, as each species has distinctive spatial requirements. Moreover, ecologically desirable solutions may conflict with scenic preferences, and accompanying visualisations may be needed in order to gauge public and political reaction.

The focal species approach has gained a degree of popularity, especially where it is coupled to visualisations conveying the likely appearance of future landscapes that would provide suitable conditions for the target species. It has reached its greatest sophistication in the Netherlands, where the creation of new landscapes has a relatively long pedigree. A significant deficiency of landscape ecological planning has conventionally been its tendency to produce a single optimum design. In the focal species approach, alternative – though not mutually exclusive – 'optima' based on different species are presented as scenarios for integrated spatial planning. This has been used to guide policy-makers on the withdrawal of land from agricultural production, the consequences of developmental and recreational pressures, and biodiversity planning (Harms et al., 1993; Lambeck, 1997). However, critics claim that it relies on undue generalisation and inadequate knowledge of species' requirements.

Whilst focal species and ecostabilisation approaches seem to emphasise defragmentation, another trademark of landscape ecology is its concern for connective corridors. This perspective finds its apogee in the 'greenway' concept, based principally on the belief that continuous linear features in the landscape assist key environmental functions, such as species dispersal and hydrological processes. However, an important quality of the greenway is that it is essentially a multi-benefit landscape and, whilst the initial motivation may be ecological, it also supports other objectives such as recreation, visual appreciation, scenic highways, pollution buffering, and heritage and cultural resource protection (Smith and Hellmund, 1993; Fabos, 2004). This is proving to be especially important in land use planning. Theoretical deficiencies in the science underlying the conduit (connectivity and connectedness) functions of vegetated linear features have made it difficult for planners to defend ecological corridors when challenged by developers. However, whilst there is limited evidence of support for the wildlife diffusion role of corridors in planning decisions, their multi-benefit nature makes it much more feasible for planners to mount a case for their defence (Dover, 2000). The greenway planning approach is not restricted to a particular spatial scale, but is intended to operate at all scales from the local to the regional. In practice, scalar differences may not so much be related to environmental characteristics, as to the degree to which community groups take responsibility for aspects of design and management, with more local greenway schemes more likely to be inspired by communities-of-place.

Landscape ecological approaches based on connectivity also lie at the heart of Forest Habitat Networks (FHNs) (Ray *et al.*, 2004). Latham *et al.* (2004) describe FHNs as entailing the strategic consolidation, expansion and reconnection of woodland cover to reverse some of the impacts of fragmentation. FHN objectives are often described from a forest management perspective, so that woodlands are linked together into coherent areas which not only function better ecologically but are also more rational to manage (Worrell *et al.*, 2003). Some users of this approach emphasise that it need not take a species-use view of habitat patches within the landscape mosaic, but can adopt a landscape structure approach in which landscape metrics, including the contiguity of patches, are measured. However, With (2002) suggests that, rather than just measure structural connectivity, the model can address the 'functional connectivity' of a landscape using a generic focal species method, where species' profiles have been chosen to represent classes of dispersal ability and area requirements, and patches' scales to represent matrix permeability for both woodland and open-habitat specialists and generalists. Since, in forests, many of the most important species are relatively immobile and thus unable to take advantage of a habitat network within the typical (c. 50 year) simulation period of a computer model, relatively mobile focal species are usually selected. Various outcomes are possible depending on local circumstances. For example, one application of the model indicated the possible buffering of riparian woodland in the Scottish Borders, as an alternative to unconstrained native woodland expansion. The researchers saw this as an adaptive approach, increasing the functional connectivity of habitats within agreed size thresholds so that, in the long term, landscapes could be managed to conserve biodiversity and, at the same time, accommodate multiple uses. FHNs also reveal scale effects, whereby smaller networks are nested within networks, characterised by species with lesser dispersal abilities and higher area requirements.

The increasing sophistication of landscape ecological methods is now leading to the emergence of more generalised normative planning models, based on the production of scientifically credible alternative future scenarios. Thus, Iverson Nassauer and Corry (2004) have investigated the use of normative scenarios in landscape ecological planning, that is, where models have been used to construct future scenarios for land on the basis of their capacity to meet explicit societal goals. The authors argue that landscape ecology is particularly apt as a basis for developing normative scenarios, as it allows scenario designers to experiment with alternative land cover patterns that are expected to have selected socially valued ecological functions. Hypothesised functions and values can then be tested against ecological, economic and cultural models or empirical data. Whilst normative models are eminently capable of incorporating stakeholder views, and even providing an imaginative basis for stakeholder participation, they demonstrate essentially the outcomes of scientists' deliberations. However, their value lies in rendering expert hypotheses about landscape pattern-process relationships explicit by using an inventive scenario design process. This enables the testing of expert hypotheses from many disciplines on the same invented landscapes, and then testing hypotheses in landscape futures that embody a high degree of realism (Iverson Nassauer and Corry, 2004). The authors propose a normative planning approach based around the issues of collecting existing data, formulating and operationalising hypotheses, generating new data, and testing hypotheses. This process is illustrated through a case study of potential alternative visions of landscape changes likely to be driven by agricultural policy in Iowa watersheds (Figure 5.1).

A similarly normative approach is reflected by the Dutch LARCH (Landscape Analysis and Rules for the Configuration of Habitat) model (Oost et al., 2000), which is being used to assess the biodiversity potential of fragmented landscapes on the basis of a selection of indicator species (Table 5.2). LARCH is a rule-based GIS expert system used for scenario analysis and policy evaluation, where habitat networks of one or more species can be visualised and the sustainability of the network assessed in terms of total network area, habitat quality and the spatial cohesion of habitat patches. In broad terms, the model is based on four basic rules, namely: the size of a natural area determines the potential number of individuals of a specific species it can contain; the distance to neighbouring areas determines whether it belongs to a network; the size of the network determines whether it can contain a viable population; and the network population must be sufficient to sustain the numerical and genetic viability of the species. LARCH requires input in the form of habitat data (e.g. a vegetation map) and ecological standards or rules (e.g. dispersal distance, population density), the latter being based on literature and simulations derived from dynamic population models (van der Sluis et al., 2001).

Van der Sluis et al., (2001) have shown how the LARCH model was applied to an analysis of the ecological network around the agricultural plains of Modena and

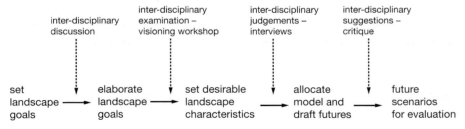

Figure 5.1 A normative approach to scenario-based landscape planning: iterative process to identify policy goals, propose desirable landscape characteristics and develop land-cover allocation models

Source: adapted from Iverson Nassauer and Corry, 2004

TABLE 5.2 THE FOUR-STAGE LARCH DESIGN PROCESS

1   Decide which ecosystems are to be improved for biodiversity. The output of this step is selection of one or more ecosystems for targeted action.

2   Decide on the goals for each selected ecosystem, and translate these into target species – as it cannot involve all species, so-called ecoprofiles are used, each representing a number of species with similar spatial characteristics and habitat requirements. The output of this step is a selection of one or more target ecoprofiles per selected ecosystem, for which ecological network improvements can be designed.

3   Generate several spatial options to achieve sustainable networks for each selected ecoprofile. A decision-tree is used to identify all possible areas where measures might improve the ecological network significantly, and then rank these to identify the most feasible and important. Strategies are to enlarge habitat patches, increase the density of a habitat network, improve the connectivity of habitat patches, and improve habitat quality in one or more habitat patches. This frequently involves participation from local experts and policy-makers.

4   The selected ecoprofiles of one or more ecosystems are integrated into an overall landscape design, to be merged with wider spatial planning perspectives.

Bologna provinces (Italy), paying particular regard to woodland, wetland and grassland. Here, LARCH was used in a planning study of an area where habitats had often become too small to sustain viable populations. An approach based on extending existing ecological networks, framed principally on the local hydrological system, was proposed. The scenario involved withdrawing areas from agriculture for nature rehabilitation to increase the connectivity of the landscape, with the main habitat increases arising from wetlands and woodlands on the floodplains. The proposals were then tested by the model, which confirmed the extent of defragmentation and improved spatial cohesion that could be achieved, albeit not all target species were able to achieve minimum viable populations. The findings led to modifications of the scenario to concentrate on particular corridors that would provide maximum benefits in terms of cohesion. The exercise was paralleled by a linked study aiming to achieve similar habitat network improvements in Cheshire (UK) (van Rooij et al., 2004).

DELIBERATIVE LANDSCAPE SCALE PLANNING

Although there are no 'polar opposites' in planning theory, the complement to normative planning is often considered to be deliberative planning. This is a rather broad term to describe a range of approaches that emphasise the contribution to planning decisions made by individuals and stakeholding groups. It assumes that decisions are reached, not only on the basis of codified expertise, but also through a 'deliberative' or 'communicative' rationality of dialogue and debate amongst those who make decisions and those who are affected by them.

There has been a growing recognition in all areas of spatial planning that ordinary people, and not just experts, should be involved in key processes. This requires that communities and stakeholders – two overlapping but distinct groups – should be engaged, both actively (e.g. in participatory design or site management) and passively (e.g. by receiving exhortation and information). In practice, notions of stakeholders and communities might be quite blurred, but a broad distinction would be that stakeholders often have a singular perspective on, and a particular and specific (perhaps even a controlling) interest in, a landscape, whereas communities are groups that are affected in more personal and diffuse ways. However, stakeholders may approximate to communities, especially where they are organised on a collective basis (for example, the 'business community'), and communities, particularly those bound together by a common interest rather than attachment to place, may appear as stakeholders.

Spatial planning requires a participatory approach for a number of reasons. First, people have a right to be involved in decisions affecting their living, working and leisure environments. Second, as we have noted, planners and their colleagues exercise a particular type of expert gaze, and need to counter this elitist tendency by taking a more inclusive approach to research and design. Third, people often seem as if they are becoming more 'alienated' from their quotidian landscapes, and participatory exercises have been advocated as a means of helping them re-engage. Fourth, 'insiders' often hold the key to long-term sustainable management, and their participation at the planning stage can often help secure their continued active commitment to achieving the outcomes of plans. In some circumstances, it may also be the case that people associated with landscapes may possess particular land or water rights, and thus have legal claims to be involved. Fifth, in the long term, it is important for social learning to take place, so that people become more aware or knowledgeable about the needs of sustainable landscapes, through being involved in decisions and actions. Finally, a central purpose of landscape scale planning is to capitalise on the ways in which people attach to and identify with a place, thereby building capacity for creative participation.

Low Choy (2002) has related participation in landscape scale planning to Ostrom's (1990) logic of collective action, which theorises the level at which the possibility of a benefit for a group is sufficient to generate collective action to achieve that benefit. In this, 'coordination' approaches entail the pursuit of a common goal through a process where people act in concert, either voluntarily or in response to the directions of a superior; 'collaboration' involves stakeholders with differing perspectives and preferences constructively exploring their differences, often making informal trade-offs and searching for solutions that go beyond their own limited vision of what is possible (Gray, 1989); and 'cooperation' occurs where all parties come together on a voluntary basis to orientate their actions towards a common issue of outcome, whilst still retaining their autonomy and being free to pursue their own goals. More specifically in relation to protected areas, 'collaborative management' (Borrini-Feyerabend, 1996) has been widely adopted as an appropriate model. In this, some or all of the relevant stakeholders in a protected area are involved in a substantial way in management activities, rather than authority being allocated entirely to specialist agencies. As a consequence, planners may need to accept a relaxation of strict conservation goals.

Pimbert and Pretty (1997), writing from a 'development studies' perspective, but with wider applicability, have noted that a deliberative approach entails dialogue, negotiation, bargaining and conflict resolution, and these should continue well after the initial appraisal and planning phases. Thus, they argue that conservation institutions and professionals need to concede some of their role as project implementers, and give greater attention to facilitating analysis and planning by local people, and to building their capacity for independent action. Echoing other frameworks such as those of Arnstein (1969) and Wilcox (1994), they identify several different styles of participation, namely:

- *Passive Participation* – where people 'participate' simply through being told what is going to happen or has already happened, and the only sharing occurs between external professionals.
- *Participation in Information Giving* – where people participate by answering questions posed by extractive researchers and project managers using questionnaire surveys or similar approaches, but do not have the opportunity to influence proceedings.
- *Participation by Consultation* – people are consulted, and external agents listen to views. Whilst these views might lead to modifications, problems and solutions are defined externally, and professionals do not concede any share in decision-making.
- *Functional Participation* – here, groups are formed to meet predetermined objectives related to the project. The brief for these groups and their role in implementation does not tend to be at early stages of project cycles or planning, but rather after major decisions have been made; although they tend to be dependent on external initiators and facilitators, they may become self-dependent.
- *Interactive Participation* – people participate in joint analysis, which leads to action plans and the formation of new local groups or the strengthening of

existing ones. It tends to involve transdisciplinary methodologies that make use of systematic and structured learning processes, and permit groups to take control over local decisions.

- *Self-Mobilisation* – participation is on the basis of taking initiatives independent of external institutions.

(Pretty, 1994, modified)

Pimbert and Pretty draw a broad distinction between two paradigms towards landscape management, which can loosely be summarised as the traditional 'blueprint' approach masterminded largely by outsider experts, and the 'learning-process' approach whereby outsiders facilitate insider groups to achieve sustainable development (Table 5.3).

Table 5.3 Blueprint and process styles of landscape management

	Blueprint	*Process*
Point of departure	expert-defined values of bio/geo-diversity	the diversity of both people and nature's values
Planning style	strategic planning	participation
Locus of decision making	centralised, ideas originate in government office	decentralised, ideas originate in local community
First steps	data collection and plan	awareness and action
Design	static, by experts	evolving through interaction between experts and stakeholders
Main resources	central funds and technicians	local people and their assets
Methods, rules	standardised, universal, prescriptive	diverse, local, varied menu
Analytical assumptions	reductionist	systems, holistic
Management focus	spending budgets, completing projects on time	sustained improvement and performance
Communication	vertical (orders down, reports up)	lateral (mutual learning, sharing experience)
Evaluation	external, intermittent	internal, continuous
Error	buried	embraced
Relationship with people	controlling, inducing, motivating; people seen as beneficiaries	enabling, supporting, empowering; people seen as partners
Outputs	conservation as a 'sector'; empowerment of professionals	conservation achieved through sustainable management; empowerment of rural people

Source: Pimbert and Pretty, 1995, modified

The benefits of participatory management in land-care have been noted to include acting in a cooperative and collaborative manner, incorporating a wide corpus of lay and professional knowledge, enhancing capacity for implementation, increasing trust between stakeholders, reducing the deadweight of enforcement, improving understanding and awareness, facilitating policy integration and increasing public commitment. However, planners must be prepared to invest substantial amounts of time and other resources in order to help develop unfamiliar skills, overcome potential opposition and maintain initial levels of consensus and energy (Selman, 2004a). Many stakeholders, particularly those who have previously been marginalised in decisions about their locality, may need considerable support in the form of community development if they are to make a positive contribution. Handley (2001) and Starkings (1998) emphasise this point in the context of greening damaged urbanic landscapes, where there can be signal challenges in securing effective design inputs and subsequent management involvement from disadvantaged and sometimes alienated neighbourhoods (Figure 5.2).

Community participation is often more likely to occur within a general national culture of collaboration and participatory action. Consequently, higher-level policy developments and sources of funding may set the climate in which local landscape management occurs. An example is the Dutch Ministry of Agriculture, Nature Management and Fisheries (2000), which has promoted a range of management and

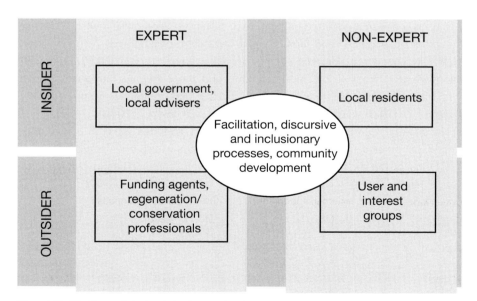

Figure 5.2 Effecting participation in landscape planning
Source: adapted from Handley, 2001; Starkings, 1998

rural regeneration initiatives across several topic areas. For instance, the department's nature management policy is based partly on traditional reserves, and partly on integration of urban and rural nature conservation, creation of ecological links across the wider landscape, and promotion of nature in ways which enhance people's well-being. Especially important opportunities for creating community partnerships appear to occur in relation to the National Ecological Network, which is intended to provide ecological connections and conserve characteristic landscape elements and heritage values. At a local level, 'urban green space networks' are being integrated into the national network through spatial planning, creating links between city parks, new housing and green areas on the urban fringe. Through this mechanism, private stakeholders can participate in decision-making processes for green space in the vicinity of built-up areas (Dutch Ministry of Agriculture, 2000). The Government supports target-oriented partnerships with an area-specific, integrated approach, and clear and accountable administrative agreements.

Increasingly, the attainment of participation by itself may be considered insufficient, and a more active learning process is sought. One of the most widely promulgated examples of this has been the Landcare movement in Australia. Although concerned initially with natural resource issues (e.g. soil and water) amongst the agricultural community, it has subsequently broadened out to include other landscape concerns and a wider cross-section of rural society. Landcare began in 1986 with a pioneer group in central Victoria, and further groups followed, generally in response to a common problem (e.g. salinity, erosion gullies) which spanned a number of properties and thus required cross-farm collaboration. The movement now comprises three elements – the National Landcare Program (NLP), community Landcare (the most visible manifestation), and the Landcare movement – and, through the National Heritage Trust, it supports 4,000 community groups involving around 120,000 volunteer members (Cary and Webb, 2000). Although its achievements regarding deep-set problems and attitudes have at times been limited, nonetheless its 'learning group' approach has widely been emulated.

One of the more difficult aspects of involving communities in cultural landscape management is that of helping them to imagine what future landscapes could look like, and how their active participation in policy options might affect this appearance. Much effort has latterly been invested in visualising future landscapes. For example, Dolman *et al.* (2001) investigated farmers' acceptance of alternative future landscape options, and what these might mean for their management operations. Consideration has been given to the necessary level of 'realism' in landscape portrayals, and the importance of representing certain elements with particular accuracy (Bishop and Rohrmann, 2003). Tress and Tress (2003) used photorealistic visualisations based on aerial and land photos as a basis of participatory land-

Figure 5.3 Scenario-based visualisations can be an effective way of generating debate about the nature and acceptability of landscape change

Source: Hehl-Lange, S., Lange, E.

scape planning. With respect to the involvement of non-experts, they found that small-scale visualisations were more appropriate and more effective in promoting communication than large-scale ones because of their realistic and detailed appearance. The researchers produced a range of visualisations, presented with a video beamer and posters, and used a questionnaire to survey reactions, as well as a variety of scenarios for an agricultural landscape – industrial, recreation and tourism, nature conservation and residential expansion. Some interesting differences emerged between lay and professional views, and between those living locally and more distantly. Notably, only the planners were favourable to residential development (and then only moderately so), whilst productive farming appealed most to locals, recreation and tourism to nearby stakeholders, and nature conservation to regional stakeholders.

Participatory approaches to landscape scale planning are dependent on being able to identify relevant stakeholders on a fair and systematic basis at an early stage. Typically, stakeholders will fall into one or more of the following categories:

- those whose interests are affected by an issue;
- those whose activities strongly affect an issue;
- those who possess information, resources and expertise needed for strategy formulation and implementation; and
- those who control relevant implementation instruments.

Borrini-Feyerabend (1996) notes that stakeholders typically:

- are *aware of their interests* in managing the area, even though they may not be aware of all its management issues and problems;
- possess *specific capabilities* (knowledge, skills) *and/or comparative advantage* (proximity, custom, mandate) for such management; and
- are *usually willing to invest* specific resources (time, money, political authority) in such management.

Their status is often determined through processes of stakeholder 'mapping' and 'analysis', often undertaken on a participatory basis.

In one mapping approach (Dick, 1997), it is recommended that stakeholders should be related to particular actions, in terms of their attitudes and influences (Table 5.4). The starting point is typically to list the general groups, rather than individuals, with particular interests. Initially, as full a list as possible is entered followed by an estimate of the stakeholder's attitude, from supportive to opposed (using a five-point scale). This estimate is then qualified by indicating confidence – for example, fully confident, reasonably confident, informed guess, wild guess – about the stakeholder's role/attitude. Then, an estimate of the influence of the stakeholder is made, typically on a three-category code: high, where a person or group has power of formal or informal veto; medium, where goals could probably be achieved against a person's or group's opposition, but not easily; and low, where a stakeholder could do little to influence the outcomes of the intended actions. This column is similarly qualified in terms of confidence. Having mapped and assessed stakeholders, the assessor must decide on the extent to which identified stakeholders should be engaged as participants – for example, involved only as informants, consulted, directly involved in decision-making, or involved as co-researchers and co-actors. Where the stakeholder is a group rather than an individual, it is necessary to decide on the style of participation appropriate, such as direct participation of everyone, or selective representation.

A similar approach is proposed by UN-HABITAT (2001), seeking to identify those people, groups and organisations who have significant and legitimate interests in specific environmental issues. It is advocated that stakeholder analysis

TABLE 5.4 KEY STEPS IN STAKEHOLDER MAPPING AND ANALYSIS

1   *Specifying issue(s) to be addressed.* Stakeholders are defined and identified in relation to a specific issue – people and groups only have a concrete 'stake' in a specific issue or topic.

2   *Long Listing.* With respect to the specified issue, a 'long list' of possible stakeholders, as comprehensive as feasible, is prepared, guided by the general categories of
stakeholder groups (e.g. public, private, and community/popular), with further sub-
categories for each. It also identifies those which: are affected by, or significantly
affect, the issue; have information, knowledge and expertise about the issue; and
control or influence implementation instruments relevant to the issue.

3   *Stakeholder Mapping.* The 'long list' of stakeholders can then be analysed by different criteria or attributes, which will help determine clusters of stakeholders that
may exhibit different levels of interest, capacities, and relevance for the issue.
Knowledge of such differences will allow systematic exploitation of positive attributes. This step should identify areas where capacity building is necessary for effective stakeholder participation, and highlight possible 'gaps' in the array of
stakeholders.

4   *Verify analysis and assess stakeholders' availability and commitment.* Review,
perhaps utilising additional informants and information sources, the initial analysis to
ensure that no key, relevant stakeholders are omitted. Assess the identified stakeholders' availability and degree of commitment to meaningful participation in the
process.

5   *Devise strategies for mobilising and sustaining effective participation of stakeholders.* Strategies should be tailored to the different groups of stakeholders: for
example, empowerment strategies could be applied to those stakeholders with high
stake but little power or influence.

Source: based on Dick, 1997

should separately identify relevant groups and interests within the public, private,
and social and community sectors. In addition, the analysis can seek out potential
stakeholders to ensure balanced representation in relation to gender, ethnicity,
poverty, or other locally relevant criteria. Cutting across these categories, the
analysis can also look at stakeholders in terms of their information, expertise and
resources applicable to the issue. The approach is designed to facilitate the
mapping of potential stakeholder roles and inputs and access to implementation
instruments, which in turn can lead to judgements about how best to maximise the
constructive potential of each stakeholder whilst also revealing obstacles that
could obstruct realisation of landscape plans. The approach is based on three key

principles and five broad sequential steps. The principles are *inclusiveness* (ensuring involvement of the full range of stakeholders, including marginalised and vulnerable groups), *relevance* (including only those who have a significant stake in the particular issue), and *gender sensitivity* (ensuring equal access to the process for women and men). The sequential steps comprise: specifying the issues to be addressed; long listing; stakeholder mapping; verifying the analysis and assessing stakeholders' availability and commitment; and devising strategies for mobilising and sustaining the effective participation of stakeholders.

A signal capability of a deliberative approach is that it can be related to the 'stories' underlying legible landscapes, which were examined in the previous chapter. Clearly, the encapsulation of shared and personal stories within landscapes creates both a profound basis for attachment to an area, and a basis on which local participants can express their concerns and visions to professional planners. The use of 'storylines' has been quite widely adopted in qualitative social science methodologies as an effective means of conveying people's experiences in a coherent and ordered manner for subsequent analysis or policy development. The approach also has significant potential within planning. For example, Sandercock (2003) has shown how stories about place have:

- a temporal or sequential framework;
- an element of explanation or coherence;
- a potential for generalisability – for seeing the universal in the particular;
- generic conventions that relate to an expected framework – a plot structure and protagonists; and
- moral tension.

In other words, they are not simply catalogues of anecdotal instances, but coherent and purposeful accounts of significant associations and experiences. We might suggest that they are particularly useful in revealing covert meanings attached to places, and thus can help outsiders share the perspectives of insiders. Sandercock (2003) advocates its role in planning, counselling caution that we should learn to deconstruct the 'official story' espoused by policy makers as well as construct the stories of other stakeholders. In England, the Countryside Agency, in collaboration with the New Opportunities Fund, grant aided a programme of urban micro-landscapes called 'Doorstep Greens'. These were evaluated by preparing stories about the differing key purposes of each Green, which range from tackling drug abuse and improving recreational access, to including ethnic minorities and creating links to the open countryside (e.g. NOF/CA, 2003).

CONCLUSION

At the heart of a landscape scale approach to planning is the opportunity for sectoral and spatial integration. This arises, on the one hand, from the scope for inter- and transdisciplinarity afforded by the multiple nature of landscape, and the need to enrol a range of subject experts and user groups. On the other hand, the adoption of landscape units as a framework for data gathering, analysis and interpretation – whether based on whole-scale bioregionalism or more limited multi-attribute zones – enables a geographical synthesis. There is a profound attraction in taking such an approach to addressing the challenges of sustainability. However, the practice of integration is generally far more difficult than the theory. A heavy investment in specific methods of joint working is invariably necessary.

Two broad planning frameworks are available for landscape scale action. Both, though, share common ground and purposes, and they can be used in combination. One is the normative approach, which is largely expert-driven and is strongly influenced by principles of landscape ecology. Historically, it has tended to borrow from other fields of ecosystem-based management; increasingly, though, it is able to draw upon an emerging suite of computer models and conceptual frameworks. Despite its 'expert-led' nature, there are significant opportunities for lay involvement, particularly where models are scenario-based and these alternative scenarios are presented in ways that enable user-groups to make informed choices.

The other broad approach emphasises deliberative principles. This recognises that cultural landscapes draw their past, present and future meanings from people's relationships to them. Consequently, landscape scale strategies need to reflect the aspirations and entitlements of insiders and outsiders. This requires a significant degree of humility from planners and scientists. Once more, it is essential to call upon specific techniques to ensure that stakeholders and the wider public are systematically involved. Overall, despite the complexities of landscape scale planning, it is reassuring that there is a growing body of experience and methods to support effective action.

This chapter has essentially considered the possibility of a landscape scale approach 'in principle'. As noted earlier, however, on top of the conceptual challenges facing practitioners, there are also major difficulties posed by the disparate and often weak powers available to give effect to landscape-centred plans. The following chapter, therefore, looks at the repertoire of delivery mechanisms available for strategy implementation. Clearly, there are a huge variety of individual instruments available across different countries, but these tend to fall into fairly consistent types of measure. It is suggested that such measures can be used in combination to assemble the range of resources necessary for implementing landscape scale objectives, though a high level of imagination and persistence will be necessary to make a significant impact on potent drivers of landscape change.

CHAPTER 6

INSTRUMENTS FOR LANDSCAPE SCALE PLANNING

INTRODUCTION

The practice of landscape scale planning has generally been undermined by the lack of a clear and robust set of policy instruments – in effect, we have often been faced with the prospect of having to plan without effective planning powers. Over the decades, 'development planning' has had weighty legislation and rafts of policy measures at its disposal, and even so has found difficulty in achieving its object-ives. New legislation and policy guidance for spatial planning is being introduced, but its emphasis is still firmly on conventional definitions of 'development', related to construction, civil engineering works, minerals and associated changes of use. Influencing the drivers of landscape change continues to rely on far weaker and more fragmented provisions. Nevertheless, across different national legislatures, there is a recurrent repertoire of legal and policy instruments that can be deployed to effect landscape scale strategies.

In respect of landscape planning *per se*, there are many frameworks, both domestic and international, that enable strategies of protection, planning and man-agement. These are often directed at 'special' sites, but attention is increasingly being paid to practices of landscape planning across the wider countryside. The European Landscape Convention, for example, is an outstanding innovation in terms of recognising the role of landscape across the 'entire territory' of countries.

With regard to integrative planning at the landscape scale, the situation is less clear. However, even here, we can point to a range of generic devices for con-trolling, inducing and informing decision-makers. Whilst the array of programmes and projects may at times seem confusing, we can identify generalities in the way that governments seek to manage knowledge, facilitate networks and partnerships, and mobilise action. Imaginative use of these instruments can create opportunities for intervention at a range of scales and in different landscape contexts.

SAFEGUARDING 'THE LANDSCAPE'

National legislatures for environmental protection and spatial planning have tended to emphasise safeguard of special features and regulation of the process of urbanisation. Strong measures are often in place to designate and safeguard 'the best' landscapes, especially where these are pristine and acquired as reserves. However, this book focuses on 'cultural' landscapes for which protection, if it is afforded at all, is more tenuous. This distinction between landscape types is made clear by IUCN's typology of protected areas (Table 6.1). Thus, the main point of departure for the current discussion is Category V, Protected Landscapes and Seascapes, which are defined as:

> ... areas of land and/or sea especially dedicated to the protection and maintenance of biological diversity, and of natural and associated cultural resources, and managed through legal or other effective means.

These are areas where the interaction of people and nature over time has produced an area of distinct character with significant aesthetic, ecological and/or cultural value, and often with high biological diversity. Their key features are:

- high and/or distinct scenic quality
- significant associated habitats
- a harmonious and enduring interaction between people and nature
- valued for the provision of environmental services (e.g. watershed protection).

Often, too, they are associated with unique or traditional social organisations, which may underpin the sustainable use of natural resources, and there are likely to be opportunities for public enjoyment through sensitive recreation and tourism. Not surprisingly, the IUCN sees their maintenance and evolution as based firmly on securing the traditional interaction of 'people and nature'.

Table 6.1 IUCN protected area management categories

Category	Principal purpose
I(a) Strict Nature Reserve	scientific
I(b) Wilderness Area	wilderness protection
II National Park	ecosystem protection and recreation
III Natural Monument	conservation of s pecific natural features
IV Habitat Species Management Area	conservation through management intervention
V Protected Landscape s/Seascape s	management intervention for conservation and recreation
VI Managed Resource Protected Area	sustainable use of natur al ecosystems

Source: adapted from IUCN, 1994 a

In addition, since 1992, UNESCO[1] – through ICOMOS,[2] its principal advisor on heritage – has embraced 'Cultural Landscapes' in the World Heritage Convention, and so some landscapes have been included in the World Heritage List. They are defined as being 'illustrative of the evolution of human society and settlement over time, under the influence of physical constraints and/or opportunities presented by their natural environment and of successive social, economic and cultural forces, both external and internal'. Selection of this elite group is based on very strict criteria – outstanding universal value, representativeness in terms of a clearly defined geo-cultural region, and capacity to illustrate the essential and distinct cultural elements of such regions – and thus they are few in number and make only a small contribution to the overall task of sustaining the wider countryside. However, the fact that a category of 'cultural landscape' is recognised at this level is of great significance in terms of the status it gives to the broader subject. This convention recognises three kinds of Cultural Landscape, namely:

- 'Landscapes designed and created intentionally by people' – such as gardens and parklands constructed for aesthetic reasons.
- 'Organically evolved landscapes' – resulting from an interaction between a social, economic, administrative and/or religious imperative and the natural environment.
- 'Associative cultural landscapes' – important by virtue of the powerful religious, artistic or cultural associations of the natural elements, rather than material cultural evidence.

International measures, as well as strengthening safeguards over important areas, have also introduced valuable terminologies which help us define the challenges of landscape planning more consistently and independently of national peculiarities. Thus, given that cultural landscapes are working landscapes, IUCN recognises that a protected landscape/seascape is most likely to comprise a mosaic of private and public ownerships operating a variety of management regimes rather than a public authority operating a single one. It is argued that these regimes should be subject to a degree of planning or other control and supported where appropriate by various incentives, to ensure long-term continuation of key qualities. Indeed, it is possible to generalise about the planning principles, management principles and management objectives for these Category V areas (Table 6.2). Likewise, the World Heritage Convention imposes on its signatories a duty of ensuring the identification, protection, conservation, presentation and transmission to future generations of designated cultural landscapes. Specifically, signatories are required to endeavour:

- to adopt a general policy which aims to give the cultural and natural heritage a function in the life of the community and to integrate the protection of that heritage into comprehensive planning programmes;
- to set up within its territories, where such services do not exist, one or more services for the protection, conservation and presentation of the cultural and natural heritage with an appropriate staff and possessing the means to discharge their functions;
- to develop scientific and technical studies and research and to work out such operating methods as will make the State capable of counteracting the dangers that threaten its cultural or natural heritage;
- to take the appropriate legal, scientific, technical, administrative and financial measures necessary for the identification, protection, conservation, presentation and rehabilitation of this heritage; and
- to foster the establishment or development of national or regional centres for

---

TABLE 6.2 IUCN CATEGORY V – PROTECTED LANDSCAPES/SEASCAPES

PLANNING OBJECTIVES

1 Planning at all levels should be based on the laws, customs and values of the society concerned.
2 A strong legal basis is required.
3 A systematic approach is needed to selection.
4 A Category V protected area should be planned with a view to links with other protected areas and the broader bioregion of which it is a part, and as a model of sustainability for potentially wider application.
5 Consideration should be given to the relevance of any international classification of protection.
6 Defensible determination of protected area boundaries is needed.
7 Planning systems should be flexible enough to accommodate existing land ownership patterns and institutional roles where these can support the aims of conservation.
8 An effective system of land use planning is an essential foundation.
9 Planning must involve participation by a range of national, regional and local interests.
10 A strong political and public constituency must be engendered in support of the area.

MANAGEMENT PRINCIPLES

1   Conserving landscape, biodiversity and cultural values are at the heart of the Category V protected area approach. (It is important to manage change in such a way that environmental and cultural values endure: change should take place within limits that will not disrupt those values.)

2   The focus of management should be in *point of interaction* between people and nature. (Management primarily addresses the linkage between people and nature, rather than just nature itself.)

3   People should be seen as stewards of the landscape. (Managers are thus facilitators and negotiators.)

4   Management must be undertaken *with* and *through* local people, and mainly *for* and *by* them. (But this must also have regard to other, non-local stakeholders, such as consumers of water supplies downstream.)

5   Management should be based on cooperative approaches, such as co-management and multi-stakeholder equity.

6   Effective management requires a supportive political and economic environment. (Broader governance structures and practices in society at large are committed to certain standards.)

7   Management should not only be concerned with protection but also enhancement.

8   When there is an irreconcilable conflict between the objectives of management, priority should be given to retaining the special qualities of the area.

9   Economic activities that do not need to take place within the Protected Landscape should be located outside it. (The key tests should be, 'is the activity sustainable?', 'does it contribute to the aims of the area?', and 'are there strong reasons for it to be located within it?'.)

10   Management should be businesslike and of the highest professional standard.

11   Management should be flexible and adaptive. (That is, it should respond to the very different social, cultural and economic situations in which it takes place: it should always be culturally appropriate and economically relevant.)

12   The success of management should be measured in environmental *and* social terms.

MANAGEMENT OBJECTIVES

1   To maintain the harmonious interaction of nature and culture through the protection of landscape and/or seascape and the continuation of traditional land uses, building practices and social and cultural manifestations.

2   To support lifestyles and economic activities which are in harmony with nature and the preservation of the social and cultural fabric of the communities concerned.

3   To maintain the diversity of landscape and habitat, and of associated species and ecosystems.

4   To eliminate where necessary, and thereafter prevent, land uses and activities which are inappropriate in scale and/or character.

5   To provide opportunities for public enjoyment through recreation and tourism appropriate in type and scale to the essential qualities of the areas.

6   To encourage scientific and educational activities which will contribute to the long-term well-being of resident populations and to the development of public support for the environmental protection of such areas.

7   To bring benefits to, and to contribute to the welfare of, the local community through the provision of natural products (such as forest and fisheries products) and services (such as clean water or income derived from sustainable forms of tourism).

SUGGESTED ADDITIONAL MANAGEMENT OBJECTIVES (PHILLIPS, 1998)

i   To provide a framework which will underpin community participation in the management of valued landscapes or seascapes and the natural resources and heritage values that they contain.

ii   To contribute to bioregional scale conservation and sustainable development.

iii To buffer and link more strictly protected areas.

iv   To encourage the understanding and conservation of the genetic material contained in domesticated crops and livestock.

v   To help ensure that the associative and non-material values of the landscape and traditional land use practices are recognised and respected.

vi   To act as models of sustainability, both for the purposes of the people and the area, so that lessons can be learnt for wider application.

Source: IUCN, 1994a, modified

training in the protection, conservation and presentation of the cultural and natural heritage and to encourage scientific research in this field.

The status of landscape as a spatial policy issue has been strongly boosted by the European Landscape Convention, which came into force in 2004. As noted elsewhere in this book, it marks a major advance in recognising the relevance of landscape planning to the 'entire territory' rather than just selected hotspots, although it continues to ensure the importance of retaining elite landscape designations. Perhaps the key element of the Convention is Article 5, under which each Party undertakes:

- to recognise landscapes in law;
- to establish and implement landscape policies aimed at landscape protection, management and 'landscape planning' (i.e. active design) through the adoption of specific measures (these are set out in detail in Article 6 and include awareness raising, training and education, landscape assessment, setting landscape quality objectives and devising policy implementation tools);
- to establish procedures for citizen participation, local and regional authorities, and other interests, in defining and implementing landscape policies; and
- to integrate landscape into its 'regional and town planning policies and in its cultural, environmental, agricultural, social and economic policies, as well as in any other policies with possible direct or indirect impact on landscape'.

Phillips (2002) has composed a useful summary of the approach taken to 'landscape' by these three major international programmes (Table 6.3)

Almost all landscape-related legislation has tended to focus on sites and areas, and very little has reflected the importance of linear landscapes which form visual and ecological connections across the wider countryside. One of the few examples of legislation directed at network landscapes is in the UK, where Hedgerow Regulations require permission from a local authority to remove most countryside hedgerows, provided they are at least 30 years old and meet at least one of a list of criteria of importance. If the local authority deems the hedge important, they are likely to issue a 'hedgerow retention notice'. The Regulations have been criticised for over-emphasising detailed

Table 6.3 Three international approaches to landscape

Initiative	Geographical scope	Types of landscape affected	Policy/management emphasis
World Heritage Convention (Cultural Landscapes)	Global	Landscapes of outstanding and universal value	Protect heritage values
European Landscape Convention	European	All landscapes, urban and rural	Protect, manage and plan landscape
IUCN Protected Areas (Category V: Protected Landscapes/ seascapes)	National/ sub-national	Important cultural rural landscapes/seascapes meriting protection	Integrate activities and enhance natural and cultural values

Source: Phillips, 2002, modified

criteria and not including a specifically 'landscape' dimension, but this may well be remedied in future revisions.

GENERIC MEASURES FOR 'THE LANDSCAPE SCALE'

Notwithstanding the importance of measures aimed at protecting 'the best' land-scapes, this section considers more generic mechanisms for the wider countryside. It notes that, despite the absence of a coherent policy and legislative 'package', a repertoire of approaches is available. Thus, whilst specific instruments for landscape scale planning may masquerade under many guises in different national systems, they tend to address similar tasks through a suite of broadly comparable instruments.

Wascher (2004) has concluded that European policies and initiatives comprise:

- protective measures for agricultural landscapes, habitats and biotopes and isolated features;
- control/prohibition of certain types of agricultural practices;
- schemes providing farmers, foresters or other land managers with positive economic incentives for adopting a particular form of land management;
- the use of land use planning to maintain cultural, scenic, ecological and his-torical importance of landscapes (including urban development on farmland, afforestation programmes, watershed schemes, etc.); and
- restoration measures for landscapes which have been degenerated or degraded.

Thus, a defining feature of landscape scale planning is that there is no convenient and consolidated set of legislation or policy that can be applied directly in order to achieve policy outcomes. Instead, we must combine a range of measures imagina-tively in order to influence action on the ground. A generalisation of the range of

---

TABLE 6.4 IMPLEMENTATION MECHANISMS AVAILABLE TO 'WIDER COUNTRYSIDE' PLANS

1   Ownership or management of land via long-term leases.
2   Regulatory controls, mainly negative.
3   Monetary disincentives to discourage production and/or undesirable uses.
4   Financial incentives to encourage production and/or desirable uses.
5   Voluntary methods – exhortation, advice, demonstration.

Source: Gilg, 1996, modified

available instruments has been proposed by the 'Gilg-Selman spectrum' (Gilg, 1996), which summarises the principal duties, enabling powers, incentives and disincentives, and advisory services that can be combined to give effect to 'wider countryside' planning (Table 6.4).

One perceptive account of governance instruments has characterised them in terms of 'carrots, sticks and sermons' – or, in more academically sanctioned language, incentivisation, regulation, and extension work (Bemelmans-Videc et al., 1998; Collins et al., 2003). Key to the notion of carrots is that government can entice private operators (e.g. farmers, firms) to pursue publicly desirable goals by offering incentives in the form of subsidies and grants. Subsidies, guaranteeing producers stable prices by cushioning market fluctuations to ensure they obtain a return at or above 'world' prices, have become increasingly difficult to offer under global trading regimes that seek to reduce market distortions. Historically, they have been used to assure large-scale producers (e.g. cereal-focused agribusinesses) of a stable and predictable investment environment, or to enable sub-economic producers (such as hill farmers) to remain in business for 'social' reasons. Grants typically comprise capital or management payments to encourage producers to invest in various ways, either in terms of fixed capital (e.g. buildings) or maintenance regimes (e.g. woodland management). These were often used for land-improvement works, such as drainage and fencing, but are now more usually targeted at conservation measures and sustainable management practices.

For example, in relation to agriculture, many European countries now make agri-environment payments to farmers. With respect to timber, the (British) Forestry Commission pays woodland grants for planting, maintenance, and appropriately timed felling, on the basis of approved plans. Many sub-national bodies such as national park authorities receive central government payments for conservation and recreation provision. Increasingly, grants are allocated on a 'challenge' basis, in which grantees will have to bid competitively for limited resources on the basis of soundly conceived proposals and matching the grant with additional sources of income.

Agri-environment schemes, given their increasingly significant role in European farm policy, have been subject to a good deal of evaluation in terms of providing value for money and actually delivering benefits to ecology and landscape. For example, Wynn (2002) examined the cost-effectiveness of biodiversity management of heather, herb-rich grassland and wetland habitats between different farm types in the context of an Environmentally Sensitive Area scheme. At the time of study, the scheme was available to farmers on a voluntary and non-discretionary basis; annual management payments were paid to compensate for actual, forgone revenue or opportunity costs, both for adhering to good farming practice (Tier 1) and for undertaking activities which improve specific habitats (Tier 2). However, on examining the extent of biodiversity gain, Wynn found that the scheme had produced few actual changes on the ground, and suggested that most payments were probably being retained as profit. Ducros and Watson (2002) similarly noted that:

> Given that the uptake of agri-environment schemes appears to be predominantly tactical (i.e. gaining payment for little effort), significant environmental changes are unlikely in the short-term.

After examining farmer characteristics and the potential to introduce a tiered system, they advocated co-management solutions (preferred by farmers above government or locally led schemes), as these establish a sense of scheme ownership within the farming community, and may result in better compliance.

Agri-environment schemes in Europe have been in something of a flux since they were first introduced in the mid-1980s, and have addressed a wide range of issues relating to nature conservation, eutrophication, landscape, cultural and historical elements and recreation value. Some have included strong elements of farmer education or a formal move to 'green accounting' systems; others have required relatively little from recipients beyond broad compliance with pre-determined principles. Some have been payable for isolated actions, others have required a comprehensive farm plan. However, this variability has been instrumental in enabling progressive moves towards a more consistent and standardised approach.

One UK scheme – with several parallels in continental Europe – has been the Environmentally Sensitive Area (ESA), which has sought to maintain and, in places, enhance the conservation, landscape and historical value of key environmental features within a designated area. Improved public access has also often been a consideration. In signing up to a time-limited management agreement, farmers received an annual payment on each hectare of land entered into the scheme (subject to a mutual five-year termination clause). Each ESA had one or more tiers of entry, with each tier requiring different agricultural practices to be followed. Typically, higher tiers had higher payment rates than the base tier, but imposed more conditions on farmers and achieved greater environmental gain. However, one of the key issues for landscape ecological planning is the ability not just to protect existing or create new habitat, but also to reconnect contiguous habitat. Thus, MacFarlane (2000) explored the scope for an additional tier of payments to ESAs, where the further funding would be linked to agreements on

Figure 6.1 The Cotswold Environmentally Sensitive Area: strong trends towards arablisation and field
enlargement have resulted in financial support for conservation measures such as
maintenance of field boundaries, sympathetic grassland management, and conservation
headlands on arable fields

Source: Sarlov-Herlin, I.

connecting habitats between adjacent farms. According to this research, many
farmers indicated a potential willingness to collaborate in ways that would enable
habitat improvements to link across farms and thus start to produce landscape
scale effects.

In the UK, the Countryside Stewardship Scheme somewhat eclipsed ESAs
during the late-1990s. This grant-aid mechanism aimed to: improve the natural beauty
and diversity of the countryside; enhance, restore and recreate targeted landscapes,
their wildlife habitats and historical features; and improve opportunities for public
access. Farmers and land managers entered 10-year agreements to manage land
in an environmentally beneficial way in return for annual payments, and grants were
also available towards capital works such as hedge laying and repairing dry stone
walls. Eligible landscape types and features included chalk and limestone grassland, lowland heath, waterside land, coastal land, upland, old meadows and
pasture, historic features (such as old orchards, parkland, traditional farm buildings), field boundaries (including dry stone walls, hedgerows, ditches and dykes),

field edges, community forests, countryside around towns and new permissive access; particular features were targeted on a county basis. Despite the high administration costs associated with local 'tailoring', this was generally viewed as a successful scheme, and it has informed the development of subsequent measures.

Greater standardisation between national schemes in the EU is emerging through the general introduction of 'entry level schemes' for compliance with a 'broad and shallow' degree of environment-friendliness, and 'higher level schemes' for more active contribution to landscape scale conservation targets. Thus, tiered 'Environmental Stewardship Schemes' are likely to become a widespread generic mechanism. Franks (2003) considers that such measures will streamline, simplify and increase efficiency and will enrol a much larger land area and many more land managers. Key policy considerations will be participation rates, levels of payment, scheme administrative costs, and the production of environmental goods.

In some countries, a further important source of support for landscape management has been the 'heritage fund', available through government or charitable organisations to encourage citizen and stakeholder involvement. The Swiss Landscape Fund (SLF), for example, was created by Parliament (though independent of any government department) in 1991, with the goal of establishing sustainable landscapes for a large part of the population, and for future generations. The fund is financed by voluntary contributions from the federal government, cantons and communes, as well as industry and private individuals, and works for the conservation, maintenance and restoration of traditional rural landscapes and threatened natural environments (Fonds Suisse pour le Paysage, undated). It aims to develop synergies between agriculture, tourism, construction and traditional crafts, as well as helping create employment in disadvantaged regions; it distinguishes itself from mainstream state subsidies by concentrating on filling gaps, facilitating alternative practices, providing demonstration projects, and giving start-up assistance. In the USA, the Conservation Fund has assisted the conservation of a number of 'working landscapes', managed by private landowners, public agencies and non-profit organisations. For example, the Valle Grande Grass Bank (New Mexico) is a partnership between ranchers, environmentalists and Forest Service personnel, which has developed into an on-the-ground demonstration project in landscape rehabilitation and sustainable ranching (http://www.conservationfund.org/pdf/casestudy.pdf [accessed 28 June 05]).

Spatial planning outcomes are also widely achieved through regulation, or *sticks*. Thus, it is frequently necessary to introduce specific controls in order to prevent damage and, hopefully, promote sustainable development: in general, 'sticks' are more appropriate to prevention and 'carrots' to promotion. Thus, there is a need to control development, pollution discharges, and environmentally damaging operations, but hopefully in a positive and constructive way. 'Stick' measures often operate by producing some sort of forward-looking statutory framework (plan), and ensuring adherence to this through either flexible or formula-driven controls, coupled with penalties for non-adherence. Frequently, consents (for development, emissions, etc.) will have some sort of 'conditions' attached to them in order to effect mitigation of adverse environmental and social effects. Within key sites, last resort controls over the destruction of landscape features may also exist – Nature Conservation Orders and Limestone Pavement Orders are examples within UK legislation.

Promoting sustainable landscape management has, ultimately, to win the 'hearts and minds' of the individuals and organisations with responsibility for achieving it – hence the importance of *sermons* within sustainability policy. In some cases, failure to attain landscape goals may mainly be due to lack of awareness, or to an ingrained culture of 'productivist' farming aimed at high volume and cheap food. Thus, government agencies and voluntary organisations seek to improve and actively promote information, demonstration sites and extension services in the belief that this can lead to improved practice. Regardless of whether sub-optimal information is a dominant or contributory cause of landscape deterioration, it is still clearly important to have high quality information services as part of an overall strategy. However, whilst there is some substance in the belief that improved information will result in improved action, equally, the existence of a 'value-action gap' (Blake, 1999) is well attested, indicating that behaviour and attitudes may be deep-seated and only changed by continued pressure and encouragement over a sustained period. Similarly, as with all sermons, there is a risk of only preaching to the converted. Regrettably, there appears to be little evidence that 'sermons' have had much effect on actively changing attitudes particularly amongst the more intensive farmers. Within an EU context, the larger and more commercially oriented farms appear to be preparing themselves for a drift towards world prices and thus are reluctant to enter voluntary environmental schemes.

The key elements of a 'sermon'-based approach are:

- publicity;
- information, either published or through internet sites;
- demonstration, typically on-site on a working farm, allowing the viewer to experience how measures can be integrated with the current business;
- extension work and integrated delivery of advisory services, often based on face-to-face visits to the land manager, but sometimes using more cost-effective methods such as discussion groups, road shows, workshops and seminars; and
- networks of knowledge.

The last of these points to more complex social learning opportunities based on multiple sources of integrated advice (e.g. face-to-face, internet-based) combined with self-help, cooperative and commercial sources. The varied and complementary role of extension services was well illustrated by Rural Delivery Review, which took place in England under the chairmanship of Lord Haskins (2003) and sought to simplify and rationalise existing delivery mechanisms. This review identified five principal failings in the delivery of rural policy related to poor accountability, failure to satisfy regional and local priorities, the existence of too many players, lack of coordination, and confused customers. The review thus proposed a rationalisation and integration, and a shift of delivery closer to the customer by devolving greater responsibility to regional and local organisations.

Thus, 'sermons' alone rarely have great effect, and often rely for their success on being combined with field-level support services to target grant-aid in ways appropriate to individual situations. Buller and Lobley (2004) identified significant weaknesses in the way that this combined approach had often operated in practice. Notably, landscape-related grant-aid has tended to be applied in a 'prescriptive' way (such as individual conservation measures in agri-environment schemes) and, whilst a 'tick-box' approach is administratively cheaper and less demanding on the recipient, it does little to change attitudes or routine practices. Similarly, agreements under agri-environment schemes have been struck in a relatively inflexible way, which creates problems when trying to match national schemes to local or farm-specific circumstances. Whilst there is usually some tolerance in what is permitted within a scheme, there are limits to the degree to which street-level bureaucrats (Lipsky, 1980) can 'bend the rules' of national schemes, and reliable and consistent advice is difficult to achieve. Flexible and tailored outcomes appear most likely where there is an effective chemistry of advice and financial assistance.

With regard to provision of advice, there is a persistent need for this to be integrated (e.g. on conservation, drainage and agronomy), but this is difficult to achieve as advisors are rarely expert in more than one area, and will either give sound advice on narrow topics or unhelpfully vague recommendations across the board. Often, the idea of a 'one-stop-shop' of environmental advice for farmers is advocated, but in practice this creates problems of providing authoritative advice across a range of topics – a 'first stop' facility, where an enquirer is never more than one 'phone call away' from definitive advice, is probably more realistic. In broad terms, multifunctional land use requires multifunctional delivery, implying an innovative approach to enrolling the target audience, and the promotion of a 'policy learning' process where field-level experience gained by advisors is fed into future scheme and delivery design.

STRATEGIC ACQUISITION

As noted in the Gilg–Selman spectrum, there is an even more interventionist approach than 'carrots, sticks and sermons', namely that of purchasing or leasing land. IUCN Category I and II areas are often purchased or leased by the highest responsible authority (typically, an agency of central government). However, this approach is costly to the taxpayer and is thus spatially quite limited, and the extensive promulgation of landscape scale effects relies on the complementary actions of the non-governmental sector. Voluntary 'trusts' have been particularly significant in this regard. For example, in the UK, the National Trusts (for England, Scotland, Wales and Northern Ireland) have long acquired land of historic and scenic interest, the extensive agricultural holdings in the Lake District National Park and the coastal lands acquired through 'Operation Neptune' being signal examples.

Recently, however, more explicitly landscape ecological strategies have been adopted. Thus, in England, the Woodland Trust – long experienced in the purchase of existing woodlands and of land for the creation of new woodland – has latterly sought a spatially coherent basis for future site acquisitions (WT, 2002). The Trust's proposals were based on a selection of widely attested landscape ecological principles. A scientific review indicated a number of site features likely to exercise a strong influence over woodland biodiversity, and some surrogate measures of woodland biodiversity that could be used to assist in site search (Table 6.5). These suggested that habitat creation should focus on buffering and extending semi-natural habitats to increase their core area and thus their ecological resilience from external impact and that enhancement of woodland biodiversity had greatest potential in areas where there was already a high density of ancient woodland. The Trust's spatial strategy thus sought to:

- Prevent further loss of ancient woodland.
- Seek the conservation and extension of all areas of old growth.
- Seek restoration of ancient woodland planted with non-native conifers to semi-natural woodland.
- Undertake and promote the buffering and extension of ancient woodland and existing semi-natural open-ground habitats in areas with a high density of ancient woodland.
- Undertake woodland-creation schemes in targeted areas, for example, where a project could contribute to a landscape scale woodland initiative such as a community forest, or to similar initiatives led by other conservation interests whose focus may be semi-natural open-ground habitats.

- Support the need to protect and maintain semi-natural open-ground habitats.
- Support the removal of secondary woodland and plantations from important semi-natural open-ground habitats, where sufficient relict features survive to enable their successful restoration.
- Seek a general reduction in the intensity of land use, particularly adjacent to semi-natural habitats.

In so doing, the intention was not to create sanctuaries, set apart from mainstream land use activities, but rather to promote woodlands that were 'part of ecologically functional landscapes'.

A comparable approach was proposed in Southwest England by a consortium of county wildlife trusts, related not only to their own reserves but also to statutory nature reserves and privately owned land (South West Wildlife Trusts, 2004). In this, they strongly advocated the need to 're-build' biodiversity, essentially through realising the potential of key habitat patches to replenish the wildlife resources of the wider countryside. Once more, maintenance of the conservation interest was based on integration with wider landscape functional-

---

TABLE 6.5 LANDSCAPE ECOLOGICAL CRITERIA FOR STRATEGIC SELECTION OF FUTURE WOODLAND SITES

SITE FEATURES OF MAJOR INFLUENCE OVER WOODLAND BIODIVERSITY

- Ancient woodland
- Old-growth woodland
- Size
- Core area
- Woodland edge adjacent to other semi-natural habitats
- Density of semi-natural habitats
- Linkage of open-ground habitats

SURROGATE MEASURES OF WOODLAND BIODIVERSITY

- Density of ancient-woodland cover
- Percentage of ancient woodland which is semi-natural
- Cumulative core area of semi-natural habitats (area of semi-natural habitats as a whole not affected significantly by edge effects from intensive land use)
- Area of old-growth woodland

Source: derived from Woodland Trust, 2002

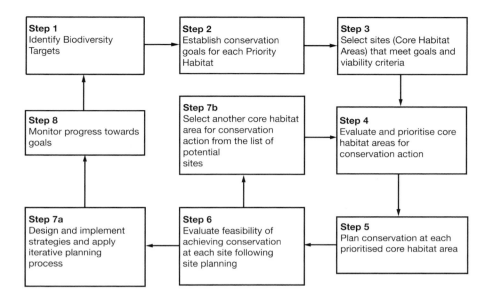

Figure 6.2 The 'rebuilding biodiversity' planning process
Source: South West Wildlife Trusts, 2004

ity, notably, water purification, flood minimisation and healthy living (Figure 6.2). Whilst neither of these approaches requires ownership of all key sites by voluntary trusts – indeed, they assume inter-dependence with wider land management activities and partnership with state, business and community – they can clearly be anchored through a network of key sites over which control can be exercised.

In the USA, Kazmierski *et al.* (2004) have noted the comparable role played by non-profit land trusts, whose ability to protect land is based partly on acquisition, but also on other types of legal and voluntary agreement. In particular, they applied a landscape ecology approach to a plan designed for the Grand Traverse Regional Land Conservancy around the Manistee River in Lower Michigan. In order to guide the Conservancy in site selection, a three-phase method was applied, comprising:

- *phase one* – develop, spatially represent and weight 'conservation drivers' (i.e. spatial representations of project objectives, such as site conservation, de-fragmentation and threat identification); conduct GIS-based overall ranking analysis; rank 'conservation focus areas' according to ecological, spatial, opportunity and feasibility criteria;

- *phase two* – examine, analyse and score all private land parcels of 16 ha or more in top three focus areas within main-priority area of search; base scores on ecological value, number of hectares with 'natural' vegetation cover, and contribution to landscape connectivity;
- *phase three* – identify and assess key threats and their sources, and overlay on 'conservation focus areas' to illustrate spatial relationship.

The exercise resulted in the identification of hotspots and, in particular, selected an amount of land small enough to narrow the Conservancy's area of search yet large enough to offer them a meaningful range of options. Further criteria were then explored, such as conservation opportunity and feasibility, leading ultimately to a hierarchy of sites for priority action.

STATUTORY PLANNING – AN OBLIQUE APPROACH

Approaches based on planning control can contribute to landscape objectives in various ways. For example, controls within protected areas tend to be stricter, with a heightened regard for 'amenity' and vernacular materials. Planning controls have a major influence over the 'middle landscape' (Rowe, 1991) of suburbia, new settlements, green belt and urban fringe. New landscape features can be created alongside construction works, either as planning conditions or as financial 'contributions' ('gain') extracted from developers. However, the weakness of central government guidance on landscape within the planning process means that plan policies have limited effect in this respect (Punter and Carmona, 1997).

Despite the presence of formal planning powers, in practice, the main influence of the statutory spatial planning system on landscape is likely to be an indirect one. In this regard, many landscape issues, despite lying outside statutory definitions of development, can nonetheless be linked to spatial planning (Selman, 2002). For example, given the exclusion of forestry from planning control, planners have sought to influence the location and nature of new and regenerated woodland through forestry and woodland strategies, whilst regional forestry frameworks now link management of the woodland estate and its associated industry to wider strategic programmes. Equally, official forestry policy in England, Scotland and Wales is being linked to spatial planning objectives related to environmental quality, recreation and access, derelict land reclamation, rural economy, and climate amelioration (Forestry Commission, 1998; Scottish Executive, 2000; WAG, 2001). Also, the UK's biodiversity strategy has been given more detailed expression through the production of local Biodiversity Action Plans (BAPs), which are essentially consensus-based multi-stake-holder plans for coordinated action. Complementary to these, English Nature experimented with 'wider countryside' spatial delivery through targeted plans aimed at consolidating fragments of key habitat to satisfy landscape ecological objectives. Thus, 'prime biodiversity areas' and the *Lifescapes* initiative (Porter, 2004) both involved mapping and implementing visions for future habitat restoration and targeted creation of new wildlife habitats across the 'wider countryside', and subsequently provided the experience for a national pro-gramme of 'area-based delivery' of nature conservation. This last venture expressly recognises the limitations of sectoral- and site-based approaches, and seeks to achieve sustainable outcomes for bio- and geo-diversity through restor-ing ecosystem functioning at the landscape scale, and to help reconnect people with nature conservation by demonstrating the link between bio-/geo-diversity and socio-economic benefit.

These various non-statutory plans suggest that, despite the limitations of statutory planning powers, the spatial planning system may be used obliquely to achieve landscape aims. Selman (2002) has argued that the prevalent sectoral approach could potentially be consolidated into integrated landscape strategies covering biodiversity, character, forestry, farmscapes, coasts and river basins. In the UK, these could become adopted within Local Development Documents, intro-duced by the Planning and Compulsory Purchase Act 2004. Such a formal linkage to the Local Development Framework would considerably increase the scope for the effective delivery of landscape scale policies, albeit existing attempts to

---

**TABLE 6.6 SPATIAL PLANNING FOR BIODIVERSITY AND
GEOLOGICAL CONSERVATION**

SUMMARY OF PRINCIPLES

i   Plan policies and planning decisions should be based upon up-to-date information about biodiversity and geological resources of the area, including an assessment of the potential to sustain and enhance those resources.

ii   Plan policies and planning decisions should seek to maintain, or enhance, or add to biodiversity and geological conservation interests.

iii   Plan policies on the form and location of development should take a strategic approach to the conservation and enhancement of biodiversity and geology, and recognise the contributions that individual sites and areas make to conserving these resources within the wider environment.

iv   Subject to other planning considerations, developments seeking to conserve or enhance the biodiversity and geological conservation interests of the area and/or the immediate locality should be permitted.

v   Local planning authorities should consider whether proposed developments can be accommodated without causing harm to biodiversity and geological conservation interests. Where there may be significant harmful effects, local planning authorities will need to be satisfied that any reasonable alternative sites that would result in less or no harm have been fully considered.

vi   Where development will result in unavoidable and significant adverse impacts on biodiversity and geological conservation, planning permission for it should only be granted where adequate mitigation measures are put in place.

vii   Development policies should promote opportunities for the incorporation of beneficial biodiversity and geological features within the design of development.

SUMMARY OF ROLE OF PLANNING STRATEGIES AND DOCUMENTS

Regional spatial strategies should:

i   Incorporate biodiversity objectives.

ii   Address regional, sub-regional and cross-boundary issues in relation to habitats, species and geomorphological processes through criteria-based policies.

iii   Seek to conserve and enhance biodiversity at the regional and sub-regional levels, including through meeting targets for the restoration and re-creation of priority habitats and the recovery of priority species populations.

iv   Identify suitable indicators for monitoring biodiversity.

Local development documents should:

i   Identify designated sites of international, national, regional, and local importance for biodiversity and geodiversity – as well as 'networks of natural habitats', linking sites of biodiversity importance and providing routes or stepping stones for the migration, dispersal and genetic exchange of species in the wider environment.

ii   Set biodiversity objectives that reflect both national and local priorities, including those which have been agreed by local biodiversity partnerships, and ensure that policies in local development documents and proposals are consistent with those objectives.

iii   Encourage the re-use of previously developed (brownfield) land but, where such sites have substantial biodiversity or geological interest of recognised local importance, look for ways of retaining this interest or incorporating it into site development.

iv   Promote the building-in of beneficial biodiversity features or elements to new developments.

Source: based on ODPM, 2005

eye on the bigger picture

connect landscape and biodiversity within development plans have met with only limited success (Bishop and Bate, 2004). Planning guidance on bio- and geo-diversity (ODPM, 2005) appears to indicate scope for improved practice within the new context of spatial planning (Table 6.6).

The oblique and indirect relationship of landscape scale issues to the statu-tory spatial planning process requires that non-statutory strategies are linked systematically to extant powers of implementation. Drawing upon the work of Healey *et al.* (2002), it may be argued that the general kinds of implementation resources available to landscape plans comprise:

- a 'knowledge' base in which issues, barriers and opportunities can be 'framed', learning can take place, and professional and lay knowledge can be merged through the use of deliberative techniques;
- a 'relational' base, defined through stakeholder analysis, that utilises the power and relationships between different stakeholders as a means of inte-grating collective aspirations for landscape management; and
- a 'mobilisation capacity', drawing upon a repertoire of implementation tech-niques and change agents.

This requires 'institutionally thick' settings for these ingredients to gel and persist. It is clear that possibilities for effective delivery and implementation of landscape scale strategies, despite lacking a single corpus of legislation and policy, are emerging. However, they pose serious challenges of 'keeping the eye on the bigger picture' whilst struggling with inter- and transdisciplinary set-tings, and operating with a fragmented repertoire of 'carrots, sticks and sermons'.

CONCLUSION

As a sectoral planning issue, the status of landscape is unquestionably rising. Major international programmes now attest to its importance, and adjure govern-ments to take steps to safeguard key cultural assets. Further, the ELC in particular recognises the need to protect, manage and plan landscape on a spatially compre-hensive basis. International programmes, as well as requiring the acclamation of top-tier areas, have established general criteria for stewarding cultural landscapes in line with sustainable development principles.

With regard to integration at the landscape scale, however, planning instru-ments are more diffuse and oblique. Even here, though, a substantial repertoire of powers is potentially available if used with commitment and imagination. Despite differences and inconsistencies between countries, generic powers can typically be identified. Agri-environment schemes, in particular, are now maturing to the point of facilitating resource stewardship at a landscape scale. New spatial planning measures offer opportunities to integrate natural environmental issues with strategies for economy and community.

There is clearly a danger of being over-reliant on measures that are unduly indirect and tangential. The intention must be to mainstream landscape as a spatial planning issue, not only to ensure effective intervention on a sectoral basis, but also to optimise the integrative potential of a landscape scale approach for wider sustainability objectives. In part, this may entail additional powers and resources. More generally, though, it requires building up the institutional thickness within a region, not by creating additional bureaucracies, but by combining resources in ways that integrate sectoral measures for spatial planning. Ultimately, success will largely be down to the determination and imagination with which practitioners can mobilise a varied repertoire of powers, including the strongest possible links into statutory planning.

An important foundation for success will be clarity over the purposes of a spatial plan. The next chapter suggests that landscape scale plans should seek to achieve ecological integrity and cultural legibility. These qualities, in turn, need to be applied to specific spatial challenges. These may be thought of as three-fold. First, there is the well-established practice of protection, where the cultural landscape already has a high level of integrity and legibility, and the tasks are essentially those of maintaining and reinforcing this condition. Whilst most effort has been directed at nationally and internationally acclaimed areas, however, there are many more ordinary settings where safeguard is equally important, albeit perhaps a higher degree of well-modulated change is acceptable. Second, in many areas integrity and legibility have been more seriously compromised, and there is a greater need to restore and re-create. The urban fringe and the legacy of past industrialisation have been widely reported in this regard, but it is essential also to consider the landscapes of new industry which, soundly planned, can create sustainable and coherent new environments. Third, we must recognise that landscape is not always a 'container' but also a network, and that we should facilitate the increased linkage and re-connection of linear landscapes. These practices are distinct, but not always separate, and often require to be combined within a single landscape strategy.

CHAPTER 7

PRACTICES OF LANDSCAPE SCALE PLANNING

INTRODUCTION

Practising landscape scale planning, as we have seen, is not a neatly identifiable task concerned with enforcing a single body of legislation in a narrow range of situations. Rather, it involves mediating decisions through the imaginative deployment of a repertoire of complementary planning instruments in pursuit of multiple objectives across numerous terrains and networks. It involves matching styles of intervention to different scales of *place* – for example, neighbourhood, district, regional, national, global – and *network* – such as greenway, sub-regional green infrastructure, and transnational 'string of emeralds'.[1] Although diverse, the tasks of landscape scale planning are broadly three-fold, namely, the protection of areas that display special qualities, the regeneration of damaged and degraded terrains, and the reconnection of linear structures to achieve a more favourable complementarity. Further, it recognises that all areas have character, and that this requires recognition, safeguard, reinforcement and celebration. It is evident that tasks vary greatly according to attributes and condition. Thus, some landscapes need special attention by virtue of their heritage qualities, and their protection will require both statutory safeguards and positive management. At the other extreme, some landscapes will need remediation before they can deliver multiple functions that sustain environmental services and human quality of life.

This chapter considers a range of challenges that landscape scale planning seeks to address. It considers three principal situations – landscapes which are deemed currently to be of 'special' quality, meriting protection in their present condition; those which display varying degrees of disintegration, such that remedial intervention is the appropriate strategy; and those that are essentially linear in nature. Different though these challenges may be, it is argued here that they share a common objective: to create landscape units and links that reveal a story of *ecological integrity* and *cultural legibility*. Here, both 'ecology' and 'culture' are used as metaphors – a shorthand for the wider natural and social systems that coalesce within landscape settings.

In the first instance, the criterion of 'special-ness' immediately raises the question of 'special to whom?' Two cases are considered here – those areas whose special-ness is principally defined by outsider groups, as possessing qualities that are outstanding in international, national or regional terms; and those areas, often overlooked, that are valued mainly by insiders who possess a more secret and intimate sensitisation to local places. The former may be thought of as 'exceptional', and the latter as everyday or 'quotidian' landscapes. However, these categories are themselves increasingly convergent for, whilst top-tier protected areas are hugely important in their own right, they are now seen not only as a ring-fenced 'best', but also as a source for replenishing the 'rest'. Thus, core areas may supply sources of native wildlife species to re-advance across the wider country-side, and may also serve inspirationally as 'greenprints' providing exemplars of sustainability which can more generally be adopted for landscapes, and their communities and economies. Increasingly, therefore, protected landscapes are seen to have a role in regenerating the wider resource, as Beresford and Phillips (2000) spell out in their 'new paradigm' for protected areas (Table 7.1).

The second situation – that of declining landscapes – takes us back to our earlier discussion of processes of polarisation and globalisation, leading to the loss of landscape coherence and cohesion. Whilst processes such as industrialisation, suburbanisation and tourism are capable of producing valid landscapes, the more normal trend has been for them to overwhelm pre-existing traces. Regions with a

Table 7.1 A new paradigm for protected areas

As it was: protected areas were...	As it is becoming: protected areas are...
Planned and managed against people	Run with, for, and in some cases by local people
Run by central government	Run by many partners
Set aside for conservation	Run also with social and economic objectives
Managed without regard to local community	Managed to help meet needs of local people
Developed separately	Planned as part of national, regional and international systems
Managed as islands	Developed as networks (strictly protected areas, buffered and linked by green corridors)
Established mainly for scenic protection	Often set up for scientific, economic and cultural reasons
Managed mainly for visitors and tourists	Managed with local people more in mind
Managed reactively within short time scale	Managed adaptively with long-term perspective
About protection	Also about restoration and rehabilitation
Viewed primarily as a national asset	Viewed also as a community asset
Viewed exclusively as a national concern	Viewed also as an international concern

Source: Beresford and Phillips, 2000

Table 7.2 Structural and functional properties of the new urbani sed landscapes

	Landscape structure	Functioning	Conflicts
Urban centre	Regeneration and revitalisation are leading to more open space, greenways, 'nature' and water. Increasing landscape div ersity.	Highly dynamic; focus upon administrative, commercial, financial, cultural and tourist functions.	Environmental conditions, social pathology, traffic congestion, inadequate open spaces
Urban fringe	Poly-nuclei agglomeration, edge cities; few green corridors and patches; loss of ecological, historical and aesthetic landscape qualities; often lacking a distinct identity of place.	Residential function predominates. Outer fringe interfaces with the rural; industrial and commercial high -tech activities are attracted to well - serviced, readily accessible areas.	Increasing social segregation, deteriorating environmental and housing conditions; increasing traffic congestion .
The 'rural' of the urban network	Highly fragmented and heterogeneous open space: 'rurban' landscapes. Dense network of infrastructures; 'green fingers ' wedge into the urban tissue.	Intensification and diversification of land use; increasingly multifunctional landscapes.	Growing dependency of rural places upon urban services; loss of identity and landscape qualities; severe landscape fragmentation.
The 'deep' rural	Traditional village centres expand; emergence of exurbs. Zonal mosaics – in Europe these are often highly forested but very patchy.	Functional urbanisation but with few services. Residential or tourist–recreational activities related to agricultural and forested land. Extensification of land use; reforestation.	Conflicts between newcomers ('urbanites') and locals. Homogenisation of the landscape.

Source: Antrop, 2004, modified

dense pattern of cities, such as in north-western Europe, develop complex urban networks, leading to extensive fragmentation of rural landscapes by urban sprawl and road infrastructures (Hidding and Teunissen, 2002), and an increasing number of *edge cities* and *exurbs* (Stern and Marsh, 1997). Some of the changes are attributable to lack of coordination and regulation but, equally, some of them are consequences of deliberate policy and planning.

Antrop (2000, 2004) has argued that new landscapes can broadly be categorised as urban centre, urban fringe, rural of urban, and deep rural, and that these display characteristic structures, functions and conflicts (Table 7.2). He suggests that understanding the heavily modified landscape in this way can help us identify, not only the key problems encountered at different points on the spectrum, but also the opportunities for forging new landscapes. Thus, in the *urban centre*, problems are associated with environmental conditions, social and economic tensions, traffic congestion, and lack of open space and green infrastructure. Yet there are opportunities associated with high-quality residential environments (waterfronts, old industrial sites, etc.) as existing spaces suitable for renovation. In the *urban fringe*, problems derive from increasing social segregation, variable environmental and housing quality, and growing traffic congestion, yet opportunities are associated with an intimate mix of land use activities with potential synergies. In what he calls the *rural of the urban network* (or the 'urban shadow zone'), problems derive from the growing dependency of rural areas on urban facilities. Here, there is a loss of identity and landscape coherence, with severe fragmentation. Opportunities, though, derive from new forms of 'rurban' agriculture, park-forests and accessible wildlife sites (often the by-products of industrial disturbance), and there are many residual qualities that can be retained and integrated. In the *deep rural*, problems are associated with physical and economic marginality; despite the conflicts between newcomers and locals, and homogenisation of the landscape, however, there are opportunities from the vast open spaces with high natural and ecological potential. Thus, in each of Antrop's domains, driving forces of accessibility, urbanisation and globalisation act in different ways, and different opportunities present themselves for landscape redemption (Table 7.3).

Despite the categories chosen for this chapter, there are no sharp boundaries between 'intact' and 'damaged' landscapes, and distinctions along the spatial, temporal and modification axes can be arbitrary. Similarly, individual reserves can form part of an international network whilst a linear system will contain small nodes that serve as local 'pocket parks'. Even special conservation areas will have some parts that are damaged and degraded, whilst urbanic areas, high on the modification gradient, will contain ecologically rich sites. Equally, the specific tasks of protecting, de-fragmenting, reinforcing, and so forth, will apply in

Table 7.3 Opportunities in the four domains of the new urbanised landscapes

	Opportunities
Urban centre	Focus on potential high -quality residential environments (waterfronts, old industrial sites, etc.) as existing spaces suitable for renovation .
Urban fringe	Growing multifunctional mix of activities with potential synergies. Fuzzy and complex edges between urban and rural can stimulate ecological and economic diversification of farming, forestry, etc.
The rural of the urban network	New forms of 'rurban ' agriculture, park -forests and 'new nature' with intensive use by urbanites. Still many 'traditional rural' qualities that can be retained and integrated in the urban shadow zones.
The 'deep' rural	Wide open spaces with high natural and ecological potential.

Source: Antrop, 2004, modified

varying measures across all landscapes. Thus, there is no simple 'scalar' principle that neatly defines a taxonomy of tasks. However, in line with the particular challenges noted above, the following cases are considered:

- protection of special landscapes
- regeneration of damaged landscapes
- reconnection of linear landscapes.

PROTECTING SPECIAL LANDSCAPES

EXCEPTIONAL LANDSCAPES

The most extensive legacy of landscape planning has been in relation to 'protected areas'. Given the emphasis of this book on 'cultural' rather than pristine or wilderness landscapes, approaches to IUCN Category V Protected Landscapes are of particular significance. A notable example of this category is that of 'national parks' in the UK, which differ greatly from the international definition of the term, but represent exemplars of sustainable working landscapes. As Phillips (2002) noted, landscape-planning practice in UK national parks has been 'designed as a partnership'. In England and Wales, the parks are living and working landscapes with an increasing focus on supporting the communities and economic activity which underpin their wild beauty. National Park Authorities (NPAs) have their own forward planning, development control functions and other executive powers, through which they discharge their statutory purposes (as defined by the Environment Act 1995), namely:

- to conserve and enhance the natural beauty, wildlife and cultural heritage of the National Parks; and
- to promote opportunities for the understanding and enjoyment of the special qualities of the Parks by the public.

If there is a conflict between these two purposes greater weight is given to conservation than to recreational needs. In pursuing these purposes, NPAs also have a duty to foster the social and economic well-being of their local communities. The government allocates 75% of the NPAs' budget direct to the individual NPA and contributes a further 25% via constituent Local Authorities. National Park Authority membership is split into three sections: a slight majority of seats are taken by county and district councillors, just over a quarter by parish council nominees, and the remainder filled by the Secretary of State to represent the national interest. Each NPA is required to produce a National Park Management Plan which sets out its vision for management and guides the allocation of its resources.

Far more recently, National Parks have been established in Scotland, following their exclusion from the founding 1949 legislation in England and Wales. The National Parks (Scotland) Act 2000 sets out four principal aims:

Figure 7.1 The landscape of Loch Lomond, at the heart of one of Scotland's recently designated national parks

- to conserve and enhance the natural and cultural heritage of the area;
- to promote sustainable use of the natural resources of the area;
- to promote understanding and enjoyment (including enjoyment in the form of recreation) of the special qualities of the area by the public;
- to promote sustainable economic and social development of the area's communities.

To date, two new authorities have been created, Loch Lomond and the Trossachs, and The Cairngorms. The former has a range of powers very similar to those of the Anglo-Welsh parks, including development control and the preparation of local plans. The latter, though, has very limited planning responsibilities, restricted to calling in certain planning applications, and (despite provisions to make bye-laws and management laws) is seen principally as an enabling and facilitating body rather than a regulatory one. In pursuing this role it is provided with a number of powers, including general permission to pursue 'anything that will help the Park Authority achieve its aims', and more specific duties and permissive powers related to research, legal agreements, grant aid, statutory rights of consultation, and promotion of understanding and enjoyment. The track record of Scottish National Parks in practice is as yet limited, but Illsley and Richardson (2004) suggest that unresolved conflicts in Cairngorm, particularly between national and local interests, will provide continuing challenges in mediating consensus over key issues.

In England and Wales, a complementary approach to landscape protection is afforded through the family of Areas of Outstanding Natural Beauty (AONBs). AONBs are extremely varied in size and character, but are essentially extensive areas, typically in relatively lowland and cultivated countryside, in contrast to National Parks, which are mainly upland and pasture. They are inherently a landscape designation, being created solely for the purpose of conserving and enhancing their natural beauty (which includes landform and geology, plants and animals, landscape features and human settlement). At the outset, it was generally assumed that stricter exercise of planning controls in these areas would suffice to retain their intrinsic qualities, but a more active management approach has latterly been advocated. Whilst this approach is clearly limited in terms of powers and funds, and is vulnerable to the emergence of local countryside conflicts, there are nevertheless many success stories involving direct land management, reduction of development pressure, and negotiated 'codes of practice' with major land use interests (Wragg, 2000).

A major advance in the stewardship of AONBs has been instigated by the requirement under Part IV of the Countryside and Rights of Way Act 2000 (CRoW) to produce Management Plans (Table 7.4). In practice, these have been produced in many areas over the years, but on a voluntary and informal basis, and not according to a standard rubric. The 'CRoW' Act also allows the Secretary of State to establish conservation boards for individual AONBs, to which certain local authority functions can be transferred, and requires authorities such as public bodies to 'have regard' to the purpose of conserving and enhancing the natural beauty of the AONB. Official guidance now emphasises the need to instil a management planning *process* based on: bringing together managers, user groups and stakeholders; promoting consensus and reconciling multiple uses, to build commitment to the management plan and its policies; and identifying which organisations, often acting in partnership, are responsible for delivering the plan's outcomes. AONB management plans are intended to address a wide range of issues. These relate in the first instance to environmental issues such as natural beauty, landscape character, biodiversity, archaeology and historic features, agriculture and forestry, mineral extraction and development, waste disposal, and water cycle and coastal management. Second, they address public understand-

---

TABLE 7.4 PURPOSES OF A MANAGEMENT PLAN FOR AN AREA OF OUTSTANDING NATURAL BEAUTY

An AONB Management Plan is a document which:

- highlights the special qualities and the enduring significance of the AONB, and the importance of its different features;
- presents an integrated vision for the future of the AONB as a whole, in the light of national, regional and local priorities;
- sets out agreed policies incorporating specific objectives which will help secure that vision;
- identifies what needs to be done, by whom, and when, in order to achieve these outcomes;
- states how the condition of the AONB and the effectiveness of its management will be monitored.

Every AONB Management Plan should have at least two elements:

1   a strategy for the AONB – an ambitious, visionary statement of policy, which identifies specific objectives and the methods through which these will be achieved;
2   a more focused statement of who will do what in order to achieve the objectives and move towards the vision.

Source: Countryside Agency, 2001

ing and enjoyment, tourism, informal recreational access to the countryside (especially in the light of legal obligations in relation to Rights of Way and open country
'Access Land'), interpretation, education, and promotion. Finally, they now must
have regard to the economic and social well-being of local communities, the local
economy and employment, housing and the built environment, transport and
traffic. This implies a dovetailing of AONB Management Plan and other plans and
policies, notably statutory development plans and community strategies (Countryside Agency, 2001).

Although the UK National Parks have a responsibility to take social and economic matters into consideration, a more explicit emphasis on local community
benefits is apparent in French Regional Nature Parks. Many rural areas in France
are faced with serious problems such as outmigration and pressures from urbanisation and tourism, and these pose significant threats to the continuation of important cultural landscapes. Since the late 1960s, one response to this has been the
'Regional Nature Park', as a solution for areas where a rich natural and cultural heritage is demonstrably threatened. A park is designated by central government –
from which it receives a 'seal' – and is jointly stewarded by regions, departments
and townships with the intention of integrating heritage preservation considerations into local development plans. Once the seal has been awarded, it is used to
promote an environmental quality image, but this must in turn be warranted by a
consistent approach to protection, management and development on the parklands. Recognition is awarded on a ten-year rolling basis and renewal is dependent
on the achievement of clear goals related to the Park's mission (Table 7.5).

In the USA, the work of the Conservation Studies Institute displays many parallels, and reflects the growing importance of cultural landscapes, as a complement
to more strictly controlled parks and wilderness areas. For example, the Lyndon B.

**TABLE 7.5 ELEMENTS OF THE 'MISSION' OF A REGIONAL
NATURE PARK**

- to protect the national heritage, particularly by appropriate management of
  nature and landscapes;
- to contribute to rational land use planning;
- to promote economic, social and cultural development and improve the quality
  of life;
- to attract, educate and inform the public;
- to conduct experimental or exemplary actions in the above fields and contribute
  to research programs.

Johnson National Historical Park contains a specific landscape, a historic pecan orchard, which is managed as a cultural resource that remains economically productive (http://www.nps.gov/mabi/csi/csihandbook/csHome.htm [accessed 30 June 05]). Here, park staff have developed a management plan for the orchard that respects its cultural and natural resource values, while continuing to produce a saleable crop each year, notably through an integrated pest-management programme and water-quality monitoring regime. Another instance noted by the Conservation Studies Institute is the Marsh–Billings–Rockefeller National Historical Park, which contains the Mount Tom Forest, a pioneering example of planned and managed reforestation. This forest illustrates more than a century of stewardship, from early scientific silvicultural practices to contemporary methods of sustainable forest management. This approach is guided by a partnership-driven, long-term Forest Management Plan, providing both a visionary framework, and more detailed measures in relation to historic preservation, natural resource protection, recreation, education, interpretation and the cultural landscape.

QUOTIDIAN LANDSCAPES

Not all inherited landscapes are outstanding – indeed, most are relatively ordinary, and often important only to the people who inhabit them. Sometimes this importance is unrecognised, and appreciated only when it is threatened. Most landscape evaluation has emphasised inherent or elitist qualities of landscape, but it may alternatively be argued that value can be based on the number of eyes that see a particular scene – hence the importance of everyday landscapes.

An example of 'quotidian' landscape management is provided by the Cheshire Landscape Trust, described as a non-membership, non-governmental organisation, working with people of all ages, helping them to care for their places. According to Gittins (2001), the Trust tries to inspire, inform, encourage, enthuse and empower local people to stand up for and celebrate their everyday environment, and their links with common nature and ordinary histories, through an approach based on partnership and ownership. The Trust aims to argue for 'the ordinary, the everywhere and the everyone' and, to this end, has created experiments and collaborations with local people, landscape professionals, politicians, artists, craft workers, farmers and landowners, social and community development workers, teachers and researchers. Central to their way of working is to see the 'landscape as a story', having a unique sense of place based on local distinctiveness. This involves trying to connect feelings and associations for place with intrinsic landscape attributes, so that personal associations link with physical factors and land uses. Much of the Trust's work has been to secure grant aid which, in the early stages, was linked to three Countryside Agency initiatives – Community Landscape Strategies, Local Heritage Initiatives and Village Design Statements. These activities resulted in a variety of practical measures such as action plans and 'supplementary planning guidance', but their capacity-building role at community level was held to be equally important. In its wider work, the Trust also promotes general community skills and landscape improvements, for example, associated with planting local fruit tree varieties and supporting biodiversity action. Gittins emphasises that this type of activity is no panacea and can have heavy resource implications in time and finance. In the longer term, though, benefits include: provision of training in landscape management, craft and action-oriented community participation skills; creation of networks for exchanging information and experience; and building bridges between different sectors (public, private, academic, statutory, voluntary and community) and disciplines.

Previously, we noted that the Welsh notion of 'bro' was very close to the contemporary idea of a sustainable cultural landscape. An initiative known as Balchder Bro (Pride of Place), co-funded by the Countryside Council for Wales and Heritage Lottery Fund, capitalised on this by challenging communities to develop ways of marking their distinctiveness. During the initial phase, three community groups, in the Dee Valley, the City of Swansea, and the Myddfai and Black Mountain area, were engaged in projects aiming, for example, to safeguard or restore local heritage assets, improve public access to and interpretation of such sites, record and communicate the oral tradition, manage local heritage assets as a community enterprise for social and economic benefit, and promote a sense of pride and place with a local identity. The initiative embraced practical schemes bringing identifiable community benefits across a wide range of issues related to investigating, explaining and caring for landmarks, landscape, traditions and culture. The departure point in all this was for local people to look at what was distinctive and special about their community, and use that as a foundation for future projects. The scheme was subsequently made more widely available across Wales.

REGENERATING DAMAGED LANDSCAPES

THE 'RURAL OF THE URBAN'

In many areas, landscape has become little more than the space between built-up areas, and has lost most traces of distinctiveness and commonly valued characteristics. In such cases, the emphasis is on the re-creation of coherence, functionality and distinctiveness rather than on protection. Key issues are that people need access to good quality landscape, preferably without having to travel too far, and that development should be set within the capacities of a particular landscape without compromising its multifunctionality.

Some of the land around towns has been formally designated – for example as 'green belt' – and is thus likely to have strong protection, either because of stringent planning controls (e.g. UK) or because development rights have been purchased by the municipality (e.g. common in the USA). Much, however, has no formal status and is prey to intense speculation. Even 'green belt' planning safeguards are not sacrosanct in the long term, and this zone can be subject to land speculation by developers and policy inconsistency by planners and politicians. Yet the urban fringe is highly accessible and important to all groups of urban-dweller, and has a particular significance for those lacking the resources and mobility to access more distant countryside.

Inevitably, much of the land around towns has weak coherence and functionality. Even green belts have been criticised for being insufficiently 'green' or functional, as well as for choking urban development and leading to dreary dormitory towns that generate car-borne commuters. New alternatives are therefore being considered, though these are strongly opposed by some groups who fear a rash of new housing in prime semi-rural locations. Clearly, green belts should not be compromised until there is a social consensus about a superior alternative which provides better recreation opportunities, more attractive scenery, better ecological connectivity and a more self-sustaining rural economy. There is a strong case for regeneration and de-fragmentation of the fringe, whether designated as green belt or not, based on landscape multifunctionality.

Kühn (2003) has reviewed some of the issues associated with the philosophies underlying green belts, in particular the 'compact city' model, which has enjoyed a resurgence within the context of the sustainability debate. One possibility – which is being echoed for other practical and strategic reasons in contemporary Dutch planning (de Roo, 2003) – is that the compact city has particular problems of juxtaposed unneighbourly land uses, and that alternative structures might be preferable. Kühn notes in particular that post-modern geographers and planners point to the antithesis of the compact city with its hierarchical pattern of a concentric grade in density from city centre to suburbs, suggesting it could be supplanted by the hybrid qualities of a synthesis between city and landscape. This pattern can, to some extent, be seen in the well-known Green Heart (Randstad) of the major Netherlands metropolitan area, which appears to be developing a rural–urban continuum where settlements are losing their rural character. Kühn identifies two main future roles for green belt zones – namely those of 'connecting' (i.e. as a space helping to mesh complementary cities in a polycentric city region) and 'separating' (the traditional role of maintaining open space between a monocentric city and its surrounding countryside).

Gallent *et al.* (2004) argue that the urban fringe possesses special characteristics, making it more than simply a transitional landscape. These characteristics centre on patterns of land use, biodiversity and leisure/development opportunity which are unique to the urban edge and to land extending away from built-up areas. They argue that the uniqueness, diversity and particular dynamics of the urban fringe merit a distinctive approach to planning and management based on a principle of multifunctionality as a framework for action and for managing and supporting diversity. Thus, they present the urban fringe as a unique mix of land uses and landscapes, rather than a mere extension of town into country, or a 'transitional aberration' delaying the onset of real countryside. Its typical features are:

1   a multifunctional environment, often supporting essential service functions;
2   a dynamic environment, characterised by adaptation and conversion between uses;
3   low-density economic activity including retail, industry, distribution and warehousing;
4   an untidy landscape, potentially rich in wildlife.

In seeking a multifunctional approach to planning the urban fringe, Gallent *et al.* cite the work of Brandt and Vejre (2003), who advocate spatial planning as the key to delivering integration and added value (across aesthetic, socio-cultural, economic, ecological and historic dimensions) through a multi-agency and participatory approach.

An example of urban fringe where there has been a genuine attempt at multifunctional planning is instanced by the National Capital Greenbelt, Ottawa, Canada (http://www.canadascapital.gc.ca/greenbelt/index_e.asp?bhcp = 1 [accessed 30 June 05]). This comprises a 20,350 ha band of open lands and forests surrounding the Capital on the Ontario side of the Ottawa River. It was first proposed in 1950 as part of an overall plan to create a green setting for the Capital, and to protect it from haphazard urban sprawl. Whereas many green belts rely on secondary measures of protection, such as planning control, the federal government since 1956 has progressively purchased this area, and about two-thirds is now owned and managed by the National Capital Commission. Key elements include the Mer Bleue Bog, an internationally significant wetland under the Ramsar Convention, and the Stony Swamp Conservation Area comprising some 2,000 hectares of woodland, wetland and regenerating field systems.

Figure 7.2 A recreational corridor in the Ottawa Green Belt

A variant on the 'girdle' of green land encircling a city is the 'green wedge'. This has become popular internationally; for example, the 'Melbourne 2030' plan (http://www.dse.vic.gov.au/melbourne2030online/content/implementation_plans/0 6_green.html [accessed 30 June 05]) comprises twelve green wedges designated around the metropolitan area for environmental, economic and social benefits (Table 7.6). In the UK, Leicestershire County Council Structure Plan (http://www.leics.gov.uk/index/your_council/council_plans_policies/structure_plan. htm [accessed 30 June 05]) proposed green wedges in association with planned urban extensions, having key roles of countryside protection and prevention of coalescence, and secondary functions of accessible recreation, positive land management, and contributing to the quality of life of nearby urban residents. Acceptable land uses in the green wedges were agriculture (including allotments and horticulture), outdoor recreation, forestry, access (footpaths, bridleways, cycle ways) and burial grounds. Intensive uses, such as mineral extraction and park and ride facilities, were only acceptable in the absence of alternative sites and subject to mitigating conditions. Nearby in Derby, a similar strategy aimed to protect and enhance the recreational, landscape and ecological value of two green wedges in the southwestern suburbs. This was backed up by questionnaire surveys to determine public aspirations for the areas and encourage voluntary action, and by policies for protection and enhancement in the City's development plan, woodland

---

TABLE 7.6 PURPOSES OF GREEN WEDGES, DERIVED FROM MELBOURNE 2030 PLAN

- areas of environmental, landscape and seascape qualities
- national, metropolitan and state parks
- native vegetation fauna habitat
- areas of productive agricultural potential
- internationally recognised wetlands
- areas with potential for wastewater recycling
- areas of significant landscape, seascapes and environmental qualities
- tourism and recreational facilities such as golf courses, beaches and horse riding
- metropolitan water storages
- waste-treatment plant and related odour buffers
- sand resources and metropolitan landfills
- airports and related flight paths
- high-quality horticultural areas
- land banks for future potential development

and parks strategies, and local biodiversity action plan. Objectives for the green wedges were to link the countryside with the urban area, maintain the identities of separate areas of the city, reduce the impression of urban sprawl, cater for casual and organised recreation, and act as buffer zones between residential communities and industry.

More generally, the Groundwork Trust and Countryside Agency (2004) instigated a policy debate about 'Unlocking the Potential of the Urban Fringe'. They proposed an ambitious agenda for delivering an urban renaissance and addressing the need for new housing, whilst promoting diversification of the rural economy to compensate for gradual declines and intermittent shocks within the agricultural economy. Complementary renewal of rural and urban areas was seen to depend on strengthening the relationship between town and country, with the rural–urban fringe thus playing a central role. Despite the nondescript nature of much of this zone, the debate centred on capitalising upon its accessibility. Thus, for example, it expected local farmers and landowners to take advantage of the urban demand for food, leisure and environmental services; equally, it anticipated that nearby communities could benefit from high quality building design, landscape design and management, sustainable transport and renewable energy. Elements were expected to include networks of new and improved parks, woodlands and other green spaces, linked to the urban centre and wider countryside by footpaths, cycle ways, river valleys, waterways, and associated green corridors. Thus, ecological and amenity infrastructure benefits were combined with an infrastructure of car-free routes to highly accessible areas. It also viewed the rural–urban fringe operating as a recreational gateway to the deeper countryside (Table 7.7).

THE INDUSTRIAL LEGACY

Many of our landscapes, which suffer from a legacy of industrial damage, are unlikely to realise their potential without substantial remedial treatment. With sufficient imagination, community consensus, reliable science and supportive policy, there is an opportunity for 'de novo' landscapes. In northwest England, where much derelict land remains as a result in particular of the deep mining industry, an initiative called 'Newlands' has been instigated to achieve multifunctional benefits through woodland establishment and provision of other site facilities. The changes are taking place within the context of one of England's relatively recently established community forests, which increasingly emphasise 'public benefit forestry' on socially and environmentally challenging sites. Developed by the Northwest Development Agency and the Forestry Commission, this £23 million scheme aimed at reclaiming large areas of 'derelict, underused and neglected' (DUN) land across

England's northwest and transforming them into community woodlands. Initially, 3,800 'DUN' sites of more than one hectare in size were identified, of which 1,600 'brownfield' sites formed the principal area of search. A multifunctional approach was used to select target areas from this list, and a specially devised 'Public Benefit Recording System' (PBRS) was used to measure the public benefit that could be delivered through site regeneration. This method identified the key issues in the locality of each site based on indicators of 'social benefit', 'public access', 'economic benefit' and 'environmental benefit'. Then, in order to maximise strategic impact, the sites were filtered according to the objectives, priorities and themes agreed by the Regional Development Agency. These themes include aspects such as more appealing gateways, transport corridors and settings for investment, and the screening of significant areas of industry. Selected sites were then mapped onto a GIS, enabling a number of other geographically-specific 'layers' to be intro-

---

TABLE 7.7 KEY POTENTIALS OF THE RURAL URBAN FRINGE IDENTIFIED BY GROUNDWORK TRUST/ COUNTRYSIDE AGENCY

- an indicator and advertisement for the quality of a town or city and its rural hinterland, especially along major access routes
- accessible and attractive respite from the stresses of urban living, with safe and enjoyable walking, cycling and horse riding, or water sports on rivers, canals and reclaimed mineral workings
- improved physical and mental health as a result of regular countryside recreation and an interaction with nature
- opportunities for hands-on learning in a variety of 'outdoor classrooms'
- contributor to the sustainable processing of waste, management of water resources and pollution control
- regulator of flood hazard, through functional flood plains and reinstated water meadows
- assisting land development and housing renewal, including installation of renewable energy technologies
- new opportunities for producing and marketing varied farm products and services, for example through farmers' markets and direct sales, helping in the process to reduce 'food miles'
- providing settings for major new residential expansions
- new and reinstated areas of woodland, wetland, meadow and a broad array of other natural habitats, bringing biodiversity up to the urban edge allowing more people to encounter wildlife and appreciate nature

Source: based on GWT/ CA, 2004

duced to give each site a public benefit based on a range of social, economic and environmental factors and attributes.

Our historic legacy demonstrates the potential of industrial development not only to occupy sites, but also to effect landscape scale transformations, often for the worse. However, there is great potential to ensure that future industry not only respects its landscape setting but also creates positive landscape scale effects. Turner (1998) has suggested that landscape planning can be used to create new landscapes associated with major economic activities and service facilities, such as reservoirs, mineral workings, agriculture, forests, transport corridors and urban extensions. By developing multifunctional plans, selecting use intensities appropriate to the setting, integrating land and water uses, and applying high environmental standards, Turner argues, we cannot only minimise environmental impacts but also produce coherent and enduring landscapes, often involving less long-term cost and maintenance than traditional measures. He implies that planning has too often been concerned with minimising negative environmental effects and too infrequently with designing positive impacts that respect the dignity and character of a place.

Figure 7.3 Site in the process of being reclaimed for 'public benefit' forestry, alongside the M62 'gateway' corridor in northwest England

An obvious example of anthropic change is that of the motorway and main road network. Apart from its striking strategic effects on the landscape, it has major implications for habitat fragmentation and connectivity. One response (Scottish Office, 1998) has been to effect improvements in the quality and efficiency of road landscape design and management through the application of natural character-istics. In seeking a strategic and wildlife-friendly approach, this draws upon an eco-logical design concept based on the analogy of a pendulum falling naturally to rest at 'Bottom Dead Centre'; for it to be raised above this level requires an energy input, and the higher the level, the greater the energy required to maintain that position. In a comparable way, the more artificial a landscape design, the greater the maintenance input required (fertilisers, management, irrigation, etc.), whereas lower energy and materials subsidies are needed for designs that work more closely with nature. Thus, the report advocated highway landscapes based on natural self-reliant principles, requiring the designer to understand:

- how and why the landscape was formed;
- how and why the landscape works;
- how and why the landscape is valued and protected, and its development controlled;
- how and why the landscape will develop.

Whilst decorative planting will have its place at times, naturalistic solutions will generally tend to be preferable in the more open countryside.

Another contemporary force in landscape scale change is that of wind turbine location. A study in Wales (Miller et al., 2002) developed a method for the spatial planning of new turbine complexes, taking account of the onshore wind resource, physical restrictions and policy constraints. This entailed the use of a rule-based model, in which potential for energy production was represented by wind speed and modified according to constraining factors, and in which information was integrated on land use, transport infrastructure, archaeology, land-scape and natural heritage. The analysis used a Geographic Information System in which map-based data were interrogated to answer 'where' and 'what if' ques-tions relating to wind energy production. Certain datasets were preprocessed to derive buffer areas around selected features (e.g. airfields, transport infrastructure) and to take account of landscape visibility from selected designations such as national parks or trails. Various classes of output were generated ranging from unavailable or highly sensitive sites to those with few constraints and favourable wind speeds. The model accommodated four themes set by the Countryside Council for Wales, namely:

- wind resource data, forming the technical basis of any assessment of the suitability of an area for the production of wind energy;
- physical constraints, which are features that will prohibit development, or require significant modifications prior to development;
- policy constraints, namely, factors that result in limiting the spatial extent of the areas subjected to subsequent consideration with respect to the wind regime; and
- additional factors which may be sensitive to the presence, or geographical distribution, of turbines, or their construction.

The land in the vicinity of Wales' three National Parks and five AONBs was looked at particularly closely to identify areas with extensive views of protected landscapes. The output was used to generate scenarios which have subsequently formed the basis of national guidelines for locating future turbine clusters.

RECONNECTING LINEAR LANDSCAPES

THE STRING OF EMERALDS

Landscape networks operate at various scales; at the most strategic level, they cross national boundaries and aim to connect key sites as a 'string of emeralds'. A notable example is EU's principal response to the Convention on Biological Diversity, the 'Habitats' Directive. Although this is quite traditional in terms of its emphasis on site-based designation and regulation, its more innovative ambition is to create a network of designated areas – NATURA 2000 – that seeks 'no net loss' of, and 'favourable conservation status' for, habitats and species of community-wide importance on a geographical basis. Thus, Member States must identify and protect Special Areas of Conservation (SACs), and protect them against deterioration and damage; as part of this, any plan or project likely to have a significant effect on a NATURA 2000 site must undergo an environmental assessment to determine whether the nature conservation interest would be damaged. If it is thought to pose a significant threat, it can only go ahead where there is no alternative location, and where implementation is of overriding public interest. Stricter criteria are applied where a site hosts species and/or habitats listed as a priority under Article 4 of the Directive. One problem with the 'Habitats Directive', however, is its continuing reliance on a 'ring fence' approach, which we have noted as now often being considered rather old-fashioned and bureaucratic. Consequently, other more 'spatial' approaches are also being pursued.

A particularly interesting example of this is the Council of Europe's Pan-European Biological and Landscape Diversity Strategy (PEBLDS), which is described as an 'innovative and proactive approach to stop and reverse the degradation of biological and landscape diversity values in Europe'. It is considered to be innovative, because it addresses biological and landscape issues together within a single European approach; and proactive, because it promotes the integration of biological and landscape diversity considerations into policies for other social and economic sectors. The Strategy effectively comprises a coordinating and unifying framework for strengthening and building on existing initiatives, rather than introducing new legislation or programmes. In brief it seeks to ensure that:

- the threats to Europe's biological and landscape diversity are reduced substantially or where possible removed;
- the resilience of European biological and landscape diversity is increased;
- the ecological coherence of Europe as a whole is strengthened; and
- public involvement and awareness concerning biological and landscape diversity issues is increased considerably.

PEBLDS is being implemented through a series of five-year Action Plans which address key issues related to forestry and agricultural practices, re-use of military and brownfield land, and industry. Several familiar arguments are used in favour of the strategy, but it is interesting to note that 'the issue of landscape diversity is as yet not adequately integrated into mechanisms aimed at protecting and enhancing the natural environment'. A particular concern, therefore, is to mainstream landscape into policy and planning and achieve policy integration.

PEBLDS is closely associated with the establishment of a Pan-European Ecological Network (EECONET) which aims to ensure that:

- a full range of ecosystems, habitats, species and landscapes of European importance are conserved;
- the habitats are large enough to enable species to be conserved;
- there are sufficient opportunities for species to disperse and migrate;
- damaged parts of the key environmental systems are restored;
- the key environmental systems are buffered from potential threats.

Using familiar arguments for promoting use of the 'landscape scale' and 'landscape units' (Table 7.8), this Network was devised as a conceptual framework for organisations to cooperate and set priorities at European level, in particular building on the Natura 2000 network and complementary initiatives, and giving coherence to national and regional ecological networks. The embryonic network incorporates many existing or candidate protected areas, and includes extensively used agricultural landscapes and other semi-natural habitats where existing land practices can be maintained in a form compatible with conservation needs. EECONET requires effective cooperation at both national and international levels, the involvement of NGOs, and voluntary partnerships of interested parties, in order to advance its proposals.

THE LOCAL WEB

At a more local level, the network comprising the dry and wet boundaries of agricultural landscapes is of pre-eminent importance. Perhaps the most significant cultural landscape of this nature is the European *bocage*, comprising a mixture of isolated trees, hedgerow trees, hedges, shelter belts, wooded zones and associated ditches. Soltner (1985) attributes *bocage* landscapes to the outcome of centuries of observation and experience by farmers to modify microclimates and protect the landscape against the rigours of climate and soil erosion. Such areas are highly prone to changes arising both from human pressures such as land consolidation (*remembrement*) and road widening, and from natural change such as ageing of trees. The two are often related, as it is typically the loss of agricultural function of historical field boundaries that leads to under-maintenance and consequent gappiness, unhealthy condition and unbalanced age structure. Soltner describes the hedge as a forest in miniature, with its edge habitats, canopy, shrubs, and herb and grass layer; in addition, hedges are often associated with ditches and earthen or stone-filled embankments. Numerous variants are found on

---

TABLE 7.8 ELEMENTS OF THE PEBLDS EECONET

- the identification of core areas to ensure the conservation of habitat types and species;
- the provision of corridors or stepping stones to enhance the coherence of natural systems;
- the creation of restoration areas serving to extend the network, providing new habitats and facilitating dispersal and migration;
- the provision of buffer zones to protect core areas and corridors in the network from adverse external influences; and
- the enhancement of the environmental quality of the countryside as a whole.
  Source: based on http://www.strategyguide.org/index.html (accessed 30 June 05)

this around the world, but they typically comprise living hedges – sometimes remnants of earlier forests – composed of introduced or native species, or dead hedges made of branches. Styles of hedges are equally varied, but are broadly based on combinations of tall trees, coppices and pollards. Soltner notes that the functional importance of *bocages* is particularly associated with microclimate regulation, hydrological control and soil conservation, ecological balance, and production, such as energy biomass and forest foods. Yet, equally, they are crucial to local quality of life, occasionally in terms of practical uses such as fuel wood, but more generally simply in terms of amenity.

Soltner sees these elements coming together in a *bocage* landscape which (although the term originated in Picardy and Normandy) is widely found across temperate and tropical lands. Typically, it is a landscape in which fields are surrounded on all sides by living hedges, and which form a *maillage* (the term 'mesh' only partially captures the sense of this term). Shelterbelts can contribute to such an effect or, in places, may be the dominant component. *Bocage* and semi-*bocage* regions are found widely in Europe, particularly across much of the British Isles, Scandinavia, north Germany, north Belgium, Galicia, the Northern Alps, Romania and in many parts of France. In these areas, there tend to be characteristic landscapes, typified by:

- a large and geometric mesh;
- a mesh of small fields (elliptical and rectangular), which often reflect the pattern of land inheritance (either to oldest son, or equally divided between offspring);
- either a relatively perpendicular arrangement of fields, with narrow parcels, or a more informal division often based on natural features such as streams and soil changes.

Further south, the *Mediterranean bocages* repeat the similar associations of *silva* (the forest, especially tall native species), *ager* (cultivated fields) and *saltus* (mainly pasture). They are also widely associated with fruit trees, including vines, olive groves and orchards. A highly characteristic form is the Tuscan landscape with a mixture of small field parcels and multiple cropping of cereals, vegetables, tobacco, lucerne, olive trees and vines. The Spanish *huertas*, by contrast, rely on intensive irrigation, yet their intimate mix of fruit trees and field crops is particularly vulnerable to intensive mechanisation. Related landscapes can also be found in the Tropics, where they are characterised by multiple functions and inter-cropping, and sometimes merge into *swidden* landscapes.

Regionally important landscapes can be linear as well as areal. Perhaps the best-known example is the American greenways programme, which is now being adopted and adapted in other countries. However, it is the US experience which is most pertinent to landscape scale issues, due to its sheer magnitude and existence of a national programme connecting to regional and local schemes. The longest greenway is the 750 km Blue Ridge Parkway, but many are very local and opportunistic, and incorporate features such as landscaped urban paths, waterways, wildlife corridors and sites, community bike paths and walking trails. The US Conservation Fund provides financial and technical assistance to support partnerships between citizens, private landowners, public agencies, corporations and nonprofit organisations. Greenways are often described as systems of 'hubs' (key spaces) and 'links' (corridors). They have a role both in creating linkages between recreational, cultural, and natural features, and in improving quality of life by providing recreational and visual amenities.

In a review of greenways, Fabos (2004) noted their multiple benefits. First, they protect ecologically significant natural systems, maintaining biodiversity and providing for wildlife migration. Second, greenway networks provide people with extensive recreational opportunities within metropolitan regions and rural areas for walking, hiking, cycling, swimming, boating and other outdoor recreational activities. Third, they provide the population with significant historical heritage and cultural values. The majority of greenways are along rivers and seashores, where in the USA an estimated 90% of heritage areas and cultural resources are located. Gobster and Westphal (2004), however, acknowledge success in technical aspects of corridor selection and design but note, particularly in urban areas, that significant problems remain in respect of public participation and ongoing management leading to perceptions of neglect and hazard. Erickson (2004) points to changing objectives for developing and protecting greenways over time, so that, whilst recreation, transportation and conservation have been the dominant arguments, it is rare for each purpose to be equally weighted. Further, modern greenways are expected to provide many other benefits, ranging from environmental education to water quality protection, so that in many cases the greenway concept is compromised between two main drivers of ecological quality and social amenity, a conflict which is exacerbated where a city lacks a clear and long-standing open space framework. Where a historical legacy of planning, strong leadership, collaboration and institutional thickness exists, it would appear to be easier to retrofit new demands into existing patterns of greenspace provision.

Particularly within peri-urban and intra-urban areas, linear landscapes can be conceived of as a green infrastructure for large-scale urban growth. Thus, English Nature (2004) argued that nodes and their network links should be planned so as to complement each other in a pervasive urban–rural web. Green infrastructure has been described as a spatial framework for maintaining and increasing biodiversity assets and providing open space for settlements, as well as performing functions such as flood storage, climate moderation and air quality improvement. A coherent, integrated network might thus include national parks and other prime landscapes, more accessible recreation zones, new and ancient woodlands, river corridors, nature reserves, new habitats and linear features. The resultant mosaic can form a linked network extending from urban centres to the open countryside, so that landscape is not 'compartmentalised'. Equally, within a context of rapid urban growth, it can help ensure that new development enhances and connects, rather than destroys and fragments, natural capital.

For example, England's Sustainable Communities 'action programme' set out to provide a 'joined-up' strategy for housing and regeneration (ODPM, 2002). Although the programme is multifaceted, perhaps its best-known element is a framework for 'rapid growth' areas coupled with measures to protect and improve the environment. The programme contains plans for building more homes in the south and east including major developments centred on new towns, motorway corridors and the 'Thames Gateway' area downstream of London. Whilst this will inevitably mean a great deal of greenfield development, there is a strong commitment to re-use and regenerate brownfield sites, and the main reclamation agency (English Partnerships) and NGO (Groundwork Trust) are allocated resources with a view to engaging participatory environmental renewal. As part of its green infrastructure, development proposals have been linked to 'biodiversity opportunity areas' which are mapped spatially to show priority areas for habitat creation, woodland linkages, wildlife corridors and sub-urban wildscapes (English Nature, 2004). Thus, for instance, the Green Grid for Kent Thameside (ODPM, 2004) is intended to permeate the area, and to comprise an extensive framework of attractive open spaces, serving both existing and new communities, linked by green corridors, footpaths and parkland. Early initiatives in the Green Grid included:

- creation of high-quality open spaces and corridors within major new residential and business developments;
- new open space, including a Country Park and initial phases of a Linear Park;
- improvements to existing urban parks and wildlife habitats; and
- plans to extend and improve sections of a major riverside walkway.

Planned major development sites are programmed to contribute significantly – for example, one quarry is intended to contain open space and water features over about a third of its area – whilst under-utilised 'brown' land is being converted into amenity uses.

CONCLUSION

Landscape scale planning practice is becoming increasingly systematic, and is no longer concerned with simply collecting a select number of protected sites. Far clearer strategies are emerging related to the condition, character, functionality and vibrancy of landscapes, and the appropriate balances between conservation, creation, strengthening or restoration which are necessary to address tendencies towards dysfunction and obsolescence.

Although site protection has dominated strategies in the past, a more differentiated suite of approaches is now acknowledged. Thus, whilst a representative series of high-quality sites will most appropriately be subject to 'conservation', other cultural landscapes will require a varied blend of planning and management instruments, drawing together public, private and voluntary bodies, in addition to land managers and communities. 'Everyday' landscapes, for instance, will be heavily reliant for their stewardship on community engagement, not least because it is local people who are most aware of their values and will have ideas about what ought to be safeguarded or enhanced, and how this might be accomplished. Fragmented peri-urban landscapes will require imaginative strategies which capitalise on their diversity and accessibility, and which create virtue out of their 'in-betweenness'. New industrial landscapes may often benefit from being considered strategically, as they may alter the appearance of wide areas, and yet can often enhance environmental capital if carefully sited and designed.

As with landscape scale planning 'principles', we can draw upon a menu of approaches in order to develop 'mix-and-match' strategies that address the complex of issues encountered in a particular territory. Whereas protected area management has a long pedigree of experience and success, other landscape strategies are more experimental and high risk. Yet there is an increasing body of experience which can be shared. Further, new approaches to spatial planning hold great promise and offer the opportunity to synthesise actions across both territories and policy sectors. Landscape scale planning practice is thus becoming more systematic, comprehensive, and differentiated in response to the challenges of different geographical settings.

The foregoing discussion indicates that, whilst practices are often embryonic and experimental, coherent approaches to landscape scale planning are becoming increasingly possible. To conclude, we reflect on the over-arching purposes behind the continuing pursuit of such approaches. The key aim, it is suggested, is to pursue 'virtuosity' within landscapes. This entails securing sustainable management of landscapes, so that they in turn become the foundation for community prosperity and quality of life, instilling a reason for continuing stewardship into the future. In this way, a mutually reinforcing virtuous circle is instigated. Such a fortunate dynamic, however, is rarely sustained spontaneously under conditions of strong external pressures; more often, these pressures, having little sensitivity to place, instigate a vicious circle of deterioration. Consequently, there is an important role for planned intervention, either to lubricate local social and economic entrepreneurship, and/or to regenerate areas of fragmentation and degeneration. Equally, though, we must be cautious not to fossilise inherited landscapes, but to discover new ways of living in them sustainably.

CHAPTER 8

THE VIRTUOUS CIRCLE

INTRODUCTION

An underlying theme of our discussion has been the operation of a vicious circle of deterioration and homogenisation leading to the progressive erosion of integrity and legibility of cultural landscapes. In places, the main driver of this vicious circle is a process of obsolescence, where the factors which gradually created distinctiveness over a period of centuries no longer have a *raison d'être* in a period of globalising economy and culture. Elsewhere, the principal driver is that of dysfunction, where discordant new land uses punctuate and fragment formerly cohesive landscapes. The main argument of this final chapter is that the object of landscape scale planning should be to re-instil a virtuous circle of sustainable development that reconnects socio-economy and landscape quality, in a way that is both self-sustaining and mutually reinforcing.

Place-making entails a constant creativity in striking a balance between the homogenising forces of 'convenience' landscapes and the heterogenising forces of multifunctional landscapes. Understanding the structural and functional properties, and the opportunities and conflicts, at a particular landscape scale can facilitate the redemption of features that make it distinctive and coherent. A key argument of this chapter is that this can be at least partly effected by 'embedding' economic activities (cf. Granovetter, 1985) back into their landscape.

This argument requires some elaboration. Globalisation has resulted in economic linkages becoming increasingly 'vertical' – in other words, trading and investment are characterised by subsumption of external capital into local economies, and top-down links and dependencies between large (even transnational) headquarters and local agents. Local economic activity has thus, in a sense, become increasingly de-coupled from its locality. For example, in a wood supply chain, much of the production is currently associated with imported timber being processed by large enterprises, perhaps close to freight terminals, with cut timber being transported to manufacturers, and finished products being exported from the region for sale. The end result is that few jobs are either created in the locality or linked directly to sustainable woodland management in the area's landscape. Embedding requires that horizontal linkages are re-emphasised, so that strong interactions occur between local land uses, companies, cooperatives and individuals. Thus, an alternative model might be for high-quality and sustainably stewarded timber to be produced, sold and processed in close proximity, so that local manufacturers could market and add value to their goods with a localised 'marque' and a high premium. Similarly, it has been widely canvassed that farming could place a far stronger emphasis on the place-related production of food which is of such distinctive quality and 'typicity' that it can both command a price premium and facilitate local processing activities that add value to the original products. This, in turn, would create a demonstrable link with high-quality landscape, and so provide a powerful and visible justification for enhanced stewardship.

We should not pretend that this will re-create the self-contained local economies of yesteryear, and most of our economic production and social discourse will, of course, continue to be non-local. What is suggested here is that the spatial re-embedding of even quite a small proportion of our activities, coupled with local implementation partnerships, can instil a virtuous circle between people and place that is sufficient to sustain landscape integrity and legibility (Figure 8.1) (Powell *et al.*, 2001; Selman, 2004b). Whilst the pursuit of re-embedding might in reality be quite a minor objective in the grand scheme of spatial planning, therefore, its consequences for landscape sustainability and place identity can be profound.

The institution of a virtuous circle foregrounds the two-fold purpose of planning both 'for' and 'through' landscape. Thus, on the one hand, we are concerned with the narrower purpose of maintaining or creating landscape distinctiveness in its own right. A classic example would be maintaining the cultural landscape of a national park. Here, the underlying causes of character loss are likely to be associated with globalising forces of food and fibre production, outmigration of long-standing residents in response to deteriorating job prospects, immigration of residents with little connection to the local economy, and unsustainable modes of tourism and recreation. Recovery could be linked to an economic strategy which supported rural enterprises that capitalised on 'place' qualities, thereby reinforcing distinctive local character and creating local job opportunities. On the other hand, more ambitiously, a virtuous circle of sustainable development could be pursued *through* the landscape. Here, the transdisciplinary approach necessary for achieving mutual reinforcement between natural, built and social capitals might be enabled by using integrated datasets, cultivating partnerships, and reconnecting communities and governance within a framework of landscape units. The multifunctionality of landscape would thus be intimately linked to quality of life, identity and shared spatial visions. Notwithstanding these exciting possibilities, there are inevitably both pitfalls and opportunities in pursuing landscape-centred approaches, some of which are addressed in this chapter.

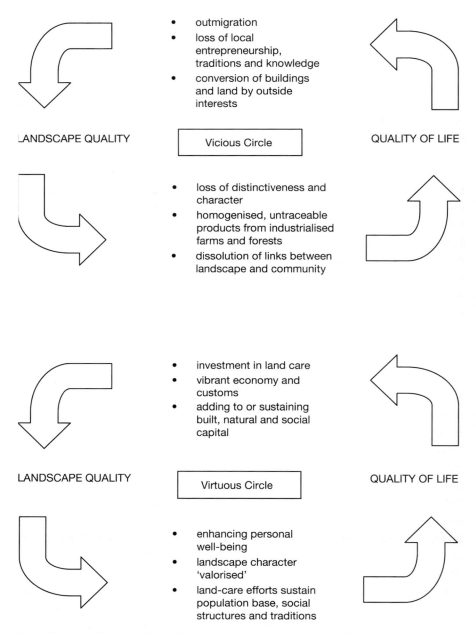

- outmigration
- loss of local entrepreneurship, traditions and knowledge
- conversion of buildings and land by outside interests

LANDSCAPE QUALITY   Vicious Circle   QUALITY OF LIFE

- loss of distinctiveness and character
- homogenised, untraceable products from industrialised farms and forests
- dissolution of links between landscape and community

- investment in land care
- vibrant economy and customs
- adding to or sustaining built, natural and social capital

LANDSCAPE QUALITY   Virtuous Circle   QUALITY OF LIFE

- enhancing personal well-being
- landscape character 'valorised'
- land-care efforts sustain population base, social structures and traditions

Figure 8.1 An outline of the vicious/virtuous circle underlying landscape condition

Source: adapted from Powell *et al.*, 2001; Selman, 2004b

PASTICHE VERSUS FIDELITY

Attempts by spatial planners to recover characteristic regional and local features are, of course, nothing new. There is a long legacy of design guidance, for example, which seeks to reinforce the identity of areas through incorporating vernacular features in new development. Whilst measures to recapture place-ness are to be applauded, there is a clear risk that strategies based on traditional processes and products will rely too heavily on nostalgia. They may even require continuous subvention from the public purse to remain viable if they lack an inherent economic rationale.

Whilst there may be particular circumstances in which faithful adherence to local building styles and materials or traditional land management may be appropriate, the general practice of landscape scale planning cannot be based on purely 'cosmetic' treatment, as this would create an unconvincing and unsustainable pastiche. Further, those who most vociferously resist homogenisation appear to be drawn very selectively from particular age, socio-economic and ethnic categories, and thus strategies for landscape protection can sit uneasily with those for social inclusion. Hence, our aim should be to draw upon the past practices and future potentials in order to promote 'regenerative' and 'autopoietic' landscapes where the links between natural systems, human settlements and economic activities are sustainable, just and self-reinforcing.

Two tests for the landscape 'fidelity' of plans are proposed here. First, the emergent landscape should tell a valid and convincing local 'story'. It should be sufficiently legible to reveal information about past and present ways of life, and to convey the sustainability of the emerging socio-economy. Understanding the nature and direction of landscape change is the first step in recovering its legibility. Different potentials are likely to exist in different types of landscape, ranging from those within or adjacent to the city fabric, to those in remote marginal areas. Whilst inherited stories generally relate to localised production, Lapka and Cudlinova (2003) suggest that future landscape stories will be more indicative of 'consumption' activities. Perhaps more fundamentally, the underlying future story might be linked to designs and behaviours that limit our ecological 'footprints' (Wackernagel et al., 1999). Thus, genuine attempts to live sustainably, although in some respects being uncompromisingly modern, might produce a spontaneous new vernacular with which people readily identify. We have already observed how new, sustainable landscapes may 'acquire' an aesthetic in the eyes of beholders who appreciate their underlying values, especially where processes of social learning thrive.

Second, integrated strategies at the landscape scale should promote practices of 'valorisation', where economic and social entrepreneurship can capitalise on the special-ness of a place. Thus, wise stewardship is repaid and real economic values accrue from retaining and enhancing landscape character and functionality. In policy terms, there appear to be four main mechanisms for stimulating this, namely:

- reinforcing and re-embedding food and timber chain linkages which re-create direct links between people, work and place;
- ensuring that the consumption values of post-industrial countryside generate inputs for landscape maintenance, including voluntary measures such as visitor payback schemes (Scott *et al.*, 2003);
- creating policy mechanisms that, from general taxation, ensure society pays a fair price for the landscape's public benefits and service functions (for example, agri-environment schemes);
- sensitising spatial and site planning mechanisms to the scope for retaining and creating distinctiveness and character.

However, important though public policies are, the contribution of governance can only be one part of a wider approach that draws in social learning, nurturing asso-ciative values, and living within the productive and assimilative capacities of the natural environment.

SPATIAL INTEGRATION WITHIN LANDSCAPES

Governance, especially where based on locally relevant partnerships, can play an important role in landscape recovery. In essence, there are three elements that define the solution space for landscape scale planning. First, there is the natural dimension of autopoietic or regenerative systems. These may be understood in terms of the dynamics and geometry of landscape ecology, and in respect of both biodiversity and hydrological functions. Second, there are the human stories of belonging, aes-thetics, production and consumption. These are often manifest in an area's charac-ter, condition, functionality and distinctiveness. Third, there is the governance dimension, where effective delivery of sustainability measures will often need to be based on boundaries that reflect the innate sub-divisions of the natural or cultural landscape, rather than artificial political-administrative units. These three can be seen to converge through the pursuit of integrated development, wherein governance structures can 'construct' advantageous circumstances for valorising a territory's natural and cultural place qualities, such that sustainable development can be intimately linked to the character, vibrancy and systems integrity of landscape units.

Thus, whilst much of the basis for landscape recovery must lie in self-sustaining endogenous activity, planned intervention has a critical role to play. Principally, this will relate to the process of regional or local embedding, which often requires government support and promotion, especially in the early stages. However, we must acknowledge the fragility of many landscapes relative to the potency of external forces of change, and the difficulty of reinstating strong and durable links between communities, land and livelihoods. Indeed, in practice, there is often a sense that policy initiatives and grant aid are unequal in scale to globalising pressures, and that many projects and programmes are ill-conceived straws in the wind which will have little enduring effect in terms of community, capacity and partnership. Intervention must thus be sufficiently robust and well funded to make a real difference, even if this means being highly selective in the choice of policy targets.

In this regard, spatial planning has an important role to play in promoting styles of development and economic activity which define and reinforce local distinctiveness. Agri-environmental policy can assist the reintroduction of local food systems, in which typicity is associated with particular breeds of cattle and varieties of crop. Here, food and its value-added products are visibly associated with a local 'terroir' and may be more trusted than mass-produced commodities through being more traceable, flavoursome, unadulterated and wholesome. Carefully targeted government support, such as start-up assistance and marketing, can help a variety of other pertinent activities. These include, for instance: high-quality goods manufactured in traditional local ways and/or from locally-sourced products, such as furniture from native hardwoods; tourism and leisure uses, especially those which possess a high degree of 'fitness' to the host community and environment (Oliver and Jenkins, 2003); and the 'unseen' revival of place, related to maintaining local stories, events and traditions, and celebrating differences of language, dialect, and folklore. Collectively, these can afford effective methods of arresting trends towards homogenisation, and of linking landscape legibility to the integrity of environmental systems.

In England, one notable initiative was the Eat the View programme (Table 8.1) (Countryside Agency, 2002). This was based on the principle that consumers' decisions have an important influence on the nature of countryside management, as some products help maintain the environmental quality and diversity of the countryside by virtue of their modes of production. Further, where products are processed and sold locally, they may be a source of new income and jobs, helping to support the local economy. Launched in 2000, the five-year programme had the following key objectives and outcomes:

- increased consumer awareness of the links between what people buy and the countryside they value;

- increased demand for locally and regionally distinctive products from sustainable systems;
- improved marketing for producers, development of supply chain partnerships, accreditation and product branding;
- enhanced marketing for producers and growers that promote the character, diversity and environmental value of the landscape.

Programmes such as this can help counter trends towards uniformity of local crop varieties and livestock breeds, and indirect effects such as the declining proportion of money spent by consumers on food that finally reaches the farmer. Similarly, sustainable management of woodlands often depends on finding new markets for native timber and other woodland products. In the High Weald of southern England, for example, coordinated marketing by land managers, craft workers, food producers and service providers has reinvigorated traditional land uses such as the production of durable hardwoods such as oak, sweet chestnut and ash.

This need to enrol a combination of 'carrots, sticks and sermons' in the pursuit of sustainable landscapes has underpinned a long-standing interest in 'integrated rural development' (IRD). However, the actual meaning of IRD remains poorly articulated, and relatively few landscape scale programmes or projects can confidently be said to have achieved genuine integration. Partly, this is because the

---

TABLE 8.1 PRINCIPLES OF THE 'EAT THE VIEW' INITIATIVE

Support products from sustainable land management systems that:

- maintain and improve the key resources of soil, water and air;
- meet animal welfare and environmental standards;
- minimise all forms of pollution;
- support the full diversity of plant and wildlife habitats across their natural range;
- consider the wider social and ecological impacts of the production and processing systems utilised;
- value and protect landscapes that are rich in local character and distinctiveness;
- help restore damaged rural landscapes;
- provide employment in new and existing businesses in the rural economy;
- provide opportunities for public enjoyment through sustainable recreation and tourism;
- strengthen relationships with local communities;
- create robust and adaptable rural economies.

Source: Countryside Agency, 2002

notion has most extensively been analysed and applied in developing-country contexts, where the role of indigenously-based multifaceted agrarian development is relatively apparent. In 'first world' conditions, where the countryside has undergone centuries of improvement and investment and where its role lies increasingly in 'consumption' rather than 'production' values, the purpose and nature of IRD is less obvious. In the UK, an experiment in the Peak District National Park in the 1980s came close to articulating the defining characteristics of IRD in cultural landscapes (PPJPB, 1990), namely:

- *Integration* (sometimes referred to as 'interdependence') – through integrating policies or developing a 'package' of linked policies designed both to harmonise different interests and to achieve economic, social and environmental objectives;
- *Individuality* – acknowledging local circumstances, reflecting an area's distinctive character, priorities, problems and opportunities; and
- *Involvement* – emphasising active inclusion of local communities, drawing upon self-help rather than reliance on external action.

More recently, the Countryside Agency (2005) suggested that *Investment* might be a '4th I', emphasising the role of pump-priming, followed by self-sustaining, endogenous growth. A further hallmark has been that, whilst individual projects within an IRD programme may not necessarily be particularly novel, IRD has involved new styles of working entailing innovative operational structures and working practices.

Latterly, our understanding of IRD has moved towards that of 'valorising distinctiveness', closely related to the principle of embedding. This involves 'identifying what's special' through surveys and inventories, and then developing policies and instilling practices which valorise these attributes. As an example, local expenditure and employment may actively be linked to wildlife. Thus, Mills (2002) found that expenditure through agri-environment schemes significantly increased off-farm contracting, whilst the RSPB (RSPB and Geoff Broom Associates, 2000) estimated that ornithological tourism on the Norfolk coast generated £6m in the area leading to around 135 full-time equivalent jobs. A number of similar studies have confirmed these patterns in relation to local and regional 'environmental economies' elsewhere.

An illustration of the scope for this approach is provided by the promotion of landscape-related regeneration in the Forest of Dean in southwest Gloucestershire, UK. This is an area with a varied landform and land cover, which has had a complex history and was a mining and manufacturing area both before and after the Industrial Revolution. This chequered history has produced a mixed legacy, combining some fine scenery with despoiled or undistinguished landscapes. In recent years, the local economy has changed from a dependency on declining industrial sectors to a more balanced one, with tourism and recreation increasing in importance, and some rise in commuting to neighbouring towns. The presence of the ancient forest with unique foresters' rights, though latterly restocked on a more commercial basis by the Forestry Commission, conveys a strong sense of identity and contains fascinating biodiversity, geology and heritage. However, there is a strong need to economically, socially and environmentally regenerate parts of the forest.

At the end of the 1990s, the Countryside Agency had come under strong pressure from locals to designate at least part of the forest an Area of Outstanding Natural Beauty, not least to prevent the encroachment of quarrying and other discordant development. The Agency was reluctant to do this, as much of the area did not meet their criteria, but instead proposed an approach based on IRD. This was initiated in a number of ways, including:

- surveys of the natural and cultural heritage in the area, notably biodiversity, landscape character and archaeology;
- a survey of local perceptions based on imaginative participatory exercises, to find out where people believed the cultural boundaries of the 'forest' to lie, and their views about its character and needs ('Dean by Definition');
- a number of local grants to encourage enterprises based on the character of the area.

One of the most successful outcomes was a project called 'Dean Oak', where local craft workers collaborated with the Countryside Agency and Forestry Commission, in order to test the market for products and artefacts made from locally grown timber, and subsequently to produce and market these. The initiative has resulted in a situation where at least a small proportion of the timber that was formerly taken outside the area for low grade end use now has value added to it locally, and is creating a visible link between landscape and economy.

The initial experiment was taken forward into a second phase – Building on What's Special (BOWS) – with a project officer acting as 'animateur' to promote further cultural and economic activity which would enhance and regenerate the area. Statutory organisations in the area, notably the planning authority, were also pressed to ensure that development and investment respected and reinforced landscape character (Countryside Agency, 2003). Thus, generally, the recovery of the area was linked to a 'valorisation' of its place qualities, potentially instilling a virtuous circle between enhancing landscape distinctiveness and promoting regeneration.

Figure 8.2 The Forest of Dean (Gloucestershire, England) – the diverse landscape offers opportunities for valorisation of 'special' place qualities as a basis of integrated rural development

PURSUING VIRTUOSITY AT THE LANDSCAPE SCALE

The intention of this book has been to represent the landscape scale as a basis for integrated, transdisciplinary decision-making, aimed at improving human quality of life within more distinctive, liveable and sustainable places. The landscape scale affords a territorial framework that can both cohere the incremental and often unco-ordinated decisions of local actors, whilst also giving particular expression to the abstract policies and programmes of high-level authorities that often lack speci-ficity and thus comprehensibility to most people. The landscape scale offers a focus for making strategic decisions in ways that are sufficiently accessible to engage local communities, and holistic enough to maintain the integrity of natural systems. Further, it provides a framework for sustainable development, wherein natural and social capitals can achieve a balance.

However, we are confronted at the outset with a profound problem: that land-scapes in a range of settings, from rural to urban, find their multifunctionality and distinctiveness compromised by various endemic and insidious processes. Thus, cultural landscapes in industrialising and post-industrial countries are widely threat-ened, sometimes by specific proposals, but often by more diffuse processes of globalisation. In some situations, these result in intensification and the attrition of previous landscape inscriptions which confer sense of place; elsewhere, processes of abandonment, marginalisation and fragmentation are apparent. Collectively, the main consequences of these trends have been deterioration in service functions – notably those related to soil, biodiversity and water quality and quantity – and in visual and associative qualities. If we are to plan at the landscape scale in order to reverse these trends, we need a clear understanding of the nature and challenges associated with particular landscape types: landscape redemption requires not merely a local technical fix, but a sophisticated and elaborate reinvigoration of natural, social and institutional infrastructure.

To date, our approaches to planning *for* landscape have mainly been concerned with scenic amenity and recreational opportunity, in particular celebrating the sublime and salubrious. Public policies have typically sought to ring-fence and protect expert-acclaimed areas. However, attention is now turning towards the functionality of landscapes – or more particularly, their multifunctionality. Thus, whilst landscape planning has, in the past, given pre-eminence to areas that experts consider to be exceptional, new spatial approaches enable the exceptional and selective to be considered alongside the everyday and inclusive. This requires that landscape is mainstreamed into spatial planning rather than perceived as a sectoral interest. Further, new definitions of biogeographic units – based on character, water catchments, time-depth and biodiversity – increasingly create opportunities for spatial planning to be conducted *through* landscapes. In this regard, landscape is seen, not so much as a pleasant commodity, but more as an integrative nexus wherein a transdisciplinary approach to sustainable development can be conducted.

In pursuing these new approaches, however, we must address some difficult issues of spatial justice. Landscape issues are widely perceived by planners as being associated with traditionalism and nostalgia, often betraying class-ridden and value-laden preferences for supposedly halcyon but unrecoverable 'golden ages'. Our human instincts often make us crave the familiar, and it is unsurprising that landscape preferences tend to be conservative and preservationist. Landscape planning policies have thus tended to be expert-driven and strongly influenced by 'polite' tastes. Public viewpoints have often only been solicited as a statistical input into methods of scenic beauty estimation. Equally, protection of valued landscapes has tended to be undertaken by top-down bureaucracies and often effected through negative restraints over land use change. These have all been, and continue to be, important. However, it is now abundantly clear that landscape scale planning must be a far more positive activity, and one which centrally involves stakeholders in choices and stewardship. Inclusion of a wide range of 'insider' and 'outsider' contributions is necessary to promote social learning about landscape, to inculcate a sense of community ownership of plans and proposals, to heal broken links between place and identity, to recognise the values associated with areas that are of both local and national significance, to understand public attitudes to landscape change, and to enrol local land managers and communities in the care of living landscapes. In adopting a more inclusive approach, experts must not only identify and engage stakeholders, but must also be prepared to integrate lay knowledge and stories with codified data and models.

Thus, the redemption of cultural landscapes cannot lie solely in top-down approaches, but in a reflexive understanding of society's changing expectations, the changing tissue of social and human capital, and the institutional thickness of public and private sector organisations. Equally, long-term sustainability at a landscape scale cannot rely on permanent taxpayer subvention or prescriptive state intervention, but must suppose the retrieval of a partnership between natural, social and institutional capital. The key paradox here, though, is that traditional cultural landscapes in post-industrial societies are rarely self-sustaining, and the links between landscape, community and economy no longer self-reinforcing. Consequently, some degree of state intervention is usually necessary to persuade land managers to pursue practices which enhance rather than erode visual and ecological distinctiveness. Just as landscape redemption cannot be seen as a technical fix, however, neither can it be seen as a simple policy fix. Many studies now attest to the limited effect that policy instruments such as agri-environment schemes have on farmers' attitudes and behaviour. Consequently, the maintenance of cultural landscapes requires approaches which retain traditional knowledge and complex network relations within and between land users and the wider socio-economy.

To achieve these outcomes, landscape-centred spatial planning will need to embrace the possibilities associated with new types of rural scenery even though some may currently be perceived as heretic or hazardous, and with emergent vernaculars reflecting sustainable settlement and infrastructure. Thus, redeeming landscape distinctiveness does not merely entail recovering lost stories, as these may have little relevance to new lifestyles and livelihoods. There is a place in landscape planning for maintaining inherited features that distinguish one place from another and convey lessons between generations about finely tuned relationships with nature; but there is little justification for spending taxpayers' money on policies to promote mere nostalgia, kitsch and pastiche. New stories and new associations between people and place are to be welcomed if they have functionality and coherence. In significant part, therefore, landscape scale planning must be an adventurous exercise, recognising that functions, rather than appearances, are ultimately what matter. In some circumstances, we will indeed continue consciously to create landscape elements for human pleasure, in the worthy tradition of ancient paradise gardens or country estates. However, as has happened spontaneously throughout the past – and notwithstanding the essential role of visionary, planned intervention – most of our landscape values will occur serendipitously, as fortunate by-products of sustainable land uses.

If this is to occur, spatial planning must seek to reinvigorate a mutuality between socio-economy and host environment. This presumes that a virtuous circle of landscape redemption – driven by multifunctionality, embedded economic activity, reflexive governance and community vibrancy – can replace a vicious circle of obsolescence and dysfunction. It seems probable that in many post-industrial countries this will rarely happen spontaneously, but will require purposeful governance. Yet this should not be seen as a cause for major extension of bureaucracy; rather, there is a need to consolidate institutional thickness and thereby accumulate flexible and effective network relations. The aim should be to assemble resources, regulate individual and collective conduct, and 'construct' advantage for entrepreneurs, in ways that promote sustainable development. Institutionally 'thick' milieux are likely to be better equipped to display the collective learning capacity and partnership capabilities necessary to make the transition to the multifunctional landscapes of tomorrow. These emerging interdependencies are illustrated in Figure 8.3.

In essence, the challenge of landscape scale planning is twofold: a purposive enterprise of making decisions based on the coherence and functionality of integral landscape units and networks; and a determination to arrest and reverse the drivers of landscape decline. Both of these require a commitment by stakeholding partners to use a cocktail of knowledge resources, relational resources and mobilisation capacities (Healey et al., 2002) to re-couple landscape dynamics to socio-economic opportunity. In the same way that the much-heralded 'death of the city' has been trumped by the city's regeneration as a cultural and information nexus, so the 'inevitability' of landscape homogenisation can be countered by positive planning based on the valorisation of environmental functionality and territorial identity. Yet this is self-evidently not just a job for the experts. Landscapes are cultural products, the visible expression of a long and close relationship between people and nature. If cultural landscapes are to persist, our plans must axiomatically draw upon the toil and imagination of local people.

Landscape scale planning will thus need to be creative and resourceful. It will need to engender integrative and transdisciplinary thinking. It will need to blend the knowledge and experience of experts with the practices and values of other stakeholders, and the providence and capriciousness of 'future nature'. It will need to plan for the processes and patterns of landscape itself, whilst developing new possibilities for delivering policies and plans through landscape units. It will need

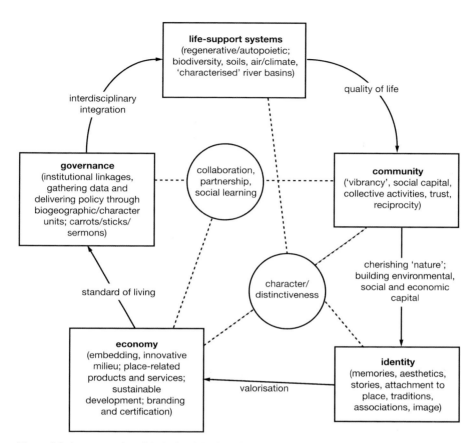

Figure 8.3 A conceptual model of self-reinforcing 'virtuosity' at the landscape scale

to be creative in its use of 'carrots, sticks and sermons', so as to assemble resources, knowledge and partners in the pursuit of deliverable strategies. And it will need to redeem cultural landscapes from insidious anonymisation by instigating measures that sustain a more 'virtuous' relationship between economy, society and environment. This may seem an unduly ambitious idea – but there is increasing evidence that it is an idea whose time has now come.

NOTES

1   INTRODUCTION: THE CHALLENGE OF PLANNING AT THE LANDSCAPE SCALE

1   IUCN is the common abbreviation for the International Union for the Conservation of Nature and Natural Resources.

2   i.e. the free services – such as pollination, water supply, salubrious air and plant growth – supplied to us by the natural environment.

2   WHY THE LANDSCAPE SCALE?

1   A similar three-dimensional representation of landscape change – comprising temporal, spatial and institutional scales – was developed independently by Bürgi *et al.*, 2004.

2   The use of terminologies for water/river 'catchment' and 'watershed' tends to differ between America and Europe, though not in ways that matter critically to the current discussion.

3   Taken from the letterhead of the International Association for Landscape Ecology.

4   COMPREHENDING THE LANDSCAPE SCALE

1   In the original wording, related to World Heritage status, these qualities are couched in terms of 'outstanding' examples.

2   A combined use of Countryside Character Areas and Natural Areas.

6   INSTRUMENTS FOR LANDSCAPE SCALE PLANNING

1   United Nations Educational, Scientific and Cultural Organization.

2   International Council on Monuments and Sites.

7   PRACTICES OF LANDSCAPE SCALE PLANNING

1   'String of emeralds' is a term sometimes used to describe a network of protected areas which are believed to serve as 'stepping stones' on diffusion or migration routes.

REFERENCES

Adams, W. (2003) *Future Nature: a vision for conservation*, 2nd edition, London: Earthscan.

Antrop, M. (2000) 'Changing patterns in the urbanized countryside of Western Europe', *Landscape Ecology*, 15(3), 257–270.

—— (2004) 'Rural-Urban Conflicts and Opportunities', in Jongman, R. (ed.) *The New Dimensions of the European Landscape*, Dordrecht: Springer.

Antrop, M. and Van Eetvelde, V. (2000) 'Holistic aspects of suburban landscapes: visual image interpretation and landscape metrics', *Landscape and Urban Planning*, 50, 43–58.

Apffel Marglin, F. and Mishra, P. C. (1993) 'Sacred Groves: Regenerating the Body, the Land, the Community', in Sachs, W. (ed.) *Global Ecology. A New Arena of Political Conflict*, London: Zed Books.

Appleton, J. (1996) *The Experience of Landscape*, Chichester: Wiley.

Arnstein, S. (1969) 'A ladder of citizen participation', *Journal of the American Planning Association*, 35, 216–224.

Austad, I. (2000) 'The Future of Traditional Landscapes: retaining desirable qualities', in Klijn, J. and Vos, W. (eds.) *From Landscape Ecology to Landscape Science*, WLO, Wageningen: Kluwer Academic Publishers, 43–56.

Baker, M. (2002) 'Developing institutional capacity at the regional level: the development of a coastal forum in the North West of England', *Journal of Environmental Planning and Management*, 45(5), 691–714.

Bastian, O. (2001) 'Landscape ecology – towards a unified discipline?', *Landscape Ecology*, 16, 757–766.

Bell, S. (1998) *Landscape: pattern, perception and process*, 81–82 London: Spon.

Bellehumeur, C. and Legendre, P. (1998) 'Multiscale sources of variation in ecological variables: modeling spatial dispersion, elaborating sampling designs', *Landscape Ecology*, 13, 15–25.

Bemelmans-Videc, M-L., Rist, R. and Vedung, E. (1998) *Carrots, Sticks & Sermons: policy instruments and their evaluation*, New Brunswick, NJ: Transaction Publishers.

Bennett, A. and Radford, J. (2004) 'Landscape-level requirements for the conservation of woodland birds: are there critical thresholds in habitat cover?', in Smithers, R. (ed.) *Landscape Ecology of Trees and Forests*, IALE-UK, 117–124.

Beresford, M. and Phillips, A. (2000) 'Protected landscapes – a conservation model for the 21st century', *George Wright Forum*, 17:1.

Bergstrom, J. (1998) *Exploring and Expanding the Landscape Values Terrain*, Faculty Paper Series FS 98–20, Athens, Georgia, USA: Department of Agricultural and Applied Economics, University of Georgia.

Bishop, I. and Rohrmann, B. (2003) 'Subjective responses to simulated and real environments: a comparison', *Landscape and Urban Planning*, 65, 261–277.

Bishop, K. and Bate, R. (2004) 'The link between landscape, biodiversity and development plans: a move towards "positive planning"?', in Bishop, K. and Phillips, A. (eds.) *Countryside Planning: new approaches to management and conservation*, London: Earthscan, 222–236.

Blake, J. (1999) 'Overcoming the "value-action gap" in environmental policy tensions between national policy and local experience', *Local Environment*, 4(3), 257–278.

Bolliger, J., Sprott, J. and Mladenoff, D. (2003) 'Self-organisation and complexity in historical landscape patterns', *Oikos*, 100, 541–553.

Borrini-Feyerabend, G. (1996) *Collaborative Management of Protected Areas: tailoring the approach to the context*, Gland: IUCN.

Botequilha Leitão, A. and Ahern, J. (2002) 'Applying landscape ecological concepts and metrics in sustainable landscape planning', *Landscape and Urban Planning*, 59(2), 65–93.

Bourdieu, P. (1977) *Outline of a Theory of Practice*, Cambridge, UK: Cambridge University Press.

Brace, C. (2003) 'Envisioning England: the visual in countryside writing in the 1930s and 1940s', *Landscape Research*, 28(4), 365–382.

Brandt, J., Tress, B. and Tress, G. (eds.) (2000) *Multifunctional Landscapes: interdisciplinary approaches to landscape research and management*, Centre for Landscape Research, Roskilde University, Denmark.

Brandt, J. and Vejre, H. (2003) 'Multifunctional landscapes – motives, concepts and perspectives', in Brandt, J. and Vejre, H. (eds.) *Multifunctional Landscapes. Volume 1: Theory, History and Values*, Southampton: WIT Press.

Brunckhorst, D. (2000) *Bioregional Planning – Resource Management Beyond the New Millennium*, Amsterdam: Harwood Academic Publications.

Bucek, A., Lacina, J. and Michal, I. (1996) 'An Ecological Network in the Czech Republic', Ecological Institute, Veronica, Brno, Czech Republic, X/11, 1–45.

Buchecker, M., Hunziker, M. and Kienast, F. (2003) 'Participatory landscape development: overcoming social barriers to public involvement', *Landscape and Urban Planning*, 64, 29–46.

Buller, H. and Lobley, M. (2004) 'Improving Rural Delivery: identifying principles for good environmental delivery'. Report of a Workshop held on behalf of the RSPB, Centre for Rural Research, University of Exeter.

Bunce, R. (2001) 'An environmental classification of European landscapes', in Green, B. and Vos, W. (eds.) *Threatened Landscapes: conserving cultural environments*, London: Spon, 31–40.

Bunce, R., Barr, C., Clarke, R., Howard, D. and Lane, A. (1996) 'The ITE Merlewood Land Classification', *Journal of Biogeography*, 23, 625–634.

Burgess, J. (1995) *Growing in Confidence*, Cheltenham: Countryside Commission.

Bürgi, M., Hersperger, A. and Schneeberger, N. (2004) 'Driving forces of landscape change – current and new directions', *Landscape Ecology*, 19, 857–868.

Buttimer, A. (1980) 'Home, reach and a sense of place', in Buttimer, A. and Seamon, D. (eds.) *The Human Experience of Space and Place*, London: Croom Helm, 166–187.

Camagni, R. (1995) 'The concept of innovative milieu and its relevance for public policies in European lagging regions', *Papers in Regional Science*, 74(4), 317–340.

Cary, J. and Webb, T. (2000) *Community Landcare, the National Landcare Program and the Landcare Govement: the Social Dimensions of Landcare*, Mimeo, Canberra: Social Services Centre, Bureau of Rural Sciences.

Castells, M. (2003) *The Power of Identity: the Information Age – Economy, Society and Culture*, London: Blackwell.

CEMAT (2003) *European Rural Heritage Observation Guide*, Council of Europe, Ljubljana, Slovenia.

Chavez-Cortes, J. (2004) 'Landscape Planning to Achieve Sustainability: the Iztaccihuatl-Popocatepetl region, Mexico', unpublished PhD Thesis, University of Liverpool.

Clark, J., Darlington, J. and Fairclough, G. (2003) *Pathways to Europe's Landscape.* Heide, Germany: European Pathways to the Cultural Landscape.

—— (2004) *Using Historic Landscape Characterisation*, English Heritage and Lancashire County Council.

Clark, J. and Murdoch, J. (1997) 'Local knowledge and the precarious extension of scientific networks: a reflection on three case studies', *Sociologia Ruralis*, 37(1), 38–60.

Claval, P. (1993) *Initiation à la Géographie Regionale* (translated by I. Thompson, 1998), *An Introduction to Regional Geography*, Oxford: Blackwell.

Cloke, P. and Jones, O. (2002) *Tree Cultures: the place of trees and trees in their place*, Oxford: Berg.

Collins, J., Thomas, G., Willis, R. and Wilsdon, J. (2003) 'Carrots, Sticks and Sermons: influencing public behaviour for environmental goals', Demos/Green Alliance for Defra.

Cooke, P. and Morgan, K. (1998) *The Associational Economy: firms, regions and innovation*, Oxford: Oxford University Press.

Cosgrove, D. (1998) *Social Formation and Symbolic Landscape*, Madison: University of Wisconsin Press.

Cosgrove, D. and Daniels, S. (1988) 'Introduction: iconography and landscape', in Cosgrove, D. and Daniels, S. (eds.) *The Iconography of Landscape: essays on the symbolic representation, design and use of past environments*, Cambridge, UK: Cambridge University Press.

Council of Europe (2000) 'The European Landscape Convention', Strasbourg.

Countryside Agency (CA) (2001) *Area of Outstanding Beauty Management Plans: a guide*, Wetherby: CA Publications.

—— (2002) *Eat the View: promoting sustainable local products*, Wetherby: CA Publications.

—— (2003) *Forest of Dean Integrated Rural Development Programme 2000–2005*, Pamphlet, Wetherby: CA Publications.

—— (2004) *The State of the Countryside 2004*, Wetherby: CA Publications.

—— (2005) *Integrated Rural Development: an approach to modernising rural delivery to achieve sustainable development*, Wetherby: CA Publications.

Countryside Agency and Scottish Natural Heritage (CA/SNH) (2002) 'Landscape Character Assessment: Guidance for England and Scotland' (authors: Swanwick, C. and Land Use Consultants), Cheltenham: Countryside Agency and Edinburgh: Scottish Natural Heritage.

Countryside Council for Wales (CCW)/Cadw (2001) *Register of Landscapes of Special Historic Interest in Wales*, Cardiff: Cadw.

Cadw/CCW (2003) *Guide to Good Practice on Using the Register of Landscapes of Historic Interest in Wales in the Planning and Development Process*, Cardiff: Cadw.

CCW/Wales Landscape Partnership Group (CCW/WLPG) (2001) *The LANDMAP Information System*, Bangor: Countryside Council for Wales and the Wales Landscape Partnership Group.

Crofts, R. (2004) 'Connecting the pieces: Scotland's integrated approach to the natural heritage', in Bishop, K. and Phillips, A. (eds.) *Countryside Planning: new approaches to management and conservation*, London: Earthscan, 170–187.

Davies, P. and Robb, J. (2002) 'The appropriation of the material of places in the landscape: the case of tufa and springs', *Landscape Research*, 27(2), 181–185.

de Roo, G. (2003) *Environmental Planning in the Netherlands: too good to be true. From command-and-control planning to shared governance*, Aldershot: Ashgate.

Department of Environment, Transport and the Regions (DETR) (1999) *Sustainable Development: the UK Government's Approach*, London: DETR.

—— (2000) *European Spatial Planning and Urban–Rural Relationships: The UK Dimension*, London: DETR.

Derby City Council (1999) 'Management Strategy for the Mickleover, Littleover and Sunny Hill Green Wedges', Derby: Derby City Council.

Devine-Wright, P., Fleming, P. and Chadwick, H. (2001) 'Role of social capital in advancing regional sustainable development', *Impact Assessment and Project Appraisal*, 19, 161–167.

Dick, B. (1997) *Stakeholder analysis*, www.scu.edu.au/schools/gcm/ar/arp/stake.html, (accessed 27 June 05).

Dolman, P., Lovett, A., O'Riordan, T. and Cobb, R. (2001) 'Designing whole landscapes', *Landscape Research*, 26, 305–335.

Dover, J. (2000) 'Human, environmental and wildlife aspects of corridors with specific reference to UK planning practice', *Landscape Research*, 333–344.

Dramstad, W., Olson, J. and Forman, R. (1996) '*Landscape Ecology Principles in Landscape Architecture and Land Use Planning*', Washington DC: Island Press.

Ducros, C. and Watson, N. (2002) 'Integrated land and water management in the United Kingdom: narrowing the implementation gap', *Journal of Environmental Planning and Management*, 45(3), 403–424.

Dutch Ministry of Agriculture, Nature Management and Fisheries (2000) *Nature for People, People for Nature*, Den Haag: The Ministry.

Eiden, G. (2001) 'Landscape indicators', in Eiden, G., Bryden, J. and Piorr, H-P. (eds.) *Proposal on Agri-Environment Indicators*, Final Report of the PAIS project, EUROSTAT, Luxembourg, 4–92.

Ekins, P., Folke, C. and De Groot, R. (2003) 'Identifying critical natural capital', *Ecological Economics*, 44, 159–163.

English Nature (2004) *Nature's Place*, 29: 4.

Erickson, D. (2004) 'The relationship of historic city form and contemporary greenway implementation: a comparison of Milwaukee, Wisconsin (USA) and Ottawa, Ontario (Canada)', *Landscape and Urban Planning*, 68(2–3), 199–222.

Fabos, G. (2004) 'Greenway planning in the United States: its origins and recent case studies', *Landscape and Urban Planning*, 68(2–3), 321–342.

Fahrig, L. (2001) 'How much habitat is enough?', *Biological Conservation*, 100(1), 65–74.

Fairclough, G. (2002) 'Europe's Landscape: archaeology, sustainability and agriculture', in Fairclough, G. and Rippon, S. (eds.) and Bull, D. (asst. ed.) *Europe's Cultural Landscape: archaeologists and the management of change*, English Heritage. 1–12.

—— (2006) 'Large scale, long duration and broad perceptions: scale issues in historic landscape characterisation', in Lock, G. and Molyneaux, B. (eds.), *Confronting scale in Archaeology: issues of theory and practice*, Dordrecht: Kluwer Academic Publishers.

Faludi, A. and Waterhout, B. (2002) *The Making of the European Spatial Development Perspective*, London: Routledge.

Finger-Stich, A. and Ghimire, K. (1997) 'Local development and parks in France', in Ghimire, K. B. and Pimbert, M. P. (eds.) *Social Change and Conservation*, London: UNRISD and Earthscan.

Fonds Suisse Pour le Paysage (FSP) (undated) Available at http//www.fls-fsp.ch (accessed 6 July 2005).

Forestry Commission (1998) *The England Forestry Strategy*, Cambridge: Forestry Commission.

Forman, R. (1997) *Land Mosaics: the ecology of landscapes and regions*, Cambridge, UK: Cambridge University Press.

Forman, R. and Godron, M. (1986) *Landscape Ecology*, New York: John Wiley and Sons.

Franks, J. (2003) 'Revised agri-environment policy objectives: implications for scheme design', *Journal of Environmental Planning and Management*, 46(3), 443–466.

Fry, G. (2004) 'Culture and Nature versus Culture or Nature', in Jongman, R. (ed.) *The New Dimensions of the European Landscape*, Dordrecht: Springer.

Fry, G. and Gustavsson, R. (1996) 'Testing landscape design principles: the landscape laboratory', in Jongman, R. H. G. (ed.) *Ecological and Landscape Consequences of Land Use Change in Europe*, Tilburg: European Centre for Nature Conservation 143–154.

Fuller, R. M., Smith, G. M., Sanderson, J. M., Hill, R. A., Thomson, A. G., Cox, R., Brown, N. J., Clarke, R. T., Rothery, P. and Gerard, F. F. (2000) *Land Cover Map 2000 Module 7 final report*, London: Department for Environment, Transport and the Regions.

Gallent, N., Shoard, M., Andersson, J., Oades, R. and Tudor, C. (2004) 'England's urban fringes: multi-functionality and planning', *Local Environment*, 9(3), 217–233.

Gibson, J. (1979) *The Ecological Approach to Visual Perception*, New York: Houghton Mifflin.

Giddens, A. (1991) *Modernity and Self-Identity: self and society in the late modern age*, Cambridge, UK: Polity Press.

Gilg, A. (1996) *Countryside Planning: the first half century*, London: Taylor and Francis.

Gittins, J. (2001) 'The work of the Cheshire Landscape Trust', paper to Landscape Research Group/Institute for Landscape Ecology workshop, Nove Hrady, August.

Gobster, P., Haight, R. and Shriner, D. (2000) 'Landscape change in the Midwest: an integrated parcelized program', *Journal of Forestry*, 98(3), 9–14.

Gobster, P. and Rickenbach, M. (2004) 'Private forest land and development in Wisconsin's Northwoods: perceptions of resource-oriented stakeholders', *Landscape and Urban Planning*, 69, 165–182.

Gobster, P. and Westphal, L. (2004) 'The human dimensions of urban greenways: planning for recreation and related experiences', *Landscape and Urban Planning*, 68(2–3, 30), 147–165.

Golley, F. and Bellot, J. (1991) 'Interactions of landscape ecology, planning and design', *Landscape and Urban Planning*, 21, 3–11.

Granovetter, M. (1985) 'Economic action and social structure: the problem of embeddedness', *American Journal of Sociology*, 91(3), 481–510.

Gray, B. (1989) *Collaborating: finding common ground for multiparty problems*, San Francisco: Jossey-Bass Publishers.

Great Britain HM Treasury (2003) *The Green Book: appraisal and evaluation in central government*, London: The Stationery Office.

Groundwork Trust/Countryside Agency (2004) *Unlocking the Potential of the Urban Fringe*, Cheltenham: Countryside Agency.

Guehenno, J. (1993) *La Fin de la Démocratie*, Paris: Flammarion.

Gurnell, A. and Petts, G. (1995) *Changing River Channels*, Chichester: Wiley.

Gwyn, D. (2002) 'Associative landscape in a Welsh context', in Fairclough, G. and Rippon, S. (eds.) *Europe's Cultural Landscape: archaeologists and the management of change*, 187–192.

Haines-Young, R., Martin, J. and Swanwick, C. (2004) *Constructing an Indicator of Change in Countryside Quality*, Final Report, University of Nottingham and Countryside Agency.

Haines-Young, R. and Potschin, M. (2000) 'Multifunctionality and value', in Brandt, J., Tress, B.

and Tress, G. (eds.) *Multifunctional Landscapes*, Centre for Landscape Research, Roskilde University, Denmark, 111–118.

Handley, J. (2001) 'Derelict and despoiled land – problems and potential', in Miller, C., *Planning and Environmental Protection*, Oxford: Hart. 115–146.

Harms, B., Farjon, H. and Jongman, R. (1993) 'Proceedings of the IALE Conference towards a Landscape Ecological Decision Making Support System for Conservation and Remediation of (Semi) Natural Habitats in Europe (LEDESS) on Agricultural Landscapes in Europe', *Rennes*, June, p. 36.

Harris, N. and Hooper, A. (2004) 'Rediscovering the "spatial" in public policy and planning: an examination of the spatial content of sectoral policy documents', *Planning Theory and Practice*, 5(2), 147–169.

Harrison, C. and Burgess, J. (2000) 'Valuing nature in context: the contribution of common-good approaches', *Biodiversity and Conservation*, 9, 1115–1130.

Harrison, P. A., Berry, P. M. and Dawson, T. P. (2001). *MONARCH: modelling natural resources responses to climate change*, Final Report to Funding Partners, Environmental Change Institute, University of Oxford.

Haskins, C. (2003) *Rural Delivery Review: a report on the delivery of government policies in rural England*, London: Defra.

Haslett, J. (2001) 'Biodiversity and conservation of *Diptera* in heterogeneous land mosaics: a fly's eye view', *Journal of Insect Conservation*, 5(2), 71–75.

Hawkins, V. and Selman, P. (2002) 'Landscape scale planning: exploring alternative land use scenarios', *Landscape and Urban Planning*, 60, 211–224.

He, X. (1998) 'Fengshui: Chinese Tradition in a Manchester Context', unpublished PhD Thesis, University of Manchester.

Healey, P., Cars, G., Madanipour, A. and de Magalhaes, C. (2002) 'Transforming Governance, Institutionalist Analysis and Institutional Capacity', in Cars, G. *et al.*, (eds) (2002) *Urban Governance, Institutional Capacity and Social Milieux*, Aldershot: Ashgate, 6–28.

Hidding, M. and Teunissen, A. (2002) 'Beyond fragmentation: new concepts for urban–rural development', *Landscape and Urban Planning*, 58, 297–308.

Hill, K. (2000) 'Visions of sustainability', in Benson, J. and Roe, M. (eds.) *Landscape and Sustainability*, London: Spon, 294–311.

Hill, M., Briggs, J., Minto, P., Bagnall, D., Foley, K. and Williams, A. (2001) 'Guide to Best Practice in Seascape Assessment', Countryside Council for Wales, Brady Shipman Martin and University College Dublin.

Hillier, J. and Rooksby, E. (eds.) (2002) *Habitus: a sense of place*, Aldershot: Ashgate.

Holdaway, E. and Smart, G. (2001) *Landscapes at Risk? The Future for Areas of Outstanding Natural Beauty*, London: Spon.

Howard, D., Petit, S. and Bunce, R. (2000) 'Monitoring multi-functional landscapes at a national scale – guidelines drawn up from the Countryside Survey of Great Britain', in Brandt, J.,

Tress, B. and Tress, G. (eds.) *Multifunctional Landscapes*, Centre for Landscape Research, Roskilde University, Denmark, 51–62.

Illsley, D. and Richardson, T. (2004) 'New national parks for Scotland: coalitions in conflict over the allocation of planning powers in the Cairngorms', *Journal of Environmental Planning and Management*, 47, 219–242.

International Union for the Conservation of Nature and Natural Resources (IUCN) (1994a) '*Guidelines for Protected Area Management Categories*', London: IUCN.

—— (1994b) '*1993 United Nations List of National Parks and Protected Areas*', Gland: IUCN.

Ison, R. and Blackmore, C. (1997) *Environmental Decision-Making: a systems approach*, Milton Keynes: Open University.

Iverson Nassauer, J. and Corry, R. (2004) 'Using normative scenarios in landscape ecology', *Landscape Ecology*, 19, 343–356.

Jackson, J. (1984) *Discovering the Vernacular Landscape*, New Haven: Yale University Press.

Jennings, M (2000) 'Gap analysis: concepts, methods and recent results', *Landscape Ecology*, 15(1), 5–20.

Jongman, R. (2002) 'Landscape planning for biological diversity in Europe', *Landscape Research*, 27, 187–195.

Kaplan, R. and Kaplan, S. (1982) *Cognition and Environment: functioning in an uncertain world*, New York: Praeger.

—— (1989) *The Experience of Nature: a psychological perspective*, Cambridge, UK: Cambridge University Press.

Kazmierski, J., Kram, M., Mills, E., Phemister, D., Reo, N., Riggs, C., Terfertiller, R. and Erickson, D. (2004) 'Conservation planning and the landscape scale: a landscape ecology method for regional land trusts', *Journal of Environmental Planning and Management*, 47(5), 709–736.

Kelly, M., Selman, P. and Gilg, A. (2004) 'Taking sustainability forward', *Town Planning Review*, 75, 309–336.

Klijn, J. and Vos, W. (eds.) (2000) *From Landscape Ecology to Landscape Science*, WLO, Wageningen: Kluwer Academic Publishers.

Klijn, J. and Vos, W. (2000) 'A new identity for landscape ecology in Europe: a research strategy for the next decade', in *From Landscape Ecology to Landscape Science*, WLO, Wageningen: Kluwer Academic Publishers, 149–162

Kolasa, J. and Rollo, D. (1991) 'Introduction: the heterogeneity of heterogeneity: a glossary', in: Kolasa, J., and Pickett, S. T. A. (eds.) 'Ecological heterogeneity', *Ecological Studies*, vol. 86, New York: Springer-Verlag, 1–23.

Kühn, M. (2003) 'Greenbelt and Green Heart: separating and integrating landscapes in European city regions', *Landscape and Urban Planning*, 64(1–2), 19–27.

Lam, N. and Quattrochi, D. (1992) 'On the issues of scale, resolution, and fractal analysis in the mapping sciences', *Professional Geographer*, 44, 88–98.

Lambeck, R. (1997) 'Focal species: a multi-species umbrella for nature conservation', *Conservation Biology*, 11, 849–856.

Lapka, M. and Cudlinova, E. (2003) 'Changing landscapes, changing landscape's story', *Landscape Research*, 28, 323–328.

Latham, J., Watts, K., Thomas, C. and Griffiths, M. (2004) 'Development of a forest habitat network for Wales: linking research with policy', in Smithers, R. (ed.) *Landscape Ecology of Trees and Forests*, IALE-UK, 224–231.

Leopold, A. (1949) *A Sand County Almanac, and Sketches Here and There*, New York: Oxford University Press.

Lipsky, M. (1980) *Street-level Bureaucracy*, New York: Russell Sage Foundation.

Liu, J. and Taylor, W. (eds.) (2002) *Integrating Landscape Ecology into Natural Resource Management*, Cambridge, UK: Cambridge University Press.

Livingston, M., Shaw, W. and Harris, L. (2003) 'A model for assessing wildlife habitats in urban landscapes of eastern Pima County, Arizona', *Landscape and Urban Planning*, 64, 131–144.

Llobera, M. (1996) 'Exploring the topography of mind: GIS, social space and archaeology', *Antiquity*, (70) 267, 612–622

Löfvenhaft, K., Björn, C. and Ihse, M. (2002) 'Biotope patterns in urban areas: a conceptual model integrating biodiversity issues in spatial planning', *Landscape and Urban Planning*, 58, 223–240.

Low Choy, D. (2002) 'Cooperative Planning and Management for Regional Landscapes', unpublished PhD Thesis, University of Queensland, Australia.

Lowenthal, D. (1997) 'European landscape transformations: the rural residue', in Groth, P. and Bressi, T. (eds.) *Understanding Ordinary Landscapes*, New Haven, CT: Yale University Press, 180–188.

Lyle, J. (1994) *Regenerative Design for Sustainable Development*, New York: Wiley.

MacEwen, A. and MacEwen, M. (1987) *Greenprints for the Countryside? The Story of Britain's National Parks*, London: Allen and Unwin.

MacFarlane, R. (2000) 'Achieving whole landscape management across multiple land management units: a case study from the Lake District environmentally sensitive area', *Landscape Research*, 25, 229–254.

McGarigal, K. and Marks, B. J. (1995) 'FRAGSTATS: Spatial Pattern Analysis Program for Quantifying Landscape Structure', Gen. Tech. Rep. PNW-351, USDA Forest Service, Pacific Northwest Research Station, Portland, OR.

McGinnis, M. (ed.) (1999) *Bioregionalism*, London: Routledge.

MacInnes, L. (2004) 'Historic Landscape Characterisation', in Bishop, K. and Phillips, A. (eds.) *Countryside Planning: new approaches to management and conservation*, London: Earthscan, 155–169.

McIntyre, S. and Hobbs, R. (1999) 'A framework for conceptualizing human effects on landscapes and its relevance to management and research models', *Conservation Biology*, 13, 1282–1292.

Macnaghten, P. and Urry, J. (1998) *Contested Natures*, London: Sage.

McNeely, J. A. (1993) '*Parks for Life: report of the IVth World Congress on National Parks and Protected Areas*', Gland: IUCN.

McPherson, G. and DeStefano, S. (2003) *Applied Ecology and Natural Resource Management*, Cambridge, UK: Cambridge University Press.

Meadowcroft, J. (2002) 'Politics and scale: some implications for environmental governance', *Landscape and Urban Planning*, 61, 169–179.

Meeus, J., Wijermans, H. and Vroom, M. (1990) 'Agricultural landscapes in Europe and their transformation', *Landscape and Urban Planning*, 18, 289–352.

Meinig, D. (ed.) (1979) *The Interpretation of Ordinary Landscapes: geographical essays*, Oxford: Oxford University Press.

Miklos, L. (1996) 'The concept of the territorial system of landscape stability in Slovakia', in Jongman, R. (ed.) *Proceedings of the First ECNC Seminar on Land Use Change and its Ecological Consequences: Ecological and Landscape Consequences of Land Use Change in Europe*, ECNC Publication series on Man and Nature, 2, 385–406.

Miller, D., de Jong, R., Morrice, J. and Horne, P. (eds.) (2002) *Summary of spatial planning of wind turbine developments in Wales*, Report to the Countryside Council for Wales. Macaulay Land Use Research Institute, Aberdeen.

Mills, J. (2002) 'More than biodiversity: The socio-economic impact of implementing biodiversity action plans in the UK', *Journal of Environmental Planning and Management*, 45, 533–548.

Millward, B. (2000) 'Governing the hollow state', *Journal of Public Administration Research and Theory*, 10, 359–379.

Morgan, K. (1997) 'The learning region: institutions, innovation and regional renewal', *Regional Studies*, 31(5), 491–503.

Muir, R. (2000) *The New Reading the Landscape: Fieldwork in Landscape History*, Exeter: University of Exeter Press.

—— (2003) 'On change in the landscape', *Landscape Research*, 28, 383–404.

Mulford, C. and Rogers, D. (1982) 'Definitions and models', in Rogers, D. L. and Whetten, D. A. (eds.) *Interorganizational Coordination: theory, research, and implementation*, Ames, IA: The Iowa State University Press, 9–31.

National Roads Directorate of the Scottish Office Development Department (1998) *Cost Effective Landscape: Learning from Nature. Landscape Design and Management Policy. A Roads, Bridges and Traffic in the Countryside Initiative*, The Scottish Office, 82.

Naveh, Z. (2000) 'Introduction to the theoretical foundations of multifunctional landscapes and their application in transdisciplinary landscape ecology', in Brandt, J., Tress, B. and Tress,

G. (eds.) *Multifunctional Landscapes: interdisciplinary approaches to landscape research and management*, Centre for Landscape Research, Roskilde University, Denmark, 27–43.

Naveh, Z. and Lieberman, A. S. (1994) *Landscape Ecology – Theory and Applications*, 2nd edition, New York: Springer-Verlag.

New Opportunities Fund and Countryside Agency (2003) 'Clifton Place Community Garden: Tackling crime and drug abuse', Pamphlet: Countryside Agency website.

Nikora, V., Pearson, S. and Shankar, U. (1999) 'Scaling properties in landscape patterns: New Zealand experience', *Landscape Ecology*, 14(1), 17–33.

Office of the Deputy Prime Minister (ODPM) (2002) *Sustainable Communities: Delivering through Planning*, London: ODPM.

—— (2004) *Creating Sustainable Communities: Greening the Gateway*, London: ODPM/Department for Environment, Food and Rural Affairs.

—— (2005) *Planning Policy Statement 9: Biodiversity and Geological Conservation*, London: ODPM.

Oliver, T. and Jenkins, T. (2003) 'Sustaining rural landscapes: the role of integrated tourism', *Landscape Research*, 28, 293–308.

Olwig, K. (2002) *Landscape, Nature and the Body Politic*, Madison: University of Wisconsin Press.

Oost, O., Verboom, J. and Pouwels, R. (2000) 'LARCH-AIRPORT: a GIS-based Risk Assessment Model', International Bird Strike Committee IBSC25/WP-RS9, Amsterdam.

Opdam, P., Foppen, R. and Vos, C. (2002) 'Bridging the gap between ecology and spatial planning in landscape ecology', *Landscape Ecology*, 16, 767–779.

Oreszczyn, S. (2000) 'A systems approach to the research of people's relationships with hedgerows', *Landscape and Urban Planning*, 50, 107–117.

Oreszczyn, S. and Lane, A. (2000) 'The meaning of hedgerows in the English landscape', *Journal of Environmental Management*, 60, 101–118.

Organisation for Economic Co-operation and Development (OECD) (2001) *Environmental Indicators for Agriculture, Volume 3: Methods and Results*, Paris: Publications Service, OECD.

—— (2003) 'OECD Environmental Indicators: Development, Measurement and Use', Reference Paper, Paris: Publications Service, OECD.

O'Riordan, T. (ed.) (2001) '*Globalism, Localism and Identity: fresh perspectives on the transition to sustainability*', London: Earthscan.

O'Riordan, T., Wood, C. and Shadrake, A. (1993) 'Landscapes for tomorrow', *Journal of Environmental Planning and Management*, 36, 123–147.

Ostrom, E. (1990) *Governing the Commons: the evolution of institutions for collective action*, New York: Cambridge University Press.

Owen, R. and Eagar, D. (2004) 'LANDMAP: a tool to aid sustainable development', in Bishop, K. and Phillips, A. (eds.) *Countryside Planning: new approaches to management and conservation*, London: Earthscan, 188–202.

Palang, H. (2003) 'How does an elephant look like? Some experiences and some more fears about interdisciplinary landscape research', in Tress, B., Tress, G., van der Valk, A. and Fry, G. (eds.) *Interdisciplinary and Transdisciplinary Landscape Studies: potential and limitations*, Wageningen: Wageningen University, Delta Series 2, 55–58.

Palmer, J. (2004) 'Using spatial metrics to predict scenic perception in a changing landscape', *Landscape and Urban Planning*, 69, 201–218.

Parris, K. (2004) 'European agricultural landscapes supply and demand: implications of agricultural policy reform', in Jongman, R. (ed.) *The New Dimensions of the European Landscape*, Dordrecht: Springer.

Peak Park Joint Planning Board (PPJPB) (1990) 'Two Villages, Two Valleys: the Peak District Integrated Rural Development Project 1981–88', Bakewell: Peak District National Park Authority.

Pearce, D. (1993) *Economic Values and the Natural World*, London: Earthscan.

Pedroli, B., de Blust, G., van Looy, K. and van Rooij, S. (2002) 'Setting targets in strategies for river restoration', *Landscape Ecology*, 17 (Supplement 1), 5–18.

Peterken, G. (2002) *Reversing Fragmentation – habitat networks as a basis for woodland creation*, Forestry Commission Practice Note.

Petts, G. and Amoros, C. (eds.) (1996) *Fluvial Hydrosystems*, Kluwer Academic Publishers.

Phillips, A. (1998) 'The nature of cultural landscapes: a nature conservation perspective', *Landscape Research*, 23, 21–38.

—— (2002) '*Management Guidelines for IUCN Category V Areas: Protected Landscapes/Seascapes*', Gland, Switzerland: IUCN.

Phillips, A. and Clarke, R. (2004) 'Our landscape from a wider perspective', in Bishop, K. and Phillips, A. (eds.) *Countryside Planning: new approaches to management and conservation*, London: Earthscan, 49–67.

Pickett, S and Cadenasso, M (1995) 'Landscape ecology: spatial heterogeneity in ecological systems', *Science*, 269, 331–334.

Pimbert, M and Pretty, J (1997) 'Diversity and sustainability in community based conservation', available at http://www.iucn.org/themes/ceesp/Publications/TILCEPA/MPimbert-UNESCOCommunityDiversity.pdf (Paper for the UNESCO-IIPA regional workshop on Community-based Conservation, February 9–12, India) (accessed 27 June 05).

Pinto-Correia, T. and Vos, W. (2004) 'Multifunctionality in Mediterranean landscapes – past and future', in Jongman, R. (ed.) *The New Dimensions of the European Landscape*, Dordrecht: Springer.

Piorr, H-P. (2003) 'Environmental policy, agri-environmental indicators and landscape indicators', *Agriculture, Ecosystems and Environment*, 98, 17–33.

Porter, K. (2004) 'The Natural Area experience', in Bishop, K. and Phillips, A. (eds.) *Countryside Planning: new approaches to management and conservation*, London: Earthscan, 91–108.

Powell, J., Selman, P. and Wragg, A. (2001) 'Protected areas: reinforcing the virtuous circle', *Planning Practice and Research*, 17(3), 279–295.

Pretty, J. N. (1994) 'Alternative Systems of Inquiry for Sustainable Agriculture', IDS Bulletin, Institute of Development Studies, University of Sussex, 25(2): 37–48.

Prigogine, I. and Stengers, I. (1984) *Order Out of Chaos. Man's Dialogue with Nature*, Boston and London: New Science Library.

Punter, J. and Carmona, M. (1997) 'Cosmetics or critical constraints? The role of landscape in design policies in English development plans', *Journal of Environmental Planning and Management*, 40, 173–198.

Purseglove, J. (1989) *Taming the Flood*, Oxford: Oxford University Press and Channel 4 Books.

Ray, D., Watts, K., Hope, J. and Humphrey, J. (2004) 'Developing Forest Habitat Networks in Scotland', in Smithers, R. (ed.) *Landscape Ecology of Trees and Forests*, IALE-UK, 216–223.

Relph, E. (1976) *Place and Placelessness*, London: Pion.

Robertson, I. and Richards, P. (eds.) (2003) *Studying Cultural Landscapes*, London: Hodder Arnold.

Rodoman, B. B. (1974) 'Polarization of landscape as a manage agent in protection of biosphere and recreational resources', in *Resources, Environment, Settlement*. Moscow: Nauka, pp, 150–162 (in Russian).

Rodwell, J. S. (ed.) (1991, 1992, 1995) *British Plant Communities*, volumes 1–5 Cambridge, UK: Cambridge University Press. Published on behalf of the Joint Nature Conservation Committee with a research team of Pigott, C. D., Ratcliffe, DA., Malloch, A. J. C., Birks, H. J. B., Proctor, M. C. F., Shimwell, D. W., Huntley, J. P., Radford, E., Wigginton, M. J. and Wilkins, P.

Rookwood, P. (1995) 'Landscape planning for biodiversity', *Landscape and Urban Planning*, 31, 379–385.

Rowe, P. (1991) *Making a Middle Landscape*, Cambridge, MA: MIT Press.

Royal Society for the Protection of Birds (RSPB) (2001) *Futurescapes: large-scale habitat restoration for wildlife and people*, Sandy: RSPB.

RSPB and Geoff Broom Associates (2000) *Valuing Norfolk's Coast: the economic benefits of environmental and wildlife tourism*, Sandy: RSPB.

Rubino, M. and Hess, G. (2003) 'Planning open spaces for wildlife 2: modeling and verifying focal species habitat', *Landscape and Urban Planning*, 64, 89–104.

Sandercock, L. (2003) 'Out of the closet: the importance of stories and storytelling in planning practice', *Planning Theory and Practice*, 4(1), 11–28.

Sauer, C. (1925) *The Morphology of Landscape*, University of California Press, Publications in Geography, 2(2): 19–54.

Schama, S. (2004) *Landscape and Memory*, London: Fontana.

Scott, A. J., Christie, M. and Tench, H. (2003) 'Panacea or Pandora's Box for conservation in the UK', *Journal of Environmental Planning and Management*, 46 (4) 583–604.

Scottish Executive (2000) *Forests for Scotland – The Scottish Forestry Strategy*, Edinburgh: The Executive.

Scottish Natural Heritage (SNH) (2001) *Natural Heritage Futures: an overview*, Perth: SNH.

Scottish Office (1998) *Cost-Effective Landscape Design and Management Policy*, Edinburgh: Scottish Office.

Selman, P. (1999) 'Changing approaches to landscape character evaluation and their implications for landscape ecological planning', in Maudsley, M. and Marshall, J. (eds.) *Heterogeneity in Landscape Ecology: pattern and scale*, International Association for Landscape Ecology (UK), 151–158.

—— (2000) *Environmental Planning*, 2nd edition, London: Sage.

—— (2001) 'Social capital, sustainability and environmental planning', *Planning Theory and Practice*, 2(1), 13–30.

—— (2002) 'Multi-function landscape plans: a missing link in sustainability planning?', *Local Environment*, 7(3), 283–294.

—— (2004a) 'Community participation in the planning and management of cultural landscapes', *Journal of Environmental Planning and Management*, 47(3), 365–392.

—— (2004b) 'Barriers and bridges to sustaining cultural landscapes', in Jongman, R. (ed.) *The New Dimensions of the European Landscape*, Dordrecht: Springer.

Shephard, R. (1984) 'Ecological constraints on internal representation: resonant kinematics of perceiving, imagining, thinking and dreaming', *Psychological Review*, 91, 417–447.

Sickel, H., Ihse, M., Norderhaug, A. and Sickel, M. (2004) 'How to monitor semi-natural key habitats in relation to grazing preferences of cattle in mountain summer farming areas: an aerial photo and GPS method study', *Landscape and Urban Planning*, 67, 67–77.

Simpson, J. (2004) 'Planning for Environmental Sustainability in the Green Belt of the Mersey Corridor', unpublished PhD Thesis, Manchester: University of Manchester.

Slocombe, S. (1998) 'Lessons from experience with ecosystem based management', *Landscape and Urban Planning*, 40, 31–39.

Smith, D. and Hellmund, P. (eds.) (1993) *Ecology of Greenways*, Minneapolis: University of Minnesota Press.

Soltner, D. (1985) *L'arbre et la haie: pour la production agricole, pour l'équilibre écologique, et le cadre de view rurale*, 7th edition, Collection Science et Techniques Agricoles, Angers, pp. 200.

South West Wildlife Trusts (2004) *Rebuilding Biodiversity: new landscapes for wildlife and people, a regional approach to landscape-scale planning for habitat restoration*, Developed by the South West Wildlife Trusts for use by the South West Regional Biodiversity Partnership.

Southworth, J., Nagendra, H. and Tucker, C. (2002) 'Fragmentation of a landscape: incorporat-

ing landscape metrics into satellite analyses of land-cover change', *Landscape Research*, 27, 253–270.

Stanners, D. and Bourdeau, P. (eds.) (1995) 'Europe's Environment', *The Dobris Assessment*, European Environment Agency, EC DG XI and Phare, Copenhagen.

Starkings, D. (1998) Unpublished BA (Hons) Dissertation, Department of Planning and Landscape, University of Manchester.

Stern, M. and Marsh, W. (1997) 'The decentered city: edge cities and the expanding metropolis', *Landscape and Urban Planning*, 36, 243–246.

Swanwick, C. (2004) 'The assessment of countryside and landscape character in England: an overview', in Bishop, K. and Phillips, A. (eds.) *Countryside Planning: new approaches to management and conservation*, London: Earthscan, 109–124.

Szaro, R., Sexton, W. and Malone, C. (1997) 'The emergence of ecosystem management as a tool for meeting people's needs and sustaining ecosystems', *Landscape and Urban Planning*, 40(1), 1–7.

Terkenli, T. (2001) 'Towards a theory of the landscape: the Aegean landscape as a cultural image', *Landscape and Urban Planning*, 57, 197–208.

Thayer, R. (2003) *Life Place: bioregional thoughts and practice*, Berkeley: University of California Press.

Tischendorf, L., Bender, D. and Fahrig, L. (2003) 'Evaluation of patch isolation metrics in mosaic landscapes for specialist vs. generalist dispersers', *Landscape Ecology*, 18(1), 41–50.

Tress, B. and Tress, G. (2001) 'Capitalising on multiplicity: a transdisciplinary systems approach to landscape research', *Landscape and Urban Planning*, 57, 143–157.

—— (2003) 'Scenario visualisation for participatory landscape planning – a study from Denmark', *Landscape and Urban Planning*, 64, 161–178.

Tress, B., Tress, G. and Fry, G. (2005) 'Integrative studies on rural landscapes: policy expectations and research practice', *Landscape and Urban Planning*, 70(1–2), 177–191.

Tress, B., Tress, G., Décamps, H. and d'Hauteserre, A-M. (2001) 'Bridging human and natural sciences in landscape research', *Landscape and Urban Planning*, 57, 137–141.

Tress, B., Tress, G. and van der Valk, A. (2003) 'Interdisciplinarity and transdisciplinarity in landscape studies – the Wageningen DELTA approach', in Tress, B., Tress, G., van der Valk, A. and Fry, G. (eds.) *Interdisciplinary and Transdisciplinary Landscape Studies: Potential and Limitations*, Wageningen University, Delta Series 2, 8–15.

Tuan, Y. (1979) *Landscapes of Fear*, New York: Pantheon.

—— (1990) *Topophilia: study of environmental perception, attitudes and values*, Englewood Cliffs, NJ: Prentice-Hall.

Turner, T. (1998) *Landscape Planning and Environmental Impact Design*, London: Taylor and Francis.

Turner, M., Gardner, R. and O'Neill, R. (2001) *Landscape Ecology in Theory and Practice: pattern and process*, New York: Springer.

Uhrwing, M. (2003) 'MISTRA and interdisciplinarity – experiences and expectations', in Tress, B., Tress, G., van der Valk, A. and Fry, G. (eds.) *Interdisciplinary and Transdisciplinary Landscape Studies: potential and limitations*, Wageningen University, Delta Series 2, 28–32.

UK Biodiversity Steering Group (1995) *Meeting the Rio Challenge*, London: HMSO.

Ulrich, R, (1997) 'Improving medical outcomes with environmental design', *Journal of Healthcare Design*, 9, 3–7.

UNESCO (1972) *Convention concerning the Protection of the World Cultural and Natural Heritage*, Paris: UNESCO.

UN-HABITAT (2001) 'Urban Governance Toolkit Series', available at http://www.unhabitat.org/cdrom/governance/html/copyright.htm (accessed 27 June 05).

Urban, D., O'Neill, R. and Shugart, H. (1987) 'Landscape ecology: A hierarchical perspective can help scientists understand spatial patterns', *BioScience*, 37, 119–127.

Ureña, J. and Ollero, A. (2001) 'Fluvial landscapes, catchment administration and land use planning: experience based on two rivers in Spain', *Landscape Research*, 26, 225–244.

van Rooij, S., van der Sluis, T., Steingröver, E. and Clarke, S. (2004) 'Applying landscape ecological methods to analyse and design ecological networks', in Smithers, R. (ed.) *Landscape Ecology of Trees and Forests*, IALE-UK, 208–215.

van der Sluis, T., Pedroli, B. and Kuipers, H. (2001) 'Corridors for LIFE: Ecological Network Analysis Regioni Emilia-Romagna – the Plains of Provincia de Modena & Bologna', Wageningen: Alterra Green World Research.

Voisey, H. and O'Riordan, T. (2001) 'Globalisation and Localisation', in O'Riordan, T. (ed.) *Globalism, Localism and Identity: fresh perspectives on the transition to sustainability*, London: Earthscan, 25–42.

Vos, W. and Klijn, J. (2000) 'Trends in European landscape development: prospects for a sustainable future', in Klijn, J. and Vos, W. (eds.) *From Landscape Ecology to Landscape Science*, WLO, Wageningen: Kluwer Academic Publishers.

Vrijland, P. and Kerkstra, K. (1994) 'A strategy for ecological and urban development', in Cook, T. and van Lier, H. (eds.) *Landscape Planning and Ecological Networks*, Amsterdam: Elsevier Science, 71–88.

Wackernagel, M., Lewen, L. and Borgstrom-Hansson, C. (1999) 'Evaluating the use of natural capital with the ecological footprint: applications in Sweden and subregions', *Ambio*, 28(7), 604–612.

Ward, J. V. (1997) 'An expansive perspective of riverine landscapes: pattern and process across scales', *Gaia*, 6, 52–60.

Ward, J., Malard, F. and Tockner, K. (2002) 'Landscape ecology: a framework for integrating pattern and process in river corridors', *Landscape Ecology*, 17 (Supplement 1), 35–45.

Warnock, S. and Brown, N. (1998) 'A vision for the countryside', *Landscape Design*, 269, 22–26.

Wascher, D. (2004) 'Landscape Indicator Assessment: steps towards a European approach', in Jongman, R. (ed.) *The New Dimensions of the European Landscape*, Dordrecht: Springer.

Watts, K (2001) 'Barriers and bridges to biodiversity action planning', unpublished PhD thesis, University of Gloucestershire.

Watts, K. and Selman, P. (2004) 'Forcing the pace of biodiversity action: a force-field analysis of conservation effort at the "landscape scale"', *Local Environment*, 9(1), 5–20.

Watts, K. and Griffiths, M. (2004) 'Exploring structural connectivity in Welsh woodlands using neutral landscape models', in Smithers, R. (ed.) *Landscape Ecology of Trees and Forests*, IALE-UK, 133–142.

Welsh Assembly Government (WAG) (2001) *Woodlands for Wales*, Cardiff: WAG.

—— (2005) *People, Places, Future – the Wales Spatial Plan*, Cardiff: WAG.

Whatmore, S. (2001) *Hybrid Geographies*, London: Sage.

Whitehead, A. (1947) *Essays in Science and Philosophy*, New York: Philosophical Library.

Wiens, J. (1997) 'Metapopulation dynamics and landscape ecology', in Hanski, I. and Gilpin, M. (eds.) *Metapopulation Biology: ecology, genetics, and evolution*, New York: Academic Press, 43–62.

Wilcox, D. (1994) *The Guide to Effective Participation*, New York: Joseph Rowntree Foundation.

Wilson, E. (1986) *Biophilia*, Cambridge, MA: Harvard University Press.

Winder, N. (2003) 'Successes and problems when conducting interdisciplinary or transdisciplinary research', in Tress, B., Tress, G., van der Valk, A. and Fry, G. (eds.) *Interdisciplinary and Transdisciplinary Landscape Studies: Potential and Limitations*, Wageningen University, Delta Series 2, 74–90.

With, K. (1994) 'Using fractal analysis to assess how species perceive landscape structure', *Landscape Ecology*, 9, 25–36.

—— (2002) 'Using percolation theory to assess landscape connectivity and effects of habitat fragmentation', in Gutzwiller, K. (ed.) *Applying Landscape Ecology in Biological Conservation*, New York: Springer-Verlag, 105–130.

Wood, R. and Handley, J. (2001) 'Landscape dynamics and the management of change', *Landscape Research*, 26(1), 45–54.

Woodland Trust (2002) *Space for Nature: Landscape-scale action for woodland biodiversity* Grantham: The Woodland Trust.

World Commission on Environment and Development (WCED) (1987) *Our Common Future*, ('The Brundtland Report'), Oxford: Oxford University Press.

Worrell, R., Taylor, C. M. A. and Spittal, J. J. (2003) *Highland Perthshire Forest Habitat Network*, Scottish Forestry, 57, 151–157.

Wragg, A. (2000) 'Towards sustainable landscape planning: experiences from the Wye Valley Area of Outstanding Natural Beauty', *Landscape Research*, 25(2), 183–200.

Wu, J. (2004) 'Effects of changing scale on landscape pattern analysis: scaling relations', *Landscape Ecology*, 19(2), 125–138.

Wynn, G. (2002) 'The cost-effectiveness of biodiversity management: a comparison of farm types in extensively farmed areas of Scotland', Journal of Environmental Planning and Management, 45, 827–840.

Yaffee, S. (1999) 'Three faces of ecosystem management', *Conservation Biology*, 13, 713.

INDEX